THE SHAPE OF THE MINISTRY

The Shape of the Ministry

by

M. A. H. MELINSKY

The Canterbury Press
Norwich

First published 1992 by The Canterbury Press Norwich
(a publishing imprint of Hymns Ancient & Modern Limited,
a registered charity)
St Mary's Works, St Mary's Plain,
Norwich, Norfolk, NR3 3BH

A catalogue record for this book is available
from the British Library

ISBN 1–85311–047–7

*Photoset by Rowland Phototypesetting Limited,
Bury St Edmunds, Suffolk
and printed in Great Britain by
St Edmundsbury Press Limited,
Bury St Edmunds, Suffolk*

DEDICATED
(WITH HAPPY MEMORIES)
TO CLERGY TRAINERS
IN LONDON, MANCHESTER,
TOKYO AND NANJING

Contents

Acknowledgements   ix
Introduction   xi

PART I – FORMATION

1 New Testament Terms for Ministry   3
2 The Authority of Jesus   11
3 Apostolic Authority   17
4 Elders and Discipline in the Early Church   26
5 Prophets and Teachers in the Second Century   35
6 Cyprian, Bishop of the One Church   42

PART II – DEFORMATION

7 The Church Established   51
8 Medieval Deformations   60

PART III – REFORMATION

9   Reformers and Counter-Reformers   73
10 The Middle Way – *Ecclesia Anglicana*   92
11 Modern Movements   101
12 Starting Afresh   114

PART IV – ORDERS OF MINISTRY

13 Deacons   127
14 Priests or Presbyters   138
15 Bishops   150
16 Models of Ministry   158

PART V – CURRENT ISSUES

17 Authority and Authorities   173
18 Ecumenical Aspects of Ministry   185
19 The Ordination of Women as Priests and Bishops   195
20 The Parish System   206
21 Teams and Groups   217
22 Specialised or Sector Ministries   221
23 Non-Stipendiary Ministry   226
24 Local Ministry   237
25 Vocation and Selection   244
26 Training for Ministry   249

Conclusion   263

Appendix 1   The Lambeth Quadrilateral   269
Appendix 2   The Lambeth Conference, 1948, on
           The Meaning and Unity of the
           Anglican Communion   270
Appendix 3   Chinese Church Order, 1991   273

Select Bibliography   277

Index   287

Acknowledgements

ANYONE who attempts to survey such a wide field as this must be indebted to other writers, especially historians, and I gladly acknowledge my debt. I have tried to check all the references to original sources, but some have escaped me.

My chief debt, however, is to colleagues, both staff and students, of the Northern Ordination Course, and in the Northern Federation for Training in Ministry, among whom I worked happily for eleven years. They generously released me for a sabbatical term so that I could work on this subject, and I am particularly grateful to the University of Manchester for awarding me, through the kind offices of Professor Tony Dyson, an Honorary Research Fellowship with its attendant privileges.

Many others have helped over the years from their knowledge and experience, including Dr Leslie Barnard, Bishop Hugh Blackburne, Canon Maurice Burrell, Archdeacon George Marchant, and Mrs Margaret Webster. Mr Kenneth Baker of the Canterbury Press has offered shrewd advice which has improved the final shape and proportion of the book.

To Mrs Kate Belcher I extend sincere thanks for an enormous amount of typing done most conscientiously over a long period.

In the area of copyright I record my gratitude to the following for permission to reproduce passages: to the Very Revd Peter Baelz for the extract on page 176; to the Right Reverend Alan Clark to quote from the ARCIC Final Report on page 186; to Professor Adrian Hastings for the quotation on page 174; to Messrs Hodder and Stoughton for the extract from *A Celebration of Faith* on page 169; to Lambeth Palace Library and SPCK for the extract from the Lambeth Conference

Report of 1948 in Appendix 2; to the Reverend R. S. Thomas for the use of his poem 'They' on pages 169–70; and to the Reverend Dr Michael Wilson for the quotation from *Hospital: A Place of Truth* on pages 148–9. If there are any other copyrights which I have unwittingly infringed I offer my apologies to their holders.

Quotations from the Bible have been made in any translation which suited my purpose for the particular passage, and I have felt free to alter the rendering if necessary. On occasion I have made up my own translation. If dissatisfied, readers are referred back to the original languages.

Introduction

SELDOM before has the Christian ministry been the subject of so much and so heated discussion not only by theologians but by all sorts of people both inside and outside the Church. A principal cause has been the fact that between 1960 and 1980 there was a remarkable loss of confidence in the ordained ministry. Between 1964 and 1986 the official figure of Roman Catholic priests leaving the ministry is 48,351, though the unofficial figure is nearer 100,000; and these men were young or in middle age. These losses were mainly in western Europe and north America, though there was some slight recovery in the late 1980s. (Hastings, 1991, p. 246).

In the Church of England between 1963 and 1975 the annual number of men ordained to the stipendiary ministry fell from 636 to just over 300, and there it remained for the next fifteen years. In 1961 there were 13,660 full-time diocesan stipendiary clergy whereas in 1981 there were 10,882. The figures for the Free Churches in England show the same trend. The situation is not uniformly dark, for western Europe is not the whole of Christendom. China emerged from the chaos of the Cultural Revolution in 1976 with the membership of the Protestant Church quadrupled over that of 1949, and since the Theological Seminary at Nanjing re-opened in 1981 it has had to turn away six or seven applicants for every one accepted.

It remains a tragic fact that the very institutions of sacraments and ministry which represent the unity of Christians in Christ continue to be the main stumbling-blocks to re-union. England witnessed the failure of Anglican-Methodist negotiations in 1969, and Scotland those between the established Presbyterian Church of Scotland and the

Anglican Episcopalian Church in 1957. The Anglican-Roman Catholic International Commission has marked out considerable common theological ground, but its reports *Ministry and Ordination* and *Authority in the Church* leave many practical issues untouched. The World Council of Churches' paper *Baptism, Eucharist and Ministry* involved virtually all the major church traditions but relegated the really contentious matters to 'deeper theological discussion'.

The question of the ordination of women to the priesthood has been the subject of keen debate for many years. Women are now ordained in many parts of the Anglican Communion, and whether or not the Church of England follows suit, discussion will become keener in the Roman Catholic Church. It is just beginning in the Eastern Orthodox Churches.

Following the extraordinary worker-priest movement in France which grew out of the turmoil of the Second World War, Anglican and Free Churches in Britain have been experimenting with various forms of non-stipendiary ministry where men and women exercise their ordained ministry while staying in their secular occupations. This has occasioned a good deal of mystification among laity and some suspicion among stipendiary clergy, but it may prove to be an important development.

Greater stress is now being put on the idea of 'collaborative ministry', with the laity encouraged to exercise their own proper ministry. Does this mean that the clergy will do themselves out of a job? Where is the border-line between ordained and lay? Why should selected lay people not preside at Communion?

These large questions, and others like them, do not admit of quick answers: they are the reason for this book. Its first half traces the theological roots of ordination in the Bible and early church, with a brief survey of its historical development to the present time (Parts I, II, and III), and its second half (Parts IV and V) deals with a number of current issues in the light of this long and rich tradition. The main perspective is Anglican, partly because it is the one best known to the author, but principally because it embraces much that is valuable in both catholic and reformed traditions. It is also world-wide.

The reader may, however, be admitted without delay to the conclusions which seem to emerge from the first half and so form the foundations for the second. They are three:

1. Ministry, and indeed priesthood, belongs to the whole People of God. Nevertheless within the Church there is an 'ordained' ministry which has the spiritual authority to maintain the Church in its apostolic-prophetic tradition. This is a constant factor.

2. The shape of the ordained ministry is, and always has been, one of 'variable geometry', a model derived from advanced aircraft design where an aeroplane can change the shape of its wings according to the demands of the flight.

3. The theological premise for discussion of the ministry is not simply Christological but must be fully Trinitarian. The argument, for example, that because Jesus was a man all ministers must be men is based on a grossly over-simplified Christology which allows no room for the operation of the Holy Spirit. There must be room for both imitation and innovation. This corresponds to the foundation of the Church on apostles and prophets. Furthermore the ministry of Jesus himself is set within the context of the kingdom of God, and so the Church and its ministry also must be set within that context, for the Church is not the kingdom.

PART I – FORMATION

1
New Testament Terms for Ministry

JESUS did not found a Church: he re-founded Israel as the faithful people of God. In those terms Paul addresses the Christians in Galatia, 'Peace and mercy be upon all who walk by this rule, upon the Israel of God.' (Gal. 6.16). If Jesus had wished to 'found a Church' he would no doubt have provided it with a constitution, with aims and objects, methods of organisation and procedure, and officers, but he did not. There are indications that the early Christians wished he had. They almost certainly wrote back into the gospels dominical authority for the two sacraments of baptism and eucharist which had become central for their corporate life (see on Matt. 28.19 and Luke 22.19). Instead he chose a small band of men to be with him during the short span of his ministry, and thereafter to depend on his continuing spiritual presence with them. The result was the Church and the ministry.

All Christians today agree that ministry stems from Jesus Christ, but there are profound disagreements about how particular forms of ministry derive from him and are related to him. Episcopal, papal, presbyterian, congregational, charismatic, and undifferentiated forms of ministry all claim their justification from the New Testament, and all, indeed, can be found there. How can these claims be reconciled? The answer is a complex one and calls for an examination of the early evidence free from the bias of ecclesiastical tradition.

The lack of a clear and comprehensive structure of church organisation and ministry is one principal feature of the New Testament evidence: the other is the remarkably secular world from which it drew its vocabulary. A brief survey of its principal terms for ministers and ministry is illuminating:

3

Doulos = slave; *douleuō* = I work as a slave; *douleia* = slavery. Paul so describes himself to the Church at Corinth, 'ourselves as your slaves for Jesus' sake'. The bite of the term is lost in all the main English versions by the use of the word 'servant'. (2 Cor. 4.5 and elsewhere). What mattered to any citizen of the Graeco-Roman world was his freedom. 'How can a man be happy if he is bondage?' asked Plato. One of a slave's more objectionable household duties was the washing of guests' feet, and John 13 gives a memorable picture of Jesus assuming this status and also laying it upon his disciples. Paul, in Phil. 2.7, urged the Christians in Philippi to have the same mind as Christ Jesus who 'emptied himself, taking the form of a slave'.

Diakonos (masculine or feminine) = waiter, servant; *diakoneō* = I wait or serve; *diakonia* = service; (whence 'deacon', 'diaconate').

The basic meaning is 'personal attendant', normally not a slave but free. He or she might wait at table, perform other household duties, or act as agent for an estate or as a confidential messenger. (See further chapter 13.) It is used in Luke 17.8 of a master ordering his man to serve him a meal. When the disciples were disputing about precedence, Jesus deliberately reverses the order:

> . . . but whoever would be great among you must be your servant (*diakonos*), and whoever would be first among you must be slave (*doulos*) of all. For the Son of Man also came not to be served (*diakonēthēnai*) but to serve (*diakonēsai*), and to give his life as a ransom for many.
>
> (Mark 10. 44–45.)

The term is used more generally in Acts 19.22 of Timothy and Erastus as two of Paul's helpers (*diakonountōn*). Paul refers to his collection for the Jerusalem church as 'gracious work which we are carrying on (*diakonoumenē*)' (2 Cor. 8.19), and sums up his apostleship with the same word, 'Inasmuch then as I am an apostle to the Gentiles, I magnify my ministry (*diakonian*) . . .'. In time, 'deacon' came to signify a regular office, closely associated with 'bishops' in Phil. 1.1 and I Tim. 3. 1–13. It is often claimed that the origin of the diaconate is to be found in the appointment of the seven in Acts 6. 1–6, but 'deacons' are not there specified, but only the duty of 'the daily distribution' (*diakonia*) and 'to serve tables' (*diakonein*). The Greek word may be either masculine or feminine and Phoebe is named as a *diakonon* of the church at Cenchreae in Rom. 16.1, and 'the women' in 1 Tim. 3.11 appear to be women deacons. The feminine form *diakonissa* does not appear until the fourth century.

Hupēretēs = a subordinate; *hupēreteō* = I serve under orders.
This term was widely used in classical and later Greek as an aide to a commander or assistant to a judge or doctor. His task was to carry out orders. Unlike a *doulos* he was a free man and exercised some power. Its original meaning is supposed to be 'under-rower' from *eretēs*, but this is disputed. It is used in the New Testament of a prison guard (Matt. 5.25), a synagogue attendant (Luke 4.20), and several times of officers of the Sanhedrin (e.g. John 18.3); apparently of the disciples by Jesus '. . . my servants would fight . . .' (John 18.36); of servants of Christ by Paul (1 Cor. 4.1); and of servants of the word by Luke in the introduction to his gospel (Luke 1.2).

Poimēn = shepherd; *poimainō* = I pasture.
The shepherd image of God is embedded in Israelite piety, and carried from there to the rulers of Israel who incur fierce criticism from the prophets, e.g. Jeremiah (23. 1–4) and Ezekiel (34). In contrast to the contempt in which they were held by rabbis, Jesus describes himself as the good shepherd (John 10. 1–30), and the Messianic Shepherd (Matt. 25. 31–46). The final pastoral charge of the risen Lord to Peter is 'Tend (*poimaine*) my sheep' (John 21.16). In 1 Peter the apostle bids the elders 'tend (*poimanete*) the flock of God that is your charge' on behalf of the chief Shepherd (*archipoimenos*) (1 Pet. 5. 1–4).

Apostolos = (one) sent out, apostle; *apostellō* = I send out; *apostolē* = apostleship.

This word was not common in written Greek. Originally an adjective, it meant 'dispatched', and then the thing dispatched, a fleet or army. A Cynic philosopher like Diogenes could describe himself as 'divinely sent' (*apostaleis*). In Rabbinic Judaism *shaliach* described the custom of using a plenipotentiary messenger, though its significance was legal rather than religious. Later rabbis were fond of the description: 'The one sent by a man is as the man himself'. This legal sense is reflected in John 13.16, . . . nor is he who is sent (*apostolos*) greater than he who sent him (*pempsantos*)'. When Paul writes in 2 Cor. 8.23, 'as for our brethren, they are messengers (*apostoloi*) of the churches', the term probably carries this neutral meaning. It becomes, however, a word of key importance as referring to the Twelve, and others, as commissioned bearers of the New Testament message, occurring some seventy-nine times. Its significance and development will be examined in the next chapter.

Leitourgos = servant; *leitourgeō* = I serve; *leitourgia* = service.

This word has a fascinating history which illustrates over the centuries a change of meaning to the exact opposite of its origin. The word comes from *laos* meaning 'people' and *ergon* meaning 'work', and was familiar at Athens as a kind of tax, compulsory or voluntary, whereby the rich performed at their own charge a public duty like equipping a trireme for the navy. In the Septuagint the word can mean 'service' in general, but more often it is used for the cultic ministry of the sanctuary. In rabbinic Judaism it refers to ministry both of the temple and of pagan cults.

In the New Testament the term appears nine times, three as a verb and six as a noun. Three times it is used in its general sense (Rom. 15.27; 2 Cor. 9.12; Phil. 2.30), in the first two referring to Paul's collection for the church at Jerusalem; three times referring to the Jewish cultus (Luke 1.23; Heb. 9.21 and 10.11); once to the present ministry of the risen Christ (Heb. 8.6); once to the fruits of Paul's ministry (Phil.

6

2.17); and once only to Christian worship, 'While they were worshipping (*leitourgountōn*) and fasting' (Acts 13.2).

All the above terms are chosen from the world of secular service in its many forms. Most of them are used by the New Testament writers in their secular meanings, though these gradually shade into particular ecclesiastical colourings. All of them denote someone of inferior social status whose prime task it is to see that someone else's will is carried out. When Greek came to be translated into Latin, the word *minister* lay to hand. It comes from *minus* meaning 'less', and it was used to refer to cup-bearers, under-officials, legal assistants and mediators.

Two terms remain which carry in themselves some idea of authority, *presbuteros* = elder, and *episkopos* = overseer. These in their Anglicised form of 'priest' and 'bishop' play a central part in the development of Christian ministry, but their origins will be briefly considered here.

Presbuteros = elder.

Age was generally thought to confer wisdom, and so Aristotle can refer to 'wise men and elders'. In Greek societies the term referred to senior groups who were not necessarily office-bearers. In John 8.9 and Acts 2.17 older people are simply contrasted with younger. In the Old Testament elders (*hazzekēnim*) are presupposed (never appointed) as heads and representatives of great clans and families. Numbers 11 tells how Moses appointed seventy elders to share the burden of responsiblity for the people, and these became a model for the Sanhedrin, the Council of Elders, the supreme ruling body of the Jews known to us in Jerusalem from Seleucid times (about 200 BC) and composed of representatives of privileged patrician families in Jerusalem. In Luke 7.3 when a pro-Jewish centurion sends elders to Jesus to ask him to heal a slave, they would have been leaders of their community and the disciplinary body of the local synagogue. In Acts 11.30 'the elders' in Jerusalem appear unannounced, resembling a Jewish synagogue council, though by Acts 15 they have extended into a kind of Sanhedrin with teaching and judicial authority for the whole Church.

Episkopos = overseer; *episkeptomai* = I oversee, care for; *episkopē* = oversight.

In secular Greek the term indicated to 'watch over' either as a guardian, protector or patron, or as a state official with technical or financial responsibilities. In the Septuagint it indicates 'oversight' of various kinds. In the New Testament *episkopos* occurs five times: of the Ephesian elders (Acts 20.28); 'to all the saints . . . with the bishops and deacons . . .' (Phil. 1.1); 'Now a bishop must be above reproach . . .' (1 Tim. 3.2); 'For a bishop must be blameless . . .' (Titus 1.7); and of Christ as 'the Shepherd and Guardian of your souls' (1 Pet. 2.25). Its later development has a long and complicated history.

Two other terms remain to be noticed, one because it refers to a recognisable religious office in the early Church, and one because, against all expectations, it does not. They are *prophētēs* (= prophet) and *hiereus* (= priest). Both were familiar enough terms in both the Jewish and the Gentile worlds, and both have a long Biblical history behind them.

Prophētēs = prophet.

The word means, in Greek, 'one who speaks for another', generally for a god. The blind Teiresias played a key role in four Greek tragedies, and the prophetess of Apollo at Delphi was the supreme religious authority. In Exodus 7.1 Aaron is appointed by God to be prophet or spokesman for his brother Moses at his interview with Pharaoh. Elsewhere in the Old Testament the word translates *nabi*. They appear first at the beginning of the monarchy in groups on the staff of religious establishments, prophesying ecstatically with the aid of music and dancing (1 Sam. 10. 5–6). In marked contrast stand the great prophets of the eighth and seventh centuries who have given their names to books, and the earliest of these, Amos, explicitly dissociates himself from the 'sons of the prophets' and their smooth words designed to please the establishment

(Amos 7. 10–17). They were all conscious of a personal call from Yahweh, and their predictions are the consequence of moral certainty, without benefit of artificial stimuli. All were bitterly critical of the sacrificial worship of the sanctuaries and two, if not three, foretold the destruction of Jerusalem and its temple (Mic. 3. 9–12; Jer. 7. 1–15; Isa. 29. 1–8). The Old Testament finishes with the promise of the return of Elijah to usher in the Day of the Lord (Mal. 4.6), and then the voice of prophecy falls silent until the ministry of John the Baptist. Jesus understands the Baptist as fulfilling the prophecy of Malachi (Luke 7.27), and himself accepts the title of prophet (Luke 13.33). Prophets figure prominently as an 'order' in the life of the early church, ranking next only to apostles (1 Cor. 12.28); Ephesians 2. 19–20 speaks of 'the household of God, built upon the foundation of the apostles and prophets'.

Hiereus = priest; *hierateuō* = I practise as a priest; *hierateuma* = priesthood; *hieros* = sacred; *hieron* = temple. (Latin: *sacerdos* = priest; *sacer* = sacred; *sacerdotium* = priesthood).

This word is astonishingly absent as an order within the early church, in view of an abundance of priests Jewish and pagan in the world around. In connection with Christians it appears only four times in the New Testament, always referring to the whole redeemed people of God: '. . . you are a chosen race, a royal priesthood, a holy nation, God's own people' (1 Pet. 2. 5–9; see also Rev. 1. 5–6; 5. 9–10; 21.6). The theme of the priesthood of Christ is worked out in Hebrews but without any suggestion of an order of Christian priesthood. Its conclusion is that the self-sacrifice of Jesus has finally abolished all cultic sacrifice (Heb. 10. 1–10).

Israel's worship was predominantly sacrificial and most of its ritual had been taken over and adapted from Canaanite use, including the three great annual festivals, but the worship of Yahweh could hardly have been more different: it originated in history, not in agriculture, with the rescue of Israel from Egypt as its *leitmotif*, and Israel's link was one of covenant and not one of nature, offered by God on terms of faithfulness

9

and moral obedience. There was a close connection between Yahweh and king, and the dominant belief of the temple worshippers was that since Yahweh dwelt there Zion must be inviolable. The splendour and music of the Canaanite-type cult satisfied the majority more than the austere imageless faith of Yahwism.

Priests were not always engaged in offering sacrifices, nor were they guardians of a dead letter of cultic law. Deuteronomy in particular is a reinterpretation of the Law in prophetic terms designed to stir the imagination and the will. (Not for nothing was Jeremiah the son of a priest (Jer. 1.1).) The early Christians, however, were quite clear that whatever terms might be suitable to describe their ministry, the world of priesthood could not provide them.

2

The Authority of Jesus

QUESTIONS about ministry are more than questions about functions. Underneath these lie issues about authority, as the religious authorities well knew when they asked Jesus, 'By what authority are you doing these things?' (Mark 11.27). Consideration of Christian ministry must begin with Jesus Christ, his ministry and his authority.

There are three main kinds of authority which people recognise: the authority of office, as in the policeman with his uniform; the authority of knowledge and skill, as in the teacher with her degree or certificate; and the authority of the personality, as in the comedian, though he may sometimes wear uniform and is certainly not devoid of skill, for the categories overlap. One of the difficulties for Christian ministry is that its authority has to be an appropriate blend of all three.

The authority of Jesus was not of the first kind. He held no recognised religious office, and spent a good deal of his time in conflict with the religious authorities. His authority was not of the second kind in so far as he held, to the best of our knowledge, no professional qualifications from the scribal schools, in contrast, for example, to the apostle Paul. His authority was a personal one, though not limited to his human personality.

Early in his narrative Mark records the unusual effect which Jesus' teaching had on the common people: 'They were astonished at his teaching, for he taught them as one who had authority, and not as the scribes' (Mark 1.22). The scribes had authority enough as the official expounders of the Law, relying for the most part on earlier interpretations, 'the tradition of the elders' (Mark 7.3f.). Jesus' interpretation,

11

however, was fresh, vital and personal, entirely in line with the inspiration of the Old Testament prophets. Its source was recognised by an unusual witness, a Roman, but God-fearing, centurion (sergeant-major) who asked Jesus to heal his batman, adding that a command only would be sufficient 'for I also am a man under authority . . .' (Matt. 8.9 // Luke 7.8).

Mark goes on immediately to record Jesus' exercise of authority in the healing of a madman in the synagogue: 'and they were all amazed . . . saying, "What is this? A new teaching! With authority he commands even the unclean spirits, and they obey him."' (Mark 1.27 // Luke 4.36). Soon after Mark reinforces the impression with the narrative of Jesus' healing of the paralysed man brought along by four of his friends. As a deliberate challenge to the scribes who were present he sets the healing in the context of the forgiveness of sins, and carries out the former by way of vindicating the latter, a claim little short of blasphemy.

The scribes react by sending an official delegation from Jerusalem with the accusation that Jesus was healing by the use of black magic: 'He is possessed by Beelzebub, and by the prince of demons he casts out demons.' (Mark 3.22 // Matt. 12.24 // Luke 11.15). Jesus comments acidly that if the Pharisees see the power of God in operation and call it the power of Satan, then indeed forgiveness is not possible for them (Mark 3.28f.). Mark lets his readers into the secret of 'Messiah incognito' by the device of having demoniacs recognise him as such because they belong to the supernatural world. The madman, bound with chains and living in the mountains, shouts at Jesus, 'What have you to do with me, Jesus, Son of the Most High God?' (Mark 5.7 // Matt. 8.29 // Luke 8.28).

The status of Jesus and the authority that went with it posed a problem even to his disciples, and it seems that he deliberately went out of his way not to provide ready answers. Near Caesarea Philippi he flung out the question, '"Who do men say that I am?" And they told him, "John the baptist; and others say, Elijah; and others one of the prophets." And he asked them, "But who do you say that I am?" Peter answered him, "You are the Christ"', though it soon became apparent that Peter had a notion of the Messiah far different from that of his master (Mark 8.27f. // Matt. 16.13f. // Luke 9.18f.).

The least inadequate category that lay to hand was that of 'prophet', and there is good evidence that many people used this of Jesus, and that Jesus accepted it, as far as it went. Mark records (11.27f. // Matt. 21.23f. // Luke 27.1f.) a head-on confrontation between Jesus and the authorities when they demand, 'By what authority are you doing these things, or who gave you this authority to do them?' (He had just cleansed the temple.) As was his habit, he turned back the question on the questioner, 'Was the baptism of John from heaven or from men? . . . for all held that John was a real prophet'. By his answer Jesus implied that his authority also was prophetic. Even some Pharisees accepted this estimate. Simon the Pharisee expostulated at his dinner party over the outrageous anointing of Jesus' feet: 'If this man were a prophet, he would have known who and what sort of a woman this is who is touching him, for she is a sinner.' (Luke 7.36f.) The disciples walking to Emmaus cannot find a better word with which to describe their dead master, '. . . a prophet mighty in deed and word before God and all the people . . .' (Luke 24.19).

It seems that Jesus accepted this estimate of himself. Luke (alone) records (13.31) a saying of Jesus which bears every sign of authenticity. Jesus, on being warned to flee from Herod, replies, 'Go and tell that fox, "Behold, I cast out demons and perform cures today and tomorrow, and the third day I finish my course . . . for it cannot be that a prophet should perish away from Jerusalem."' There follows immediately his bitter lament over the doomed city.

Foresight is one of the characteristics of prophecy, but only because it follows as a clear deduction from insight. So Jesus predicts the end, both of Jerusalem, and in particular of the temple (Mark 13. 1–2 // Matt. 24. 1–2 // Luke 21. 5–6). It seems fairly certain that he predicted on three occasions his own coming death (Mark 8.31; 9.31; 10.33 and parallels), and that he believed that death was not going to be the end. At the Last Supper he says, 'Truly I say to you, I shall not drink again of the fruit of the vine until that day when I drink it new with you in the kingdom of God' (Mark 14.25 // Matt. 26.29 // Luke 22.18). Earlier he had warned his disciples that they too would have to drink his cup and be baptized with his baptism (Mark 10.39 // Matt. 20.23). As for Jesus' insight into the hearts of the men and women with whom he had to deal, instances in all four gospels abound. They are summed up in John 2.25, 'he knew what was in man'.

The gospels do not provide much evidence about the nature of the divine inspiration. Jesus hears the divine voice at his baptism, repeated at the transfiguration, assuring him of his divine standing, but how much was seen or heard by bystanders on each occasion it is hard to know. One passage, from Q, is remarkable, and is so unlike all the other synoptic material that it has been called 'a bolt from the Johannine blue':

> At that time Jesus declared, '. . . All things have been delivered to me by my Father; and no one knows the Son except the Father, and no one knows the Father except the Son and anyone to whom the Son chooses to reveal him.' Matthew continues, 'Come to me, all who labour and are heavy laden, and I will give you rest. Take my yoke upon you, and learn from me; for I am gentle and lowly in heart, and you will find rest for your souls. For my yoke is easy, and my burden is light'
> (Matt. 11. 25–30; cf. Luke 10. 21–22).

Here is that close personal knowledge of God which lies at the heart of the prophetic experience, but closer than any prophet knew. It is not a prize to be hoarded, but the gift of the Son for his disciples. It constitutes a transformation of life, and is not a new code of rules. Unlike the Law of Moses it is a yoke which sits lightly because it is perfectly adjusted to every human need. This is vividly depicted in the Sermon on the Mount (Matt. 5–7) where Jesus revises the Law of Moses out of all recognition. He gives instead brilliant sketches of what life looks and feels like under God's rule. In that service, penetrating to the intents and thoughts of the heart, people find their perfect freedom.

His own personal authority sounds through the Sermon in the repeated formula, 'You have heard that it was said to the men of old . . . But I say to you . . .' This emphasis on the first person is underlined in the Fourth Gospel with the formula, 'Truly, truly (*amēn, amēn*), I say to you . . .'. The use of *amēn* in this way is unusual, and in the gospels it is used exclusively to strengthen important declarations of Jesus, when it becomes the New Testament equivalent of the prophetic 'Thus saith the Lord'.

The authority which Jesus claimed was not to remain his private possession. He gathered a group of disciples around him, and in good time he sends them out to exercise his delegated authority. All three synoptic gospels record a mission of the twelve (Mark 6. 1–13 // Matt. 9.35 // Luke 9. 1–6) and Luke knows of a further mission of seventy (or seventy-two) (Luke 10. 1–20). The briefing was simple: 'He called the twelve together and gave them power and authority over all demons and to cure diseases, and he sent them out to preach the kingdom of God and to heal' (Luke 9. 1–2). Both Matthew and Luke include the saying, in either its positive or negative form, 'He who receives you receives me, and he who receives me receives him who sent me' (*ton aposteilanta me*) (Matt. 10.40 // Luke 10.16).

The final commission given to the disciples by the risen Lord on the first Easter Day as recorded by John (20.23) is to receive the Holy Spirit and with it the power to forgive or retain sins. This commission is the same as that given to Peter in Matt. 16.19, and to the twelve in Matt. 18.18. The issue of binding or loosing became one of key importance in the life of the early church.

The mysterious authority of Jesus which impressed all who met him and which finally led to his death (for it undermined the authority of the Pharisees as custodians of the Law and the authority of the Sadducees as custodians of the temple) is matched by the mysterious title Son of Man which Jesus chose for himself. It has been the subject of innumerable scholarly works, but the results are not now much clearer. Two features, however, stand out. First, the humanity. The original Aramaic *bar nasha* means simply 'man' or 'the man'. There can be no doubt about Jesus' total self-identification with the human race. Second, however, is an eschatological reference which appears twice in Mark (13.26 and 14.62). At his trial Jesus is recorded as saying in answer to the high priest's question whether he is the Christ, the Son of the Blessed: 'I am; and you will see the Son of Man sitting at the right hand of Power, and coming with the clouds of heaven'. In the background is the vision of Daniel (7.13f.) where he sees one like a son of man coming with the clouds of heaven to the Ancient of Days to be given an everlasting dominion over all peoples. The title was not apparently used of Jesus after his death and resurrection. It appears only once in the New Testament outside the gospels, and that in a vision of the ascended Christ (Acts 7.56).

The authority of Jesus did not fit into any category of human authority because its origin was with God. The nearest human category was that of 'prophet', but that was inadequate. If Jesus could say of John the Baptist, '. . . to see a prophet? Yes, I tell you, and more than a prophet . . .' (Matt. 11.9), how much more does that apply to himself. He was conscious of being sent forth by the Father with the Father's authority. What of the authority of those whom he sent forth?

3

Apostolic Authority

THE New Testament is not a handbook of church order, any more than it is a handbook of morals, but important guidance about church order (and about morals) may be gathered from its pages. The evidence is fragmentary and of different types. Luke sets out in Acts to give a continuous history of the main stream of early church development, but it was published at least a generation after Pentecost, and presents a somewhat idealised version of that development. Paul, on the other hand, was an apostle *par excellence*, but quite an exceptional one. The authorship of some of the epistles is disputed but we shall assume that Galatians, 1 and 2 Corinthians, Philippians and Romans (at least) are to be attributed to the apostle.

The young church grew out of the earliest Christian community as it proclaimed the good news that God had raised Jesus from the dead. This fact, sealed by the gift of the Spirit, formed the basis of the apostolic proclamation of Jesus' Messiahship, and those who heard the good news were bidden to turn around in their view of life and join the Christian community by baptism. (See, for example, Acts 2. 1–42). There was a sense of tremendous joy, enthusiasm and close community, but all were not equal. The twelve (and their names are given by Luke in Acts 1.13) were earlier than the church, with an antecedent authority, and one of their first tasks was to choose a successor for Judas Iscariot to complete their number. This process was never again repeated, for example after the martyrdom of James, the brother of John (Acts 12.2). It seems that the twelve as a group did not play a central part in ruling the early church, despite Luke's idealised reconstruction of the story in the early chapters of Acts, and that they finally disappeared by disbandment or death. When Paul is recalling for the Galatian Christians his earliest days as a Christian he says (Gal. 1. 16–19);

> I did not confer with flesh or blood, nor did I go up to Jerusalem to those who were apostles before me, but I went away into Arabia; and again I returned to Damascus. Then after three years I went up to Jerusalem to visit Cephas, and remained with him fifteen days. But I saw none of the other apostles except James the Lord's brother . . . Then after fourteen years I went up again to Jerusalem . . . and I laid before them (but privately before those who were of repute) the gospel which I preach among the Gentiles . . .

It is remarkable that Paul does not mention the twelve on either occasion, and that among 'the other disciples' he includes James the Lord's brother who was not one of the twelve. John states specifically (7.5), '. . . for even his brothers did not believe in him', and so James must have been converted subsequently, perhaps at the resurrection, for the traditional list which Paul recounts contained an appearance to him (1 Cor. 15.7). The same list concludes, 'then to all the apostles' although the twelve have already been included. Stories of the missionary journeys of the other members of the twelve, as for example, that of Thomas to India, are legends of the second century and later, as are their martyrdoms, apart from Peter and Paul, James and John. The twelve find their eternal memorial in the holy city Jerusalem coming down out of heaven from God, 'whose walls had twelve foundations, and on them the twelve names of the twelve apostles of the Lamb' (Rev. 21. 10–14).

Undoubtedly Peter was the leading figure in the tradition of both gospel and church. The nickname 'Peter' (in Aramaic *Cephas*) bestowed on him by Jesus (Mark 3.16) bore witness at least to his potential rock-like character, though scholars are almost unanimous in affirming that the words of Jesus recorded in Mark 8 and Luke 9, 'And I tell you, you are Peter, and on this rock I will build my church' are a later

ecclesiastical elaboration. Peter was the first to see the risen
Christ, according to Paul, Luke and John, and with this act
of faithful recognition the Christian Church began. He
believed that he had been entrusted with a special mission to
the Jewish world, as Paul had to the Gentile (Gal. 2.7), though
Acts stresses his care for Gentiles as well (8.14; 10.1f.; 15.7).
Paul records his personal approval for the crucial change from
a Jewish to a universal mission (Gal. 2.7). Peter was certainly
the central figure of the early community in Jerusalem, and
Acts portrays him as its leader and spokesman, as for example
at the crucial debate about circumcision for Jewish Christians
(Acts 15). But he was no oriental potentate, nor even the first
bishop of Rome. Paul later in his letter to the Galatians (2.9)
refers to 'James and Cephas and John, who were reputed to
be pillars', and goes on to describe a painful confrontation
with Peter at Antioch where 'the pillar' had not lived up to
his reputation but had deferred to James and the circumcision
party. Peter left Jerusalem (Acts 12.17) for an unstated desti-
nation and disappears from the scene. We do not know for
certain the manner of his death, but Clement of Rome in his
First Letter (ch. 5) holds up Peter and Paul together as martyrs for the faith. Other early tradition located his death at
Rome.

James, the Lord's brother, designated by Paul 'an apostle',
plays an interesting part as leader of a strong Judaistic party
in the church at Jerusalem, whose spokesman he is in Acts
15. Other of the Lord's relatives are also mentioned: at the
very beginning of his story Luke links the twelve with 'the
women and Mary the mother of Jesus, and with his brothers'
(Acts 1.14). Paul also knows of missionary journeys carried
out by these brothers: 'Do we not have the right to be accompanied by a wife, as the other apostles and the brothers of the
Lord and Cephas?' (1 Cor. 9.5). These persons had a unique
standing as blood-relatives and clearly could have no successors.

In a similar way the first apostolic generation could neither
be continued nor renewed. Their commission was based on a
personal experience of the risen Christ, but such appearances

were not constantly repeated. The commission was similar to that experienced by the Old Testament prophets, but now it springs from the risen Jesus who is a present reality for ever and for everyone, and whose Spirit is the Spirit which was promised at the End. Bishops succeeded apostles, but they did not call themselves apostles. The authority of the apostles is subordinate to the unique authority of Jesus. He abides in them, works in them, and employs them. The New Testament does not know of an apostolic 'office' as such with a clear-cut organisation and manner of working, though the first apostolic men governed their communities and were held in honour. We may detect warnings against the dangers of power in the gospel injunction:

> But you are not to be called rabbi, for you have one teacher, and you are all brethren. And call no man your father on earth, for you have one Father who is in heaven. Neither be called masters, for you have one master, the Christ.
>
> (Matt. 23. 8–10)

In all the Johannine literature, gospels and epistles, apostleship is not mentioned. That there were strains and tensions in the early community there is no doubt, but we should avoid importing modern ideas of ecclesiastical parties or hierarchy.

We have only one detailed description of what it felt like to feel and think and act as an apostle, and that is from Paul's own hand, and he is in every sense an exception:

> Last of all, as to one untimely born, he appeared also unto me. For I am the least of the apostles, unfit to be called and apostle, because I persecuted the church of God.
>
> (1 Cor. 15. 7–8).

From such an unlikely background he, the Pharisee of Pharisees, was forcefully summoned by the Lord to be *the* apostle to the Gentiles. By what authority did he perform this extraordinary mission? He had to defend it against many challenges, especially those Christians who still felt the need to defend a Judaistic legalism. In the first place the call came from the Lord directly and personally. Luke recounts that episode in detail no less than three times (with variations) in Acts 9, 22, and 26. In the second place Paul saw himself to be one of the apostolic community centred on Jerusalem. It needed three years of meditation in the desert for Paul to realise what this call was going to mean to him, for it implied nothing less than a reversal of everything he had been brought up to hold most precious. After that he went to Jerusalem to confer with the leaders, and subsequently organised a collection for the poor church there, an act to which he attached great importance as repaying a debt of gratitude to the primitive community and as marking a bond of unity between the churches (Gal. 2.10; 1 Cor. 16.1f.). His congregations are no independent guilds because they are all united with each other and with the original Jewish congregation. But this connection carried no sort of subordination, least of all to the Judaisers. Against those who pull rank he writes with severe irony,

> From those who were reputed to be something (what they were makes no difference to me; God shows no partiality) – those, I say who were of repute added nothing to me. . .
>
> (Gal. 2.6).

Paul is well aware that his own personal qualities must match the gospel with which he is entrusted. In 2 Corinthians 11–12 he has to stand up to slanderous assertions that he is unspiritual, infirm and unreliable, and he makes his defence, but as if his heart were not in it. In any boasting he speaks as a fool; and his main boasting must be about his weakness, for that is where God's strength lies. He lambasts the spiritual self-indulgence of the supposedly perfect (1 Cor. 4. 8–9).

How does this affect the authority he has for his congregations? He is their founder, their spiritual father (1 Cor. 4.15), their nursemaid (1 Thess. 2.7); they are his joy, his crown (Phil. 4.1), his letter of recommendation (2 Cor. 3.2); their relationship will reach fulfilment on the day of the Lord Jesus (2 Cor. 12.14). In the meantime he has to decide and regulate, reprove, ignore, threaten. He claims the right to be supported, and also the right to forego support if he wishes (1 Cor. 9.4f.). But although his authority is of the highest it carries no spiritual control or subordination: 'Not that we lord it over your faith; we work with you for your joy, for you to stand firm in your faith (2 Cor. 1.24). He cannot give orders; he cannot create a norm; he can only recall them to prior teaching so that they can re-affirm it freely (Rom. 15.15). If he bids them imitate himself that can only be because his imitation is of Christ (1 Cor. 11.1).

On particular moral issues Paul takes for granted long-standing moral commandments. The classic case concerns marriage in 1 Cor. 7. Paul accepts without question Jesus' teaching about divorce, but he sharply distinguishes from it his own advice about the separation of unbelieving partners. Again, concerning the unmarried, Paul gives what he is careful to say is his opinion, that in the particular circumstances of that time it is well for a person to remain as he or she is. He again emphasises his own judgement about a woman remarrying after the death of her husband. He concludes on a note of humble confidence, 'And I think that I have the Spirit of God'.

Even on essential matters of faith Paul will not exercise unqualified supremacy. His children are also brethren, and the apostle is servant (*doulos*) for Jesus' sake (2 Cor. 4.5). They are co-workers (2 Cor. 6.1), co-strivers in prayer (Rom. 15.30), co-encouragers (Rom. 1.12), co-prisoners (Rom. 16.7), co-rulers (1 Cor. 4.8), co-sufferers (1 Cor. 12.26), co-diers and co-livers (2 Cor. 7.3). Even his verdict on the incest at Corinth is not quite unilateral: 'I have already pronounced judgement in the name of the Lord Jesus . . .' (1 Cor. 5.4). And later in the same epistle, on the subject of eating food which had formed part of an idolatrous sacrifice, 'I speak as to sensible men; judge for yourselves what I say'. His authority as an apostle is to build up the congregation, and this can only be done by candour, love and patience.

The only limit for Paul is where Christ and his gospel is being betrayed, and all Paul's warnings are reminders, not imperatives, recalling the indicative of what God had done in Christ and how he had called them to his service. Paul never calls the apostles the foundation of the church; Christ alone is that (1 Cor 3.11; but see Eph. 2.20). The emphasis on the unique importance of the apostolic office is post-Pauline.

How then did this remarkable organisation without constitution or rank actually work? For Paul, the organising principle of the congregation is the Spirit, the sign of whose presence is freedom, leading to loving service. (His argument is fully worked out in 1 Cor. 12–14.) No one is completely useless, and in any case the weaker call for greater honour. Every Christian is charismatic, having some spiritual grace, even if not one of the outstanding ones like prophesying, teaching, performing miracles, healing, helping, administering, or 'speaking in tongues'. These were valuable as gifts of God to the community, but what was of vital importance was the power of sanctifying love, because that alone could ensure that there was no discord in the body and that members might have the same care for one another.

The gifts of prophecy and teaching are closely linked with the apostolate, and are highly esteemed by Paul for building up the congregation. We may suppose (for we have no definition provided) that the New Testament prophet, like his Old Testament predecessor, was one who claimed to speak from the Lord with direct personal authority words of encouragement, admonition, censure and promise. (This was different from the gift of teaching which was concerned with the handing on and interpretation of a received Christian tradition.) The prophets, however, stand under apostolic authority, and are to be tested against the pattern of faith (this is the apparent meaning of Romans 12.6, '... if prophecy, in proportion to our faith'), just as the prophets of the Old Testament could be (see Deut. 13.5). 'Let two or three prophets speak, and let the others weigh what is said' (1 Cor. 14.29). This is not democracy but the discerning of spirits which itself is one of the spiritual gifts (12.10).

Paul never appeals to one group in a congregation as if it were responsible for the spiritual well-being of others. He does mention *kubernēsis* (a Greek spelling of the Latin *gubernatio*) which means literally 'steering' and can be translated 'governing', but the term carries none of the managerial overtones associated with it today and comes last in the list of gifts in 12.27. Paul knows of, and recommends, no organising of worship nor a president at worship: they are to wait for one another (11.23) and each shall bring his own spiritual contribution. There appears to be no financial officer since Paul has to make his own arrangements for taking the collection (16.2). There is, in short, no élite, but all members are equally involved in the corporate whole where the Spirit alone is sovereign.

Nevertheless in some congregations an embryonic system of 'elders' had already come into being. Those were Judaeo-Christian churches, whereas Paul's mission did not start from Jerusalem or Galilee but from Antioch, where we hear of no presbyters but only teachers and prophets (Acts 11.27; 13.1; 21.10). In churches of Paul's own foundation traces appear of other offices coming into being. His letter to Philippi, probably one of his latest, is addressed to '. . . all the saints . . . with the bishops and deacons . . .', but this translation would be less misleading if it were 'overseers and servants' because the terms have certainly not yet acquired the sacral overtones which they were so potently to develop. No further reference or appeal is made to these officers in the letter.

This Pauline version of a church as a free fellowship animated by the varied contribution of spirit-based ministries did not die with him. The Epistle to the Hebrews, the *Epistle of Barnabas* and the *Didachē* (the last two variously dated between AD 70 and 130) still bear witness to it, but it is apparent that the first fine careless rapture is fading. Signs of stress and fatigue are appearing: Hebrews is concerned with apostasy (6.4f.) and has to exhort backsliders to regular church attendance (10.25); liturgy is becoming prescribed, as with the arrangements for baptism laid down in *Didachē* 7 and for the eucharist in 9–10. False teaching has to countered, and Hebrews bids the congregation to remember its leaders and submit to them (13. 7–17). The *Didachē* is much concerned with false prophets who are trying to make a living out of it by moving on from place to place. Such a person's ministry is to be tested: he should not be expected to stay for more than three days; he should not ask for money; his manner of life has to accord with his teaching; but if he speaks in the Spirit (that is, in tongues) that is a proof of his genuineness (11). Every true prophet who desires to settle is worthy of his food. A more stable ministry, however, is encouraged:

> Appoint for yourselves therefore bishops and deacons worthy of the Lord, men who are meek and not lovers of money, and true and approved; for unto you they also perform the service of the prophets and teachers. Therefore despise them not for they are your honourable men along with the prophets and teachers.
>
> (*Didachē*, 15)

The epistle which bears the title of 1 Peter is markedly different. It is addressed to 'the exiles of the dispersion' in Asia Minor, and seeks to rally churches threatened by a coming persecution. The new Christian self-consciousness is given classic expression: 'But you are a chosen race, a royal priesthood, a holy nation, God's own people' (2.9). But the congregation is now stratified into elders and the younger. The former are bidden, by a fellow-elder, to tend the flock of God 'not for shameful gain but eagerly, not as domineering . . . but being examples'; and the younger are to be subject to the elders, (5. 1–5). Here is a notion of community very different from Paul's, and it is noteworthy that this document, issued to the churches of the Pauline mission field, should be published in the name not of Paul, the apostle of Antioch, but of Peter, the apostle of Jerusalem.

4

Elders and Discipline in the Early Church

JEWISH elders were entirely bound by the Law and the Tradition; for them prophecy played no active part. Christians, however, are under a new sovereignty of God. The Lord who frees from legalism is the reality of the future, as he is also present in the Spirit, as he is also an objective fact of the past, and his words and deeds, especially the resurrection, must be attested. The elders represented that tradition and were natural leaders. Only Paul is out of step; he knows of no leading class or group, though he knows the tradition well enough, but bases everything on the life of the Spirit. The next generation could not keep this up, with growing numbers, the threat of heresy, and flagging zeal, though the adoption of a new system is not necessarily a less spiritual step. Luke tries to understand the gospel according to Paul, but champions unPauline elders. In Acts 20 he portrays the apostle at Miletus summoning the elders of the Church of Ephesus, but in verse 28 they are designated *episkopoi*, and so it seems that Luke fuses the two traditions of Pauline bishops with Petrine elders and pastors.

The Epistle of James, with its strong Jewish background, refers only to elders or presbyters and not to bishops and deacons. It expects elders to be called to minister to the sick and probably to exercise a ministry of absolution, though this is also shared by the wider church (5. 13–18). For Paul, healing was simply one of the gifts of the Spirit. In 1 Peter the congregation is divided into natural, not spiritual, categories: slaves and masters, wives and husbands, younger and elders who are later appealed to as 'shepherds'. In Revelation the summation of this hierarchical grading is magnificently

26

portrayed in the twenty-four elders seated on their thrones wearing golden crowns (4.10). Other evidence, on a more mundane level, is forthcoming in two documents from Rome, probably in the last decade of the century (though the second may be later). The first, the *First Epistle of Clement* is contained within the New Testament in Codex Alexandrinus, and the second, *The Shepherd of Hermas* is similarly found in Codex Sinaiticus: so both enjoyed considerable respect in the early church. The first was written by bishop Clement in the name of the Roman church to the Christian brotherhood of Corinth where a feud had broken out and presbyters, appointed by the apostles or their immediate successors, had been unlawfully deposed. The second records a series of teaching visions by the divine Shepherd to Hermas for the Christians in Rome. In both the leading men are called both bishops and presbyters but the terms are not identical. The bishop's office is now a permanent position of recognised standing, whereas the office of elder is more fluid, varying from appointed rulers to those respected for age and wisdom (*1 Clem.* 3). In an important passage Clement writes

> And our apostles knew through our Lord Jesus Christ that there would be strife over the name of the bishop's office. For this cause, therefore, having received complete foreknowledge, they appointed the aforesaid persons, and afterwards they provided a continuance, that if these should fall asleep, other approved men should succeed to their ministration. Those therefore who were appointed by them, or afterwards by other men of repute with the consent of the whole church, and have ministered unblameably to the flock of Christ . . . – these men we consider to be unjustly thrust out from their ministration. For it will be no light sin for us if we thrust out those who have offered the gifts of the bishop's office unblameably and holily.
>
> (*1 Clem.* 44).

Certain elders, therefore, are appointed to the office of bishop the most obvious feature of which is 'to offer the gifts', that is, to preside at the eucharist, though it should not be assumed that this was their only, or even primary, function: the term denotes general oversight.

The shape of the Pauline community has therefore been combined, as in 1 Peter, with the presbyteral system, and again the element of order has taken precedence over the element of spirit. Here for the first time the presbyteral system is explicitly defended as a part of the apostolic tradition, with a significant appeal to the cultic provisions of the Old Testament as if these had been enjoined by Jesus:

> . . . while they follow the institutions of their Master they cannot go wrong. For unto the high-priest his proper services (*leitourgiai*) have been assigned, and to the priests their proper office (*topos*) is appointed, and upon the levites their proper ministrations (*diakonai*) are laid. The layman (*ho laikos anthrōpos*) is bound by the layman's ordinances.
>
> (*1 Clem.* 40).

For Paul the cult was dead: for Clement it is an essential datum of the faith. Here indeed may be located the origins not only of the three-fold clericalised ministry but also of canon law. Clement's appeal for a sense of due order is reinforced by an appeal to nature (20) and to the Roman army (37); it has been detached from any specifically Christian meaning.

This presbyteral/episcopal system is already traditional in Rome by Clement's time, and must also have taken over in Asia Minor and Syria because we find it in Ignatius, Polycarp and the Pastoral Epistles. Ignatius was the second or third bishop of Antioch and he wrote seven letters in the first decade of the second century while on his way to Rome and the amphitheatre under guard, having been condemned to death. From two halting-places in Asia Minor he writes to five local churches as well as to the church of Rome, and to Polycarp, bishop of Smyrna. The outstanding feature is the advanced state of hierarchical order, with a strong conception of monarchical episcopacy. The clergy are sharply divided into grades, with the presbyterate as the bishop's council, his 'spiritual garland', and below them deacons, servants of the Church of God:

> . . . let all men respect the deacons as Jesus Christ, even as they should respect the bishop as being a type of the Father and the presbyters as the council of God and as the college of apostles. Apart from these there is not even the name of a church.
>
> (*To the Trallians*, 2–3).

Here are clearly reflected the early stages of a three-level clergy, but Ignatius' understanding of it is quite different from the legal structure of 1 Clement. For him the whole Church is united with the Christ of Colossians, and this unity is manifested in a system comprising the episcopate, presbyterate and diaconate. He is fond of using musical images of harmony, that the presbytery be attuned to the bishop even as its strings to the lyre, so that all may form a harmonious chorus taking their key-note from God (*To the Ephesians*, 4). This structure, firmly unified in love, is closely connected with the idea of a universal or catholic Church:

> Let no man do anything pertaining to the church apart from the bishop. Let that be held as a valid eucharist which is under the bishop or one to whom he shall have committed it. Wheresoever the bishop shall appear, there let the people be; even as where Jesus may be, there is the universal (*katholikē*) Church. It is not lawful apart from the bishop either to baptise or to hold a love-feast; but whatsoever he shall approve, this is well-pleasing also to God.
>
> (*To the Smyrnaeans*, 8).

We may detect here administrative complications arising from the increasing size of city congregations. Originally the bishop was the one who presided at every eucharist, but now it is becoming necessary for the bishop to depute this prime responsibility, presumably to his presbyters. It seems, however, that he can still keep in personal touch with each member of his congregation because he writes to Polycarp (ch. 5), 'It is proper for men or women marrying to make their union with the consent of the bishop, so that the marriage may be according to the Lord and not according to lust'. In the same paragraph he calls all his fellow Christians his brothers and sisters.

To whom is the bishop responsible? Ignatius appeals neither to a clear definition of ministry (he never mentions the fact that he is a bishop), nor to the traditional scriptures. He calls himself regularly at the beginning of each letter 'God-bearer' (*theophoros*), but he also uses this term for all Christians (*To the Ephesians,* 9). His final appeal is to the Spirit of God, and under this inspiration he 'cried out' and 'spoke with a loud voice, with God's own voice' when he was among the Christians at Philadelphia (ch. 7). His is a distinctive combination of spiritual and official, perhaps owing something to the enthusiasm of Antioch. It has little in common with later Roman ideas but exercised a great influence on Eastern Orthodox development.

The other important document of the period consists of the group of Pastoral Epistles, the letters in the New Testament ascribed to Paul and addressed to Timothy and Titus. But they breathe a very different air from the Pauline corpus. Style, doctrine, and the stage of church organisation all point to a considerably later date, well into the second century, though the letters may well contain pieces of earlier tradition, some even from Paul himself. It is likely that they are the product of a bishop/presbyter of Asia Minor designed for local churches as something of a systematic treatise on church order (and the device of ascribing authorship to a well-known personality of former times was then considered in no way dishonest). It is assumed that the church is already ordered, and rules are set out, similar to those in 1 Peter, for mutual relationships between older and younger, masters and slaves, and husbands and wives. This is now 'sound doctrine' (Titus 2.1). Widows have now become a regular order in the church and rules are given for their enrolment and conduct (1 Tim. 5. 9–16). (This was to become a great burden on the clergy in later times, as John Chrysostom knew.) In particular, the epistles are concerned with the way in which the offices of bishop, presbyter, and deacon are to be carried out. 'Bishop' is always mentioned in the singular, indicating that monarchical episcopacy is now the prevailing system. Where bishops and deacons are mentioned, generally presbyters are not, and this may reflect a conflation of two different traditions; the clumsy transition in Titus 1. 5–7 from 'presbyters' to 'bishop' supports this contention.

The bishop is beginning to rise above his fellow-elders over whom he has judicial authority (1 Tim. 5.19). His office is above all one of teaching, principally to guide Christians away from gnostic 'myths and endless genealogies which promote speculations' to 'the divine training that is in faith' (1 Tim 1. 3–5), which is not separable from prayer (1 Tim. 2.1) or from the exercise of discipline (Titus, 1.11). No reference is made to the conduct or leading of worship.

The epistles raise for the first time the question of the spiritual relationship between office-holder and office, a fundamental question of pastoral theology, posed and dealt with by one who is a genuine shepherd of souls. The office of bishop is a noble task (1 Tim. 3.1f.) and it seems possible that candidates could apply for it. Youth was no bar (1 Tim. 4.12), and purely natural abilities are among the qualifications, including a good reputation. Some maturity in the faith is necessary. Candidates for the diaconate should undergo some probationary testing. The quality of their family life is an important indicator both for bishop/presbyters and for deacons. There is now an official rite of 'ordination' seen as a sacramental act for the bestowing of power and the gift of the Spirit (2 Tim. 1.6).

This is not a part of the Pauline tradition; it springs, rather from the soil of the presbyterate and its Jewish background. On the other hand, the Pastorals' concept of office is saved from undue authoritarianism by two limitations; first the person ordained does not become thereby immune from error and sin, and may indeed make shipwreck of the faith (1 Tim. 1. 18–20); second, the organisation of spiritual leadership is not seen as self-contained sacred law, as it is in 1 Clement. It is 'sound teaching', the genuine apostolic tradition, which gives the office its meaning.

The presbyterate was not automatically to be found everywhere. The author of the Second and Third Letters of John describes himself as 'the elder' but this carries no connotation of membership of a presbyterate. He is rather a prophet or teacher of the earlier type, one of those 'elders' to whose witness Papias and Irenaeus appealed. The letters are noticeably lacking in details of ministerial organisation. Diotrephes (who is presumably a bishop) does not acknowledge the elder's authority, and the writer proposes to come in person to confront the offender with the testimony of the truth.

The question of the authority to forgive sins and its relation to ecclesiastical office became a matter of major importance in the second and third centuries, and it is certainly present in the earliest strata of the tradition. The right to forgive in God's name is claimed as the new possibility open to Christianity as distinct from Judaism. The First Letter of John has sin as a principal theme, in the depth of the Christian paradox that on the one hand 'if we say we have no sin, we deceive ourselves (1.10), and on the other, 'No one born of God commits sin; for God's nature abides in him, and he cannot sin because he is born of God' (3.9). The letter, however, makes no mention of particular rules for the good ordering of church life.

The commission to bind and loose is given by Jesus to the disciples in Matt. 18.18, and in that paragraph a disciplinary process is sketched for a brother who has sinned, though how the proceedings worked we do not know. No reference is made to the nature or severity of the sin; the sentence is final; and the sentence is of the whole church with the aim not of punishment but of forgiveness, to win back the erring brother. Such a procedure is conceivable only in the very simplest community.

The other gospel passage referring to 'the power of the keys' is Matthew's version of Peter's confession containing the words (significantly absent from the other evangelists):

> And I tell you, you are Peter, and on this rock I will build my church, and the powers of death shall not prevail against it. I will give you the keys of the kingdom of heaven, and whatever you bind on earth shall be bound in heaven, and whatever you loose on earth shall be loosed in heaven.
>
> (Matt. 16. 18–19).

Is it possible that Jesus intended to 'found' his Church upon Peter? The scholars are deeply divided. The whole Lucan-Pauline presentation of the outworking of the gospel in the Church does not portray Peter as the foundation-stone of the Church. The passage is best understood as a mark of veneration by a congregation founded by him, perhaps on Syrian soil.

The *Shepherd of Hermas* is an extended penitential sermon, but repentance is left to the individual; there is no programme of discipline and no mention of excommunication, expulsion or punishment. Even Ignatius has nothing to say about excommunication or re-admission of penitents, and his silence cannot be accidental. As for heretics, Christ alone can loose their sin; they should be avoided (*To the Ephesians*, 7).

The *Epistle of Polycarp* and the Pastoral Epistles reflect the same situation. The Pastorals provide more detail about action to be taken against heretics. The church official is called to be the guardian of sound doctrine and take his stand against disobedient workers of mischief (1 Tim. 6.4f.). The most severe measures to be taken against heretics (if Hymenaeus and Alexander were heretics) was that they should be 'delivered to Satan', a procedure reminiscent of that in 1 Cor. 5, as a punishment expected to result in sickness or death. Quite apart from heresy we see in the Pastorals a marked development in the process of church law. In 1 Tim. 5. 17–22 the bishop is naturally thought of as judge, or at any rate president of a church court. His sentence must be a spiritual one, and its penalties must now acquire the character of ecclesiastical penance. Mention of the laying-on of hands at first brings to mind proper care in ordination, but the immediate context suggests rather the formal act of restoration of a sinner. If that is so, then this passage is the first witness to a public act of absolution carried out by the head of a congregation.

This brief, almost casual, instruction of 'Paul' gives no hint of the enormous importance which the power of the keys was to play in the next century. It does, however, indicate that the Pastorals are later than the *Epistles* of Ignatius and the *Shepherd of Hermas*. They belong to the very end of the sub-apostolic period. First, however, the Church was confronted with another crisis, that over Gnosticism, which compelled it to consider the teaching tradition upon which its concept of authority was based.

5
Prophets and Teachers in the Second Century

THE early emergence of the presbyteral system is not be accounted for simply in terms of practical usefulness or social pressure. Elders could not have won the recognition that they did had not something in their position corresponded deeply to the spiritual needs of the Church. In particular Christians were concerned with the handing on of the faith from one generation to the next. In the second century this becomes crystallised as the apostolic succession of bishops, and attempts have often been made to trace this back to the apostolic period itself, but this is to ignore the important intervening development.

As time went on the concept of tradition became more complicated, and questions had to be asked about true and false teaching. There is no question here of a radical contrast between tradition and spirit, a notion familiar only in medieval and modern times: both orthodox and gnostics were sure that the sacred tradition can only be understood and set forth by the Holy Spirit, and so the man who hands it on must be not only informed but also transformed, must be, as in orthodox Judaism, a spiritual man.

The Catholic Church, however, differed from the heretical sects in not entrusting their tradition to chance spiritual leaders. The responsibility fell to the elders of each community, though this did not exclude free teachers, as apostles did not exclude evangelists. Close to the Lucan tradition of a harmonious church is that of the Pastoral Epistles whose dominant concern is the safeguarding of the apostolic tradition, though with no dogmatic principle yet formulated. The only unofficial teachers known are false ones, who meet with fierce condemnation (1 Tim. 4. 1f.; 2 Tim. 3 and 4; Titus 1.9f.). Even Ignatius of Antioch, the champion of episcopal authority, lays no claim to any doctrine of apostolic tradition or succession. Clement of Rome speaks in juristic terms of Christ sending the apostles and the apostles appointing the first bishops or elders, but he does not link the office with the preservation of tradition.

The critical stage in the doctrinal development of 'tradition' and 'succession' occurs in the middle of the second century, not in the sphere of catholic Christianity but in the gnostic sects with their cult of the free teacher. The earliest and clearest evidence comes from the *Letter to Flora* written by the gnostic Ptolemaeus (in Epiphanius, *Panarion*, 33.7) who values 'the apostolic tradition (*apostolikēs paradoseōs*) which we too have received by succession (*ek diadochēs*) after the canonising of all the words in the teaching of our Saviour'.

This concept of tradition (*paradosis*) and succession (*diadochē*) originated in the philosophical schools of the ancient Greek world as a guarantee of the purity of the teaching deriving from an original master. The young Catholic Church did not at first take kindly to this concept. The author of the Pastoral Epistles in contending against gnostic myths, does not talk of 'tradition' but rather of a 'deposited trust' (*parathēkē*), namely the apostolic teaching (1 Tim. 6.20). So too the Epistle of Jude (v.3) contends for 'the faith which was once for all delivered to the saints'. In the same scriptural vein Papias, Clement of Alexandria and even Hippolytus of Rome appeal to the elders who have been acquainted with the apostles or their disciples ('elders' here meaning simply seniors in the faith). Eusebius (*Ecclesiastical History*, 5.20.1) values Irenaeus towards the end of the second century because that bishop in his youth had heard Polycarp speak and Polycarp could go back to the apostle John and the first sub-apostolic generation.

The new and Catholic form of this concept hardened into the succession of monarchical bishops, as is clearly set out around AD 180 by Hegesippus, a Christian man of letters from the east, fragments of whose work are preserved by Eusebius. He aimed to present 'the undistorted tradition of the apostolic preaching', and to that end travelled to Rome by way of Corinth. He approved what he found and tried to demonstrate the guarantee of purity by compiling a list of bishops of Rome from Eleutherus, his own contemporary, back to the apostle Peter. The term *diadochē* now assumes the technical sense of 'a list of bishops'. Tertullian, a few years later in N. Africa, uses the same argument, giving it a more legalist colour (*De Praescriptione Haereticorum*, 37.20.32).

Hippolytus, bishop of Rome in the early third century, is called to expose the errors of heretics, and his main weapon is the concept of tradition:

> No one will refute them except the Holy Spirit handed down in the Church, whom the apostles first received and passed on to men of orthodox belief. We are their successors, and share in the same gifts of high priesthood and teaching . . .
>
> (*Refutation of all Heresies*, 1 pref. 6)

In Hippolytus also we meet for the first time a clear understanding of ordination as sacramental, with special grace for each office, and a sanctifying power in episcopal consecration. Although, however, consecration is taken to convey a special gift of the Holy Spirit, a confessor or a man who demonstrably already has a gift like healing can be admitted to the ranks of the clergy without further ordination (*Apostolic Tradition*, 10.1). It is apparent that that the pneumato-charismatic and the official-sacramental conceptions here exist side by side without great strain. This growing sacralisation of ordination is important not only for the ministry but also for church politics. Only one generation leads on to Cyprian, but that is a world away.

One early set of possibilities was explored but found to have no future, that of the Ebionite Judaeo-Christian congregations in Transjordan. Elders and bishops are little regarded: what matters is the class of teachers forming a tightly organised Christian rabbinate who see Jesus as the new Moses. The traditional writings are protected by minute regulations and oaths. The law has triumphed over the Spirit. There could be no future for such a church because it had lost its soul.

By contrast, around the year AD 172 there exploded in gentile Phrygia, in Asia Minor, a volcanic renewal movement drawing its name from its founder, Montanus. (That Montanus himself claimed to be the Paraclete in person was a broadside of later propaganda.) The movement predicted the imminent end of the world, and called for a rigorous holiness of life as a challenge to growing worldliness. These features, coupled with the frenzy which seized ecstatic leaders, caused the Church much disquiet and required it to try to differentiate between genuine prophecy and demonic possession.

The tests used in the early Church were dogmatic and ethical. False prophets are predicted in Mark 13.22, and encountered in Acts in the persons of Elymas (13.6) and Simon Magus (8.18). Possession itself is no guarantee of true prophecy, though there was a reluctance to test a prophet speaking in the Spirit, an unforgiveable sin according to *Didachē* 11. That writer prefers to test against his deeds: 'Every prophet teaching the truth, if he does not do what he teaches, is a false prophet'. There was also the stern test enjoined in 1 John 4. 1–3: '. . . every spirit which confesses that Jesus Christ has come in the flesh is of God, and every spirit which does not confess Jesus is not of God.' This writer sets forth the love of the brethren as the other side of the coin, and counterfeit currency must be withdrawn.

The Montanists were clearly not heretical: even Hippolytus has to admit that their dogma is Catholic, and Tertullian, no mean theologian, joined them. The ecstatic phenomena, however, were disturbing, not least to the Greek philosophical mind which profoundly distrusted passion because it upset the philosophical calm necessary for the exercise of reason. Tertullian himself wrote a work, unfortunately lost, in seven volumes, *On Ecstasy*, in which he argued against the 'psychics' (the merely natural people) of the Catholic Church, that one who really experiences God's glory is bound to lose his reason because he is eclipsed by the power of God. This hardly agrees with Paul's estimate in 1 Cor. 14 of speaking with tongues as one of the least gifts.

Montanism was officially condemned before 200 AD and eventually became an obscure rigorist sect, and from this time began official ecclesiastical mistrust of all the more pronounced forms of enthusiasm and ecstasy, suspect as forms of demonic possession. Raptures and visions are forced out of the Church into heresy (until monasticism creates a new home for them), and the words 'prophecy' and 'charisma' disappear from circulation.

Their place in the Church was taken by teaching, though this function underwent marked change during the second century. The first teachers are closely linked with prophets (Polycarp is described in the *Martyrdom* (16.2) as *didaskalos apostolikos kai prophētikos*), but Justin and Tertullian are both proud to continue to wear their philosopher's cloak after their conversion to Christianity, and both remain, so far as we know, laymen. In the later second century the teacher rents his own premises, gathers his own students, and launches out as a man of letters, sometimes causing concern to local Christian congregations. The outstanding figure is Clement of Alexandria, spiritually and intellectually a Greek, with an amazing familiarity with the literature and philosophy of the ancient world and with the mystery cults.

He became the first theologian to detach Christian doctrine from its 'salvation-history' and proclaim it as a new 'religion' with its own dogma and way of life, with the implication that it can be appropriated individually. He is not concerned with apostolic authority. His exegesis of Jesus' words is often wrong-headed and he quite mistakes Paul in such basic matters as the nature of the gospel, freedom, and the Spirit. He gives little value to the sacraments or to penance or to the official life of the Church. Alexander, bishop of Jerusalem, referred to 'the holy Clement, who was my master and benefactor', but the Church had not yet perceived why Clement's attitude to tradition and authority, based on pagan philosophy and philosophical idealism, was in the end incompatible with the faith it was designed to conserve.

A greater than Clement was Origen who started not as a cleric but as a layman, and founded the first ecclesiastically approved catechetical school at Alexandria around the year 200 AD. He sought ordination as a presbyter but was refused by bishop Demetrius on the grounds that he had castrated himself when young (taking literally the injunction of Jesus in Matt. 19.12). In later years he moved to Caesarea, was ordained there, and entered vigorously into church life. His father was killed in a persecution in 202, and Origen himself was imprisoned in the Decian persecution in 250, was subjected to prolonged torture, and died a few years later. Despite his outstanding intellectual gifts and his martyrdom he was never canonised.

His understanding of the Church does not start from a consitution but from the concept of each congregation as a world of spiritual gifts in which every Christian can share even without the help of official mediators (*Against Celsus*, 6.48). It is desirable that spiritual gifts should fit ecclesiastical offices, and nowhere does Origen consider the possibility of a teaching profession apart from the clergy. What is new and special in his description of the clerical vocation is the need for spirituality because every Christian is called to be spiritual, and so the cleric's own spirituality must shine out as a guide to this higher life. The cleric must therefore be an ascetic, as was Origen himself, detached as far as possible from worldly concerns, so that he may devote himself wholly to the study of God's word. So Origen presses repeatedly for the conscientious payment of church dues so that the priest will be free for God. But monastic flight he sees as a temptation, indeed a sin (*Homily on Jeremiah*, 20.8).

How do the clergy of Alexandria measure up to Origen's ideals? Most of the bishops, according to him, are worldly-minded, avaricious, haughty, quarrelsome, self-assertive, both too harsh and too complaisant, forming cliques or even anti-churches to keep themselves in office (*Homily on Genesis*, 16.5; *on Isaiah*, 7.6, etc.). Clergy use sordid methods of intrigue and demagogy to seize at office, especially the highest and most lucrative, that of bishop (*Homily on Numbers*, 9.1; 22.4; *on Leviticus*, 6.3). Clergy brag about their seniority, and do their best to see that their children or relatives will succeed them (*Homily on Numbers* 22.4). They are just like the Pharisees of old (*Commentary on Matthew*, 11.9; 16.5) – the first time this comparison appears in Christian literature.

Origen never questions the hierarchical organisation of the Church; it is a sacred datum. The function of the clergy is to instruct, intercede, and take their people's sins upon themselves so that they may make atonement for them (*Homily on Numbers*, 10.1). Origen found it all there in the Old Testament – by analogy. But he brings the gnostic idea of perfection into the context of office, and so he develops his critique along pietisitic lines, with a nostalgic yearning for the ideal age of Christians' first love in the days of the small persecuted church. To celebrate a solemn liturgy before a congregation – in the last resort anyone can do that. What matters more is the real possession of virtue and the hidden spiritual wisdom of the heart (*Homily on Leviticus*, 6.6). His view of priesthood is neither catholic nor protestant, but private, pietistic, and pastoral.

At bottom, Origen does not take seriously the distinctive character of office in the church, nor the authority which lies behind it. He does not see everything depending on the word of forgiveness spoken to the penitent in Jesus' name, but is more concerned with the constant spiritual progress which a penitent may make with the help of his minister. The concept of the gnostic teacher has been radically ecclesiasticised and projected on to the office-holder. This was not seen as a threat to ecclesiastical office: Origen had many episcopal disciples. The next period combines again the cultic notions of office with the political, and the ground for this development was prepared by Origen.

6
Cyprian, Bishop of the One Church

CYPRIAN is a younger contemporary of Origen, and they both belong to the Roman world of north Africa, Origen in Alexandria and Cyprian in Carthage; but whereas Origen, influenced by Clement, was essentially an easterner in thought, Cyprian was a westerner, a pupil of Tertullian the lawyer. Son of a rich and respected family, Cyprian was educated in Carthage and became a successful public speaker. About the year 246 he became a Christian and soon afterwards a presbyter. Within three years of his conversion he was elevated to be bishop of Carthage, the greatest and most influential church in Africa, and remained so until his martyrdom in 258.

It was a tumultuous decade. In 250 the emperor Decius launched his persecution against the Church, the first comprehensive attempt to exterminate the Christian faith. Cyprian found it diplomatic to retire from Carthage in order to continue his cure of souls. Many lapsed under the trial, and when the persecution finished in 251 the bishop was faced with the problem of re-admitting apostates to the church. The rigorist party demanded the old rule that apostates be and remain excommunicated, while the laxist party demanded their re-admission with little or no discipline. Cyprian remitted the matter to a council of north African bishops whose eventual decision was to to judge each case on its merits and after due discipline to admit those who were penitent, although lapsed clergy were inhibited from exercising their ministry. The two extreme parties set up rival bishops of their own, as did the rigorist party in Rome under the presbyter Novatian who was consecrated at the hands of sympathising bishops. There

followed the years of a great plague and then a new controversy about heretic baptism in which the previously friendly
relations with the Roman see turned to bitter hostility, and
Cyprian, in order to maintain his case, strengthened his episcopal network right across the east. Persecution broke out
again, but Cyprian and his church stood firm, and on 14
September 258 the bishop went bravely to his execution like
a Christian Roman.

He is the first theologian to give the Church a thematic
treatment of its own, and a high theology it is. She is the
mediatrix of all salvation and can never be the true Church
except as the undivided Catholic Church. Neither episcopal
ordination nor the sacraments have any meaning outside the
true Church. She has a clear hierarchy of classes: at the
bottom, brothers and sisters, then virgins and ascetics, then
martyrs and confessors, then clergy, and at the head, bishops.
There is a sharp distinction between clergy and laity: the
clergy are the picked officials whose leader and standard is
the bishop, a system established by Christ and already in
being in the time of the apostles (*Letters*, 3.3). (The following
references, unless otherwise stated, refer to his *Letters*.) Without the office of bishop there is no Church, for 'not only is the
bishop in the Church, but the Church is in the bishop, and if
anyone is not with the bishop, he is not in the Church' (66.8).

At heart, Cyprian's thinking is sacral-juristic and sacral-
political, in a tradition going back to *1 Clement*. The liturgical
element is greatly intensified and interwoven with juristic conceptions. Now clerical ordination must always be confirmed,
after due election by the prescribed bodies, by a special sacramental act. For the first time it is this which makes a priest a
priest, as a result of which he can pass on spiritual gifts in
baptism or penance, and as a bishop he can ordain new clergy,
can offer the eucharistic sacrifice, and make effectual inter-
cession for others. No layman is competent for these things.
Earlier, a confessor proved he was endowed with the Spirit
and so was admitted to the clergy at once, but now he has to
be ordained. The legal system may not be disturbed by the
Spirit.

For Cyprian, priesthood has no effectual power independent of official position: it has no indelible character of its own. That concept emerged from the struggle with Donatist ideas of personal holiness, whereas Cyprian saw a priest's position rooted spiritually and politically in the Church. The bishop is the model, and through him all ecclesiastical measures must be carried out (33.1).

Nevertheless the power of bishops is not absolute, or at least not absolutist. 'From the moment I received my episcopal office I made it my fundamental principle to undertake nothing simply on my personal decision without your counsel and the assent of the church' (14.5). The bishop is bound by sacred tradition but he must have the courage to act on his own responsibility, for example, in time of persecution. In particular Cyprian stresses the importance of collaboration with fellow-bishops. Each individual bishop exercises the full episcopate; nevertheless it does not belong to him alone but he possesses it only in solidarity with other bishops: '*Episcopatus unus est cuius a singulis in solidum pars tenetur.*' (*De Unitate*, 5). Cyprian protests solemnly in a great council of the African church against the insolent presumption and folly of the bishop of Rome's boasting of his special succession from Peter, and of a resulting higher status which would allow him to dictate to his episcopal colleagues (see also 71.3; 74.1). In fact as president of this council and by virtue of his intellectual superiority, Cyprian played the part of an African pope, but he stresses that his following is voluntary. In the Catholic Church there is no tyrannical compulsion, no regulations laid down by an individual and also no arriving at conciliar decisions by majority votes. Each bishop has equal rights to express his own opinion and act on it. Christ alone will be his judge (69.17; 71.3; 72.3; 73.26). The Church will not collapse if there are occasional differences of practice, but she would disintegrate without the peace and cohesion of the episcopate.

But what if the bishops cannot agree, or are wrong? Cyprian takes unanimity for granted. He believes in the episcopate as he believes in the Catholic Church as the sphere of the Spirit's working (and the Spirit is seldom mentioned in any other context). That the bishops throughout the world will be unanimous is simply taken for granted (55.8); it can never and will never happen that the bishops acting as a whole should fall into error (67.8). The bishop's office is, in short, indefectible, but Cyprian is no papalist (far from it), nor is he a conciliarist (as understood in the Middle Ages), though the beginnings of that movement may be found later in African opposition to Justinian and the Pope dependent on him. In this mutual love the primitive concept lives on, but it must be admitted that it is now limited to leaders; real freedom is no longer a real option for ordinary Christians. Freedom is now not to be found in God's continuous redemptive work but it is contained in a human system in which law and official discretion, not faith, have the last word.

Cyprian takes for granted the teaching authority which goes with ordination, and the matter seems to him straightforward. The principles of Biblical, doctrinal or ethical understanding are either known already, or are plain to see, and Cyprian knows of no class of free-lance teachers who might conflict with the episcopal office. He puts great emphasis on the authority of the clergy, and particularly of the bishop, referring regularly to the bishop, though not to the presbyter, as *sacerdos*. Outside the Church there is no salvation, but within it access to the sacraments is free and open. Since there was little private pastoral work the community life of the congregation is important, and of this the bishop is the focal point and revered head; he is still more their servant than the bishop of the Middle Ages. In the matter of penance the sentence passed on the apostate or malefactor, being a matter of life or death, is for the bishop alone – in Christ's place (*iudex vice Christi*, 59.5).

Cyprian concludes the process begun in the Pastoral Epistles and continued through Hippolytus, by setting aside the claims of the congregation and its special representatives, the martyrs, to re-admit penitents or even to intercede on their behalf, a policy which he forced through in the face of violent resistance. The power of the keys has, for Cyprian, changed inwardly from the evangelistic to the moralistic, and outwardly from the directly spiritual to the official expressed in sacramental form: re-admission is *sacrificio et manu sacerdotis*, that is, by the bishop's eucharistic sacrifice and laying-on of hands. Significantly, this laying-on of hands can also be done by a presbyter and if need be by a deacon with the bishop's commission (18.2) There is absolutely no evidence of a priestly absolution

The real problem, what if the decision is wrong?, appears to be only peripheral. It is covered by the Last Judgement which will be infallible, and in any case the absolving power does not have the same binding power to commit God to forgive; it provides only the prior condition for salvation, making it possible but not certain that pardon will ultimately be granted (55.17); only the martyrs are free from this anxiety (55.20). No one appears to have noticed the enormous implications of this decision once it was extended from being a measure of church discipline to becoming a comprehensive understanding of the original power of the keys. A long and painful process of development had to take place before people fully realised the dangers here for the Christian conscience, emerging in the west through medieval monasticism. In the east the line of development was already different, having been treated in Greek theology in a more idealist and pietistic fashion.

Cyprian, bishop and martyr, is guided by a Roman self-consciousness, political if not military, which sustains him and his presbyteral senate, and this image has dominated the ecclesiological thinking of the Roman Catholic Church to this day.

The end of the third century AD is a good point at which to pause and look back over a period which may properly be considered 'classical' for the study of the Christian ministry, for during that time the foundations were laid which were to last for a thousand years, to the arrival of Scholasticism in the thirteenth century. The question of ministry itself presupposes the question of authority. Ministry does not derive from the sacraments: both ministry and sacraments derive from Christ as gifts for the building up of the Church. The New Testament evidence is striking in the way it avoids a cultic interpretation of priesthood, with no place for the word *hiereus*, priest, meaning a section or class of Christians set aside for cultic purposes, yet by the middle of the third century Cyprian has a clerical class sharply differentiated from the laity, headed by the bishop without whom there is no Church.

The classical period, then, is one of great movement and change, with the Church showing remarkable versatility in adjusting itself to new demands. Such a flexibility was built into its very foundation by Jesus. He bequeathed to his followers the gospel, the good news of the kingdom, a tradition which they had to hand down to subsequent generations, and also his Spirit, his own personal presence, who would animate both the message and also the community which it was bound to form. All problems about authority, and so all problems about ministry, circle around these two determinative poles: to neglect the Spirit is to opt for ecclesiastical authoritarianism; to neglect the tradition is to end up with shapeless enthusiasm. The first three centuries well illustrate the Church's varying circuit around these two poles, but the predominant tendency is towards the first rather than the second.

By the time of *1 Clement*, at the end of the first century, the patriarchal has gained over the pneumatic, and bishops have acquired a legal status as cult officials, with priests now set over against the laity. Order is valued for its own sake and has become detached from specifically Christian meaning. Here we see the beginnings of Roman Catholicism.

Ignatius also, early in the second century, holds a high doctrine of the episcopate and the three-level clergy, but for a very different reason, the sake of holy fellowship. He is ecclesiastical but never clerical, blending official with spiritual. Here are the beginnings of Eastern Orthodoxy.

The Pastoral Epistles put emphasis on the teaching office, and here are the seeds of the Reformed tradition, though the Pastorals also witness to a rite of ordination and the early stages of canon law.

47

Towards the end of the second century, with Montanus, the Spirit burst upon the Church with pentecostal fervour and alarming ecstasy, winning over a tough-minded theologian like Tertullian. Here is the first of several 'charismatic' movements which have disturbed the Church of God when it has forgotten or sat light to its proper inheritance of the Spirit.

At the end of that century and in calmer spheres their place is taken by teachers like Clement of Alexandria who combined a deep loyalty to scripture with insights from the Platonic philosophical tradition. In their quest for the deeper mystery they end up with a personalist and individualist spirituality in which the Church plays no necessary part. Here are the prototypes of those many intelligent and devout people who attend adult education classes in religion but see no need of membership of the Church.

Such are the main markers in the development of the concept of spiritual authority, and along with it, of the ministry, in the first three centuries. They point in different directions, as they witness to complex origins, and advocates of each system can fairly claim to find their roots in the New Testament. The only possible solution is to do justice to the whole evidence of the New Testament, and indeed of the whole Bible. The united Church of the future can only embrace what is sound in all these traditions, along with their accompanying tensions, and learn to live with them by the grace of the Lord Jesus Christ in the fellowship of the Holy Spirit.

PART II – DEFORMATION

7

The Church Established

THE factors which have helped to shape the Church's ministry have been both theological and sociological, with a good deal of interplay between them. The fourth century saw a major shift in the social context of the Church with respect to the Roman empire. The Edict of Milan, published in AD 313 following the conversion of the emperor Constantine, provided for complete religious toleration, and restored to Christians property confiscated during persecution, with state compensation for those who suffered. The Edict of Thessalonica, published by Theodosius in 380, ordered that the faith taught to the Romans by St Peter should be accepted by all nations. Under Constantine Christianity and the empire were allied; under Theodosius they were united. These drastic changes were bound to influence the way the clergy saw themselves and the way others saw them. But first some theological developments need to be considered.

The principal theological tool which lay to hand was the Old Testament, and its allegorical use by Christian thinkers and leaders had a powerful and baneful effect on the theory and practice of ministry. The concept of a three-fold ministry undoubtedly owes much to categories of high-priest, priest and levite, reaching its climax with Cyprian's regular use of *sacerdos* for a bishop despite the New Testament's studious avoidance of this kind of terminology. Inevitably there accompanied this title concepts of sacrifice appropriate to the Old Testament cultus – despite the fact that the New Testament steadily proclaims that in Christ the old cultus had been superseded. Tertullian, around AD 200, had spoken of the bishop as *sacerdos* or *sacerdos summus* (high-priest), but without explanation as if it were already familiar. He occasionally applies *sacerdos* to the presbyter also (*De Virginibus Velandis*, 11.1). He also uses the term *altare* for 'altar' but without drawing any theological conclusion.

At the heart of priesthood, both Jewish and pagan, lay the function of offering sacrifice, and soon this became a dominating concept for interpreting the eucharist. From an early date Christian writers claimed that the Christian cult was not about offering material things like animals but the 'pure offering' of Malachi 1.11. Early in the second century the *Didachē* links this notion of offering with the eucharist: 'On the Lord's day come together, break bread and hold eucharist, after confessing your transgressions, that your sacrifice (*thusia*) may be pure . . .' (14.1). Closely linked with this is the 'offering of the gifts' (*prosphorein ta dōra*), that is, the presenting of the bread and wine for blessing. Justin sees both types of offering combined in the eucharist (*Apology*, 6.7), as does Irenaeus (*Adversus Haereses*, 4. 29–31).

Generally speaking, the Fathers held and taught a view of the eucharist which was both realist and also symbolic because symbols were signs of reality to be apprehended by faith. Cyprian was the first to work out something like a theory of eucharistic sacrifice based on the high-priesthood of Christ:

> . . . certainly that priest truly discharges the office of Christ who imitates that which Christ did; and he then offers a true and full sacrifice in the church to God the Father when he proceeds to offer it according to what he sees Christ himself to have offered.
>
> (*Letters*, 63).

He tries to remain faithful to scripture; he insists that the primary offering is that by Christ himself; and at the heart of the sacrament lies the co-inherence of the people with their Lord. Nevertheless, by using this kind of sacrificial language Cyprian opened the way to the distortions of medieval western Christendom and the deformations of ministry which accompanied them.

Augustine, a century and a half later, who owed much to

Cyprian, maintains a sensitive and many-sided approach to the mystery. He is careful in his definition of sacrifice: 'A true sacrifice is whatever work is accomplished with the object of establishing our holy union with God' (*De Civitate Dei*, 10.6). 'The visible sacrifice is the sacrament, that is, the sacred symbol of the invisible sacrifice' (10.5). So Christ is both offerer and offered, and inherent in his self-offering is the self-offering of his people: 'The most splendid and excellent sacrifice consists of ourselves, his people. This is the sacrifice the mystery of which we celebrate in our oblation' (19.23).

In the east John Chrysostom wrote his treatise *On the Priesthood* about AD 385 (though it reflects the concerns of a bishop rather than those of a presbyter): the terms used throughout are *hiereus* and *hierosunē*. His indebtedness to the Old Testament is vividly illustrated from a passage on the glory of the priesthood:

> When you see the Lord sacrificed and lying before you, and the high-priest standing over the sacrifice and praying, and all who partake being tinctured with that precious blood, can you think that you are still among men and still standing on earth?
>
> (3.4).

In the social context, for the first four centuries no distinctive dress marked off the clergy. In the catacombs at Rome one picture probably portrays an ordination where the seated bishop and two standing presbyters all wear the customary toga and tunica, while the ordinand has the tunic only. By the end of the third century, however, the clergy are sufficiently distinct to warrant special canonical provisions. At the Council of Elvira in Spain, held about 305 and attended by nineteen bishops and twenty-six presbyters, several canons relate to 'clerics': the eighteenth punishes sexual immorality of all clergy with life-long excommunication; the nineteenth forbids all clergy to leave their place in order to engage in trade; the twentieth imposes deposition and excommunication for usury; and the thirty-third requires all clergy who minister at the altar to abstain from their wives and not beget children.

Standards of sexual morality for the clergy are now becoming a matter of acute controversy. The Church found it hard to demand celibacy in view of the clear example of married apostles, not least Peter, but it was given to a profound and ultimately Manichean, suspicion of sexual activity, which culminated, disastrously, in the later teachings of Augustine. The matter, it seems, was debated at the first ecumenical Council of Nicaea in 325 but no canon was published. According to three ancient historians the Council wished to forbid all clergy who were married at the time of their ordination to continue to live with their wives. This was strongly opposed by Paphnutius, an unmarried Egyptian bishop with a monastic background, who declared that marriage and married intercourse are of themselves honourable; that not all could live in absolute continency; and that intercourse of a man with his lawful wife may also be chaste. It would therefore be sufficient if, according to the ancient tradition of the Church, those who were ordained without being married were prohibited from marrying afterwards, but those clergy who had been married were not to be separated from their wives. The Council, we are told, was so impressed by this argument that it decided to leave the matter to the conscience of each cleric. The western Church moved, eventually, to a rule of celibacy, but the eastern Church to this day allows marriage for priests but not for bishops.

Other forces which shaped the ministry in the first three centuries concern the size of congregations and the physical arrangements for worship. It is hard to realise that for most of that time Christians did not build special buildings for their services, though they adapted existing ones. 'We have no temples and no altars', declared the apologist, Minucius Felix, about the year 200, a fact so remarkable that it constituted grounds for accusing Christians of atheism. Nevertheless as early as AD 150 buildings at Rome made over for the purposes of worship are mentioned by pope Pius I (*Ad Justum Epistolae* (1.2), and the term *ecclesia* is used in exactly the same localised way as the modern 'church' by Clement of Alexandria (*Strōmateis*, 7 and Tertullian (*De Idololatriā*, 7).

In the third century the house-church was still the norm. At Dura Europos on the Euphrates we have an actual example of a house built shortly after 200 and modified in 231 for use by a Christian congregation, providing a room large enough for some fifty people. It continued to look like a private house, and the eucharist was still a domestic ceremony (Rostovtzeff, 1938). We have an account of a raid on a Christian church in Cirta, the capital city of Numidia, north Africa, on 19 May 303, under the edict of the emperor Diocletian. The mayor with two clerks went to the house where the Christians used to meet and required the bishop, Paul, to hand over 'the writings of the law' and other property: this included church plate with two gold and six silver chalices, and large stores of male and female clothes and shoes. This was done in the presence of the clergy, three priests, two deacons, and four sub-deacons, as well as a number of diggers. There were also six readers to whose homes the mayor went to collect the copies of the scriptures. (Stevenson, 1957, p. 287–9.)

The provision of charitable care was to become a major concern for bishops in later years. Just after 250 a letter of Cornelius, bishop of Rome, refers to the official list of those who received a regular stipend from that church:

> . . . there were 46 presbyters, 7 deacons, 7 sub-deacons, 42 acolytes, 52 exorcists, readers and janitors, and over 1500 widows and persons in distress, all of whom the grace and kindness of the Master nourish.
>
> (Eusebius, *Church History*, 6.43.11.)

Of course Rome was exceptional for its size and importance, but a century later in the east John Chrysostom laments the difficulties caused to bishops by the care of widows, virgins, and the sick (*On the Priesthood*, 3.16).

It has been calculated that towards the middle of the third century there were about 25,000 Christians in Rome: so if the 46 presbyters were divided between them, that would produce a ratio of about one to 550. There is evidence from the catacombs that in the second century Christians had developed a definite parochial organisation in the capital, expanded by pope Marcellus (308–310) who presided over twenty-five *tituli* or parishes. Each probably had its own subterranean cemetery with a sacred building above it.

In the larger cities, as the number of Christians expanded, the bishop had to delegate some of his duties to presbyters and deacons, notably that of presiding at the eucharist, but in north Africa in Augustine's time (early in the fifth century) the bishop reserved to himself the right to preach. Here again we must remember that in those African provinces alone there were some 300 bishops (with another 300 rival Donatist bishops), the majority of whom were in small towns numbering only a few thousand in population. Christianity spread more slowly into the countryside, and the development of 'country-bishops' (*chorepiscopi*) is late and they remain shadowy figures.

With the triumph of Constantine, not only were confiscated houses and lands restored, but bishops were provided with money, property, and materials to build new churches (not to mention the Lateran palace which was handed over to bishop Miltiades in 312 as an episcopal residence). When the emperor wrote to bishop Macarius of Jerusalem about his plan for a site for the Holy Sepulchre, he instructed him to build the finest basilica yet seen. The term is significant, and he does not bother to explain it. The secular basilica was a large public meeting-place, used for law-courts among other purposes, which was given a religious association by the presence of a statue of the emperor. A Christian basilica was simply another such, with devotion to Christ as God taking the place of the imperial cult. A standard plan for these emerged by the end of the fourth century, consisting of a simple oblong room with parallel colonnades which give the impression of converging on the altar placed towards the far end. This was the focal point around which clergy and laity gathered for the celebration of the liturgy, each in their prescribed place. In the centre of the semi-circular apse, roofed by a half-dome, the bishop had his seat (*cathedra*), on either side of which were the seats for the presbyters. The deacons were grouped around the altar which might stand on the chord of the apse or in the body of the hall well down the nave.

In north Africa, whose provinces had the highest proportion of Christians in the population, there had been few basilicas before 260, though in Cirta, Numidia, there was one before the time of Domitian in 284. The earliest yet discovered, at Castellum Tingitanum in Mauretania, can be dated to 324 and was of fair size with a floor covered with mosaics of a high standard. The city of Theveste in Proconsularis province (modern Tunisia) provides the finest surviving example of a fourth century basilica remarkable for its size and richness of ornament. From Augustine himself we learn that Hippo Regius, (the modern Annaba on the coast of Algeria) had three Catholic basilicas (one built by Augustine himself), two chapels, and a Donatist basilica. At Thamugadi, where the conflict between the two sides was very bitter, remains have been found of no fewer than seventeen churches, chapels and monasteries of varying dates and allegiances.

The debt (for better and for worse) which the Church owes to the Roman empire may be glimpsed in the terms which it borrowed from Roman officialdom. Tertullian is the first known writer to use the term *ordo* of the clergy. The word means a 'class' in Roman society, the upper ones being knights (*equites*) and senators (*senatores*), and the lower the *plebs* or common people. The ceremony of admission to an upper order was *ordinatio*. Here, perhaps unconsciously, are sown seeds of clerical privilege implicitly set over against the laity, which before long are to become all too explicit. The 'province', which is still the largest ecclesiastical unit in the Anglican Communion, comes straight from *provincia*, the main Roman unit of imperial government. The Roman 'diocese' (*dioecēsis*) was a group of five or so provinces, created by Diocletian, whose chief officer was a *vicarius*, directly responsible to the emperor, who heard appeals from provincial courts and had the task of supervising the collection of food supplies to Rome.

Every *municipium* had its own town council (*curia*), and we know the exact composition of that of Thamugadi, a medium-sized African town, from an inscription of about 363. It comprises thirty-nine officers: two *sacerdotales*, thirty-two *flamines*, four *pontifices*, and three *augures*, all of which are titles of pagan priesthood transferred to the cult of the emperor. The titles had been emptied of any religious significance and fourth century Christians felt no more compunction about being *flamines* than twentieth century ones feel about being freemasons. The list also mentions thirty who were excused municipal burdens though they had not held office, because some professions like shippers, teachers and doctors were exempt. At the bottom of the list come eleven *clerici* who must be local Christian clergy. The term was legally defined by Constantine, and by the same law clergy were given immunity from all civic burdens:

> Those who devote their religious ministry to the divine cult, that is to say, those who are called clerics (*clerici*), shall be entirely excused from all their duties.
>
> (*Codex Theodosianus*, 16.2.2.)

Christianity was born and nurtured, under the providence of God, in the Roman Empire. If it had expanded eastwards into India and China in a comparable way one can only begin to imagine how different its subsequent history would have been.

By the last quarter of the third century the church had become a familiar part of the urban scene over much of the Mediterranean world and bishops were regarded by the authorities as important leaders. Among the bishops, collective opinion was not to be subordinated to that of any one bishop, for all bishops belonged to one sacerdotal body, as Cyprian had reminded his colleagues. Nevertheless an order of precedence was evolving among the senior bishops, with Rome already recognised as the principal bishopric in both east and west, though they disagreed about its significance. In Rome the bishop's authority was extending throughout the hundred-mile radius which was administered by the Prefect of the city. In 251 bishop Cornelius held a council of sixty bishops who must have been drawn from that area, and the Council of Nicaea in 325 confirmed the authority of the bishop of Rome over the surrounding area. By this time Rome had become the reference point for the west as a whole.

The first bishop to attempt a definition of the relations between church and state was not a pope, but Ambrose, bishop of Milan from 373 till 397, where the emperor had his headquarters. At the age of thirty-four, and as a provincial governor and a layman, he was acclaimed by the crowd in Milan cathedral, and in defiance of the canons of Nicaea he was rushed through all the ecclesiastical grades in eight days. By the end of his twenty-four years' episcopate, he had guided western Christianity towards many of its characteristics which endured through the Middle Ages: asceticism as a Christian way of life under episcopal control; the rights of church over state; the application of Christian-Platonic exegesis to scripture; and the moulding of liturgy and hymnody to congregational life. He also baptised Augustine.

Harassed by the great Christological controversies of the fourth and fifth centuries which were rending the empire, the emperors were ready to resort to any authority which would serve as a unifying force, and amongst these the see of Rome was pre-eminent. So in 378 the emperor Gratian supported the bishop of Rome's claim to authority over the other bishops in the west by granting to Rome the right to hear appeals by bishops over the heads of their metropolitans. In 445 Valentinian III laid down that 'whatsoever the authority of the apostolic see has sanctioned, or shall sanction, shall be the law for all'. Leo I (440–461) gave finality to the concept of the Petrine monarchy, and was happy to resume the title *pontifex maximus* which the emperors had discarded. His claims rose as the empire declined. Barbarian Germanic tribes, driven by the Huns, were fanning out across the provinces. Rome itself was sacked by Alaric in 410, and by 442 Spain and north Africa had fallen to the Visigoths and Vandals. The imperial government was ready to underwrite any authority which could hold together a crumbling empire. When in 452 pope Leo went out with a senatorial embassy to parley with the Huns, and three years later tried to persuade the Vandals to spare Rome, interests of Church and empire had become inseparable.

8

Medieval Deformations

THE Middle Ages may best be considered not as a period between two civilisations but rather as the time when church and society were one. The collapse of the Roman empire was a long and complicated business but it was complete in the west by the seventh century. It was to give way to the Holy Roman Empire in the form of the Roman Catholic Church, with the pope replacing the emperor, and many of its features survive to the present. As it attempted to shape the whole of society, so it was in turn shaped by features of that society, not least in matters of ministry.

From the seventh century only the orthodox and the obedient could enjoy the full rights of citizenship. The Church was a compulsory society, entered by baptism, and it had the full apparatus of a state, with laws, taxes, a great administrative machine, and power of life and death. Its final sanction was excommunication, but it had no police or dependable army, and its agents had limited powers of initiative. We need to trace briefly its development, and we borrow R. W. Southern's (1970) three divisions of time.

1. *The Primitive Age, 700–1050.*

Western Europe only survived as a Christian society because by 700 Islam had reached the limits of its conquest, having occupied Sicily and most of Spain. Plague, famine and destruction had reduced the population, and most people lived in small settlements depending on primitive agriculture. The spiritual tone for four centuries, from the eighth to the eleventh, was set by the Benedictine movement whose monasteries stood as mighty symbols of stability in a very uncertain age, offering a foretaste and a guarantee of eternal life. Sprituality was well earthed, not least in the cult of relics which, from the eighth century onwards, became the object of vast commerce. The pope was the guardian of the (alleged) body of St Peter and so could speak with his direct authority. Charlemagne's throne at Aachen was full of cavities holding relics.

The seeds of division between eastern and western Christendom were already present at the beginning of the Middle Ages but the conquests of Islam had removed three of the five ancient patriarchal churches of Alexandria, Antioch and Jerusalem. In 729 the Greek emperor sent pope Gregory II an order forbidding him to place pictures of martyrs or angels in churches under his jurisdiction, and the pope turned to the new nations of the west. In 800 Charlemagne was crowned by pope Leo III as first 'Holy Roman Emperor', but in creating an emperor the pope created a rival, even a master. The clearest example of papal claims is seen in the infamous document *The Donation of Constantine*. It is a forgery purporting to be a letter from the emperor in 315 to pope Silvester I granting to the Vicar of St Peter pre-eminence over all other churches (including the four eastern patriarchal sees), and transferring to the pope the imperial power in Rome, Italy, and all western provinces. (It was probably written about 750.)

2. *The Age of Growth*, 1050–1300.

The first seventy years of this period saw great changes, with growth of population and capital wealth, the establishment of new villages and towns, and the decline of the Greek and Moslem empires. The clerical hierarchy now asserted their claim to be the only channel of supernatural authority, and by the end of the eleventh century only clergy had the benefit of the advanced scholastic training which provided the necessary tools of government. The clergy also achieved exemption from secular law-courts and secular taxation, and the exclusion of secular 'interference' in ecclesiastical appointments. If ever the clerical ideal was realised, it was during the early part of the four-teenth century. In 1050 canon law as a science had hardly begun; by 1300 it was a closed system. The first attempts in theology at an overall systematic statement may be dated to the late eleventh century; the greatest and last of the medieval systematisers, Thomas Aquinas, died in 1274. In 1050 the Benedictines were the only religious order; by 1300 there were orders of hermits, military orders, Canons Regular, the Cistercians, and the four great orders of friars.

Although in the west papacy was the source of unity and strength, it proved to be the greatest divisive force in Christen-dom, eventually sundering east and west. The crucial date was rightly seen by Gibbon as 1054 when the patriarch of Constantinople was excommunicated by the pope's legates. But the Greeks were doomed by the tide of Islam. They turned to the west for help but in 1422 pope Martin's reply was in effect, 'Submit to us or be destroyed'. Constantinople fell in 1452 and with it the problem of the rival patriarchate. Pope Pius II hastened to make overtures to the conqueror: 'Be baptised, and no prince in the world will be your equal in glory and power. We will call you Emperor of the Greeks and of the Orient . . .'. But Mahomet II was not another Constantine.

In their quest for spiritual authority to back their claims, from the middle of the fourteenth century the popes began to assume to themselves the title of 'Vicar of Christ', soon defined in precise terms of universal sovereignty. By the end of that century Innocent III proclaimed:

> We are the successors of the Prince of the Apostles but we are not his vicar, nor the vicar of any man or apostle, but the vicar of Jesus Christ himself.
>
> (Migne, *Patrologia Latina*, 214.292.)

The theory was vigorously translated into practice, as may be seen by the growth in the machinery of papal government after about 1120. The annual average number of papal letters from about 1030 to 1130 remained at 35, but then rose steadily to 3,646 a year under John XXII (1316–1324). Business was mainly concerned with the dispensing of benefits and justice. The former was the chief method of obtaining loyalty and the latter the chief method of maintaining it. By 1150 papal jurisdiction had permeated the lowest level of ecclesiastical structure as a matter of routine.

The great and uncontrollable flood of litigation had one beneficial result in defining large areas of everyday life. The papal court gave priests security of tenure and a minimum income, together with rules for dress, ordination, duties, status, crimes and punishments; and it gave to the laity a general and not too onerous discipline from baptism to masses for the dead. The rulers of Europe, however, were finding that they could use ecclesiastical wealth to finance the growth of secular government by using clerks in holy orders, and soon voices were beginning to ask whether the Church was a conspiracy between secular and ecclesiastical authorities for the exploitation of ecclesiastical wealth; whether perhaps the pope was not anti-Christ. The voices were destined to grow louder.

3. *The Age of Unrest*, 1300–1550.

In 1323 the pope condemned the Franciscan doctrine of poverty, a sign of the new Europe which was growing out of control. Life was becoming urbanised with towns of 50,000 not uncommon. They presented a threat both to the soul and to society since, as Thomas Aquinas declared, 'trade encourages too much talk and exposes a community to bad morals and false opinions' (*De Regno*, 2.3). After 1300 the papal system became the victim of its own success, and overelaboration led to confusion and the devaluation of the spiritual currency, as seen most glaringly in the matter of indulgences. This exercise of the papal 'plenitude of power' began in 1095 when Urban II announced that participation in the crusade would be counted the equivalent of all other penances – a plenary indulgence. By the middle of the fourteenth century wealthy persons were able to buy indulgences at their dying from their confessors. There was no limit to the bottomless treasure of Christ's merit available, at a price, from the successors of St Peter.

Similarly, papal attempts to control the whole ecclesiastical system rose and fell. One underlying principle had been recognised from the earliest days, that the local community had some say in a minister's appointment, but how this was to be carried out had never been very clear. As for the election of a pope, only one man could claim to represent the clergy and people of the west – the emperor, and in the tenth and eleventh centuries he did. But there was a problem of communications, and the pope lost out to the men on the spot, the clergy and people of Rome, which meant in fact the cardinals and nobility, and this led to a long series of dynastic struggles.

The election of bishops proved a harder problem. From the eighth to the eleventh century they were mostly chosen by the ruler, since kings had a semi-sacerdotal character. In the twelfth century, however, the Roman lawyers discovered a letter written in the fifth century by Leo I to the bishop of Thessalonica pointing out that the bishop was not called to a plenitude of power but only to a share of the pope's responsibility, and so from then on in practice the bishop was the local deputy of the pope. In 1335 Benedict XII reserved to his own disposition every kind of appointment from patriarch to parish priest, 'even if they have been or ought to be filled by election or in some other way . . .' (*Extravagantes Communes*, 3.2.13, quoted by Southern, p. 158). In fact, however, the pope could only make his power effective with the consent of secular rulers, and in time they took over the whole business of ecclesiastical appointments.

There was no limit to the pope's plenitude of power. Clement VI, on becoming pope in 1342, offered the expectation of a benefice to all poor clerks who came to the papal court in the first months of his pontificate, and a hundred thousand came. His offer vastly increased the legal process since this was only the first step, and it greatly strengthened lay control because the rest depended on friends and money. By the fourteenth century papal administration had reached its limits. It was a remarkable system but it had basic defects which tended to stimulate those types of secular influence which it was designed to minimise.

'Christendom' was a magnificent ideal, the sacralisation of the secular. What actually happened included a good deal of the reverse process. It affected the patterns of ministry, but its effects are clear in other areas of doctrine. When Anselm, Archbishop of Canterbury, sets out his understanding of the atonement in *Cur Deus Homo*, written a year or two before 1100, he sees it in the context of the outraged dignity of God:

> In the order of things, there is nothing less to be endured than that the creature should take away the honour due to the Creator . . . Therefore the honour taken away must be repaid, or punishment must follow; otherwise, either God will not be just to himself, or he will be weak in respect of both parties; and this it is impious even to think of.

> (Chap. 13.)

Anselm here owes more to feudal conceptions of authority, sanctions and reparation than to the Bible (which is very little mentioned in his book) or indeed to the tradition of the Church.

The twelfth and thirteenth centuries also saw a fundamental shift in the understanding of ministry not uninfluenced by feudal concepts. Originally the *titulus ecclesiae* was the local Christian community to which a man was appointed by his ordination. Canon 6 of the Council of Chalcedon made it quite clear that a man could not be ordained *in vacuo*: 'No man is to be ordained without a charge (*apolelumenōs*), neither presbyter, nor deacon, nor indeed anyone who is in the ecclesiastical order . . .'. This ruling was valid down to the twelfth century. In 1179, however, the Third Lateran Council radically reinterpreted the term *titulus* to mean the guarantee of a livelihood: '*sine certo titulo de quo necessaria vitae percipiat*'. No doubt some such financial provision was needed given the chaos of previous centuries, but this step served to sever the old link between call and community.

Furthermore, now that almost everyone was baptised, the boundary between 'church' and 'world' shifted from baptism to ordination. As a result, priesthood was seen more as a personal state of life or status than as service to and in a community. Ordination conveyed *potestas*, and this individualistic view opened the way to practices like private masses which would have been unthinkable to early Christians. This process was aided by a convenient semantic shift from *corpus verum Christi* to *corpus mysticum Christi*. In the ancient Church it was universally held that a man was ordained to preside over the former, meaning the church community; in the Middle Ages the terminology slipped into the latter, meaning his presiding over the eucharist. In brief, in the early Church a minister was appointed to preside over a community, and so naturally he presided over its eucharist; now in the thirteenth century he is ordained to preside over the eucharist, and he might not even have a community over which to preside. The consequences of this change were drastic.

So much for the 'grand design'. How did it actually work out on the ground? We may take, as a sample, church life in England in the thirteenth century (though it is not entirely typical) using material from J. R. H. Moorman's detailed study bearing that title. That century witnessed the building of Westminster Abbey and the founding of the universities of Oxford just before 1200 and of Cambridge just after. It was a society in which every person was under the power of church and state, but in which the peasant had no voice. The Church exacted from each person a good part of his livelihood, and claimed absolute control over his whole life, here and hereafter.

The parochial system of England is often attributed to Archbishop Theodore (668–690) but his contribution was mainly to do with dioceses. The earliest mission centres were monasteries, but in time local landlords came to build churches on their own estates for themselves, their tenants and their serfs, and it is from their manor boundaries that our 'parishes' originated. In the thirteenth century the total number seems to have been around nine thousand five hundred, with an average population of three hundred each in the country and two hundred in the towns. The parochial system has never really been at home in towns where boundaries are more arbitrary and loyalties less clear. The local priest had a dual loyalty, to his bishop and to his lord who claimed the right to appoint. The bishop reserved the right to institute men, but the registers are full of examples of children of ten years old and upwards being instituted, and of men being appointed to benefices who had no intention of living or serving there. Behind the whole system lay the over-riding and much resented papal claim to provide men for benefices: in 1292 Peter de Sabaudia, a kinsman of the pope, was provided with a canonry at Lincoln although he was under age and already held the treasurership of Llandaff and prebends and canonries at York, Salisbury and Hereford.

Half the parishes in England were rectories, but many of the rectors were absentees, and three-quarters of them were not in priest's orders. Some regarded their post as a spiritual cure but others simply as a useful source of income. The lords of the great land-owning families who were also patrons of many livings, found these a useful provision for their sons, and dispensations could be obtained for acquiring several benefices. When Bogo de Aare, a son of the Earl of Gloucester and Hertford, died in 1291, he held two canonries, three dignities in cathedrals and twenty-four parishes. His total income must have been in the region of £2,200 (the 1990 equivalent being about £3,300,000).

By the end of the thirteenth century, however, half the parishes of England were served by vicars. Local lords were reluctant to give more land to monasteries, and so, instead, they gave the living to a nearby monastery so that the abbot became the rector and collected the income on condition that he appointed a vicar (meaning 'one in his place') to serve the parish church. In 1296 the new Cistercian Abbey at Whalley, Lancs, made a profit of £173 (= £311,400) by this arrangement.

Clergy incomes were very uncertain and in 1222 the British bishops laid down a minimum stipend for a perpetual vicar of five marks a year (= £6000), slightly less than the average wage of a skilled workman. Some vicarages were worth a great deal more, but the majority were in the region of four pounds (= £7,200) a year, out of which the vicar was expected to provide for an assistant priest and clerk, pay for the repair of the church, and provide hospitality and charity.

England was swarming with clergy. Moorman calculates, (pp. 52–3) on a close examination of ordination figures, that there were at least 40,000 secular (or non-monastic) clergy, as well as some 17,000 ordained monks and friars, in a population of about three million, that is to say, a ratio of one secular cleric for every eighty-five people. With about 9,500 parishes, this produces an astonishing figure of just over four ordained men for every parish in England. (The ratio in 1986 was about one to 5,200 people.) In his statutes of 1238 Robert Grosseteste laid down that 'in every church where funds permit there shall be a deacon and a subdeacon to minister therein as is fitting: in other churches there must be at least one adequate and suitable clerk who, properly attired, shall assist in the divine office.'

An incumbent was generally provided with a simple house comprising hall, two bedrooms and a kitchen, with a bakehouse and brewery, and generally a range of farm buildings. It was not uncommon for a clergyman to keep half a dozen cows and fifty sheep, and thus to share in the daily cares of his parishioners. The house could accommodate three or four celibate men, and a boy was often employed to do the housework. The rule of celibacy proved too much for many clergy, and many vicarages housed a consort, sometimes married, but more often not. Ailred, abbot of Rievaulx, was the son, grandson, and great-grandson of priests.

It is not true that everyone went to church on Sundays, and even fines failed to persuade. The outward incentives in worship were not strong. The services were in Latin, and priests were accused of mumbling. Lay people seldom received communion, and then only of bread because the chalice was falling out of use (for no known reason). They seldom heard a sermon, and sang no hymns. There were no seats for the congregation and no pulpit for the preacher, at least until about 1340. The arrival of the friars posed a major threat to the parish clergy, for these travelling evangelists provided lively entertainment with wit and repartee in which the congregation was invited to join. The most direct spiritual influence which the priest exercised lay in the sacrament of penance which was much more than a mere confession and absolution, because the clergy were taught to conduct a thorough investigation into the most secret places of people's lives.

The standard of education of the clergy was generally low. In 1220 the Dean of Salisbury examined the seven clergy of the parish of Sonning, Berkshire, and found that the first could understand little Latin and knew by heart no part of the divine office and none of the psalms. The others had conspired to refuse to answer the dean's questions and so he had to write them off as insubordinate as well as illiterate, and all but one were suspended from office. The facilities for receiving education were meagre. The universities of Oxford and Cambridge were only just beginning to make their influence felt, and the possession of a degree was no indication of religious knowledge. Theology was a post-graduate course taken only by a few, whereas the study of canon law was extremely popular because it provided the legal qualification for high administrative position. The cathedrals and collegiate churches maintained grammar schools, and most large towns could claim a school of sorts, but if a boy lived in a country village he probably had to make do with what he could pick up from the parish priest.

The medieval church was wealthy and had it within its power to offer its clergy a reasonable livelihood had it not been for the scandals of pluralism and monastic appropriations. The Church was clear that clergy needed financial independence for their ministry, and this was provided by their possession of glebe land belonging to the benefice, and the right of tithe (which lasted into the twentieth century). This amounted to an ecclesiastical income-tax of ten per cent levied on all income in cash or kind, together with absolute

spiritual power to enforce its collection. At Sturminster Newton in Dorset the house and glebe were worth £4 (= £7,200)
and the tithes about £10 (= £18,000), a total rather higher
than the average. In addition the rector was entitled to certain
fees and offerings, and in town or city parishes he was almost
entirely dependent on these: at St Stephen's, Norwich in 1303
the tithe was worth only 5 shillings (= £375) whereas the
offerings amounted to £11.15.0 (= £17,625). Far too much
money, however, found its way into the already full purses of
monasteries or absent pluralists.

Wherein lay the weakness of the system which allowed such
conditions to exist so widely? The iron of feudalism had
entered deeply into the Church's soul, stemming from the
pope and his curia, with the final sanction of excommunication, but the system was vitiated at its centre by papal
willingness to grant dispensations for ready cash to influential
persons. So the relation of priest and people could only be an
authoritarian one, and on this understanding of clerical power
many sought ordination for unworthy reasons: for security,
for prestige, for comfort.

History does not record how many clergy grew worldly,
slack or dissipated, but life was rough, hard, and dull, and
some recourse to the dice or tavern is understandable. Many
of them were men of simple faith without much education and
perhaps without much imagination, but they kept the faith
alive and handed down the tradition, in however distorted a
form, which Christians now enjoy.

PART III – REFORMATION

9

Reformers and Counter-reformers

1. *Martin Luther.*

WHEN in 1524 Martin Luther finally discarded the habit
of an Augustinian friar, and in the following year married
Catherine von Bora, a former Cistercian nun, he cracked
the whole medieval edifice of the 'double standard'. The call
to the cloister demanded of Luther the complete surrender of
his life, but God had powerfully shown him through the
scriptures that the following of Christ is not a privilege for
the select few, but an obligation for all. He had found in
the Bible, understood in the light of his profound religious
experience, an absolute authority over against the papal
system, but this put him in a difficult position about the
ministry because appeal to the scriptures yielded no final
preference for any one form of organisation. Such an appeal,
also, requires an ability to interpret scripture, and this raises
the old question of authority in a new form, a question still
very much alive.

Four years earlier he had published his major policy document, *To the Christian Nobility of the German Nation Concerning the
Reform of the Christian Estate*, in which he wrote,

It has been an invention that pope, bishops, priests and
the monastic people are called the spiritual estate, and
nobles, masters, artisans and farmers are called the secular estate. All Christians are truly of the spiritual estate

73

(*Standes*), with no difference among them but that of office (*Amtes*).

(*Works*, 44. 128.)

He held a high doctrine of secular calling, requiring that possessors of secular authority, provided that they were baptised Christians, be considered priests and bishops 'and count their office as one belonging to, and useful to the Christian congregation.'

He also reverted to an ancient tradition in attaching great importance to a minister's being called by the community:

> Because we are all priests of equal standing, no one must push himself forward and take it upon himself, without our consent and election, to do that for which we all have equal authority. For no one may dare take upon himself what is common to all without the authority and consent of the community . . . Therefore a priest in Christendom is nothing else but an office-holder. As long as he holds office he takes precedence; where he is deposed, he is a peasant or a townsman like anybody else.
>
> (*Works*, 44. 130.)

Luther goes on to dismiss the Roman idea of 'indelible character' as 'just contrived talk and human regulation'. Nor can there be any privilege at law for ministers. In his *Babylonian Captivity of the Church* of 1520 he challenged head-on the medieval doctrine of the sacraments including ordination. Does it convey sacramental grace? Luther denied that it did because he could find no warrant for it in the New Testament, and 'the word of God is incomparably superior to the church'. The ordination of priests led only, in his view, to 'that loathsome tyranny of clerics over laity'. He also rightly observed that in the New Testament the term 'priest' is always used of the whole people of God whereas 'ministers' are designated by secular terms (*Works*, 31. 356).

But who or what is the community which has this power? It may mean the local congregation, and that Luther defined as one where the pure gospel is preached, or it may mean an ecclesiastical superior including a secular officer who is acting for the Church. Luther himself, when in the midst of personal troubles, consoled himself with the fact that he had been called to his office by the magistrate, and he would brandish this call like a spear before the devil (*Works*, 51. 73).

Luther gave the fullest rein to congregational responsiblity when he was sure that they were of his mind and that the candidate was one of whom he approved. In other circumstances he took a very different view. His former colleague, Karlstadt, had left Wittenberg and moved to Orlamünde. He was a radical reformer and considered Luther's treatment of the congregation too gentle. In August 1524 Luther's visit to Orlamünde led to a direct confrontation with him: 'For you were certainly not called. Or who asked you to preach?' (*Works*, 15. 341–7). Soon after, Karlstadt was forced to leave the place at the dictate of the Saxony government authorities: we do not know what part, if any, Luther had in the decision. The next year he attempted to settle the controversy by publishing *Against the Heavenly Prophets in the Matter of Images and Sacraments* (*Works*, 40. 75–223), and here he spoke not about the congregation but about 'the mob':

> One can see very well that when God orders a congregation to do something, and names the people, he does not want it done by the mob without the authorities, but by the authorities with the people ... Now, however, they plot without knowledge of the prince, elect pastors and appoint them as they themselves please.

In that same year, 1524, the Peasants' Revolt had broken out. Luther was terrified of a breakdown in public order and sought safety in the 'godly prince'. A union of Swabian princes sent their army against the peasants and the rebellion was mercilessly stamped out. He continued to pursue his old ideals of congregational freedom, but they are circumscribed by a fundamental reliance on civic authority, allied to his own supervision or that of his 'superintendents' without whom no congregation was permitted to appoint or dismiss preachers. Luther had in fact initiated his own system of bishops, himself being the archbishop, with the 'godly prince' as the final court of appeal. Ordination now becomes a public confirmation of the call; it does not have an absolute character but draws its meaning from service to a particular community (he uses the terms *call* and *ordain* synonymously). In 1535 he freely composed his formula for ordination not following the Roman rite but consisting of scripture readings, prayer and the laying-on of hands.

Luther's reforming zeal had indeed restored important features of primitive Christian faith and order which had become sadly obscured in the medieval tradition. He rediscovered that grace was God's gracious relationship with sinners through Christ, and not a kind of supernatural fluid to be ecclesiastically channelled and tapped. He rediscovered the importance of the scriptures for all Christians, and restored the ministry of the word alongside that of the sacraments. And he rediscovered the importance of spiritual responsibility in the life and affairs of the local congregation. All this was undoubted gain. But there were problems, particularly in the area of authority, both spiritual and secular. Luther's reforming work stemmed from a deep spiritual experience revealing to him that the essence of the gospel is that faith alone justifies without works. This manner of presentation alone could be called 'the pure gospel', and its reception had to be accompanied by a kind of religious experience similar to that of Luther's *Turmerlebnis* (Tower experience). Of this presentation and this experience the minister must be guarantor. In fact this compression of the gospel message to one burning-point produces strains and distortions both in the understanding of the gospel and in the experience of those who wish to believe.

Luther was still a product of the sixteenth century, and of sixteenth century Romanism at that. His interpretation of the Bible suffered from many of the limitations of contemporary scholarship and could be questioned, as he discovered to his discomfort. His concept of 'Christendom' was absolutely essential. Having dispensed with papal authority he found that he needed a final earthly authority, not least in matters to do with the appointment of ministers. He located this in the territoral prince whom he assumed would be both Christian and reformed, and whom he was prepared to accept as *summus episcopus*. When the noble was a conscientious Christian the argument carried some weight: when the ruler was an Adolf Hitler it collapsed in ruins.

2. *John Calvin.*

Born in 1509, a quarter of a century after Luther, John Calvin belongs to the second generation of Reformers. If Luther stands with the giants of religious intuition alongside Augustine, Calvin is in the line of doctors of the Church, doing for Protestantism in his *Institutio* what Aquinas did for Scholasticism in his *Summa*.

The first edition of the *Institutes of the Christian Religion* was published in 1536 when its author was twenty-six, and subsequently revised and expanded in 1539 and 1543, reaching its definitive form in 1559. It set out to be a statement of the fundamental truths of the Christian religion from the Reformed standpoint. He maintains a high doctrine of the Church for 'Scripture pronounces that outside the unity of the Church there is no salvation' (1. 539). Calvin's arguments against the rigorist separatists of his day (*ésprits phrénétiques* he called them) are just the same as those used by Rome against Calvin, and so he has to define the way of differentiating the true from the false church. In the edition of 1543 the visible church is embodied in and rigidly organised around a fourfold office of the ministry, a great structure resting on scripture and ancient usage, cemented with a sense of order and discipline (not for nothing had he switched from theology to law at the university).

He sets himself to find scriptural authority for a fourfold order of pastors, teachers (or doctors), elders and deacons; but his theory rests on no word of Christ, and of the Pauline evidence he has to abandon more than half as being provisional and temporary:

77

> Those who preside over the government of the church in accordance with Christ's institution are called by Paul as follows: first apostles, then prophets, thirdly evangelists, fourthly pastors, and finally teachers. Of these only the last two have an ordinary office in the church; the Lord raised up the first three at the beginning of his kingdom, and now and again revives them as the need of the times demands.
>
> (4.3.3.)

In fact Calvin never arrived at a definitive classification. In a later passage (4.4.1) he lists only three types of ministers: first, pastors and teachers; second, elders charged with the censure and correction of morals; and third, deacons who have the care of the poor and responsibility for alms. This represents a drastic reading back into scripture of Calvin's own ecclesiastical arrangements both in Strasbourg and in Geneva. Elders are not mentioned in the 1536 edition, but he saw them at work in Basle and Strasbourg, and set out his theory of the presbytery in the 1543 edition. But the details are not clear since sometimes the office of pastor and elder are merged.

Calvin, like Luther, did not hesitate to appeal to secular examples of organisation to maintain peace and concord. Calvin insists that jurisdiction in city and in church are separate but complementary, and he certainly assumed that the magistracy would be Christian and Reformed. While he was re-writing the *Institutes* he was actively engaged in restoring order to Geneva. He arrived there on 13 September 1541 and the same day demanded from the magistracy the setting up of a commission of pastors and advisers to draft an ecclesiastical constitution. He had in fact decided to write it himself, and by 20 September the preparatory work was done. But there were objections from the civil councils who wished to maintain their prerogatives. So, for example, Calvin had to settle for a celebration of Holy Communion once a quarter instead of once a month as he desired, and to dispense with the laying-on of hands at the installation of new pastors. The magistracy also demanded a share in the initial choice in the nomination of pastors, not being content merely to rubber-stamp the pastors' selection.

The most serious divergences had to do with the Consistory, the body to which Calvin intended to entrust ecclesiastical discipline. This was to have been composed of the pastors and twelve councillors nominated with their agreement who would have the right to censure or excommunicate any members of the community who had offended against right doctrine or morals. The magistracy saw this as trespassing on its competence to control public morality, but Calvin affirmed that ecclesiastical discipline, based on the 'power of the keys' should go side by side with civil justice. The councils drew the line at excommunication which was the corner-stone of Calvin's system. Calvin won the day, but the final article in the *Ecclesiastical Ordinances*, published on 20 November 1541 was so ambiguous that it caused him incessant quarrels. The document was to become the foundation on which Calvin was to build his church. It was of divine right, since, as stated in the preamble '. . . we see it is taken from the gospel of Jesus Christ'. (*Works*, 10a. 16. n.1.)

How did these ministerial principles work out in the countries to which Calvinism spread, in particular France, the Netherlands, and Scotland? Ministers were required to reside in their parishes, and absenteeism was almost unknown, as was pluralism. Ministers were generally forbidden to engage in trades or professions or hold state appointments. Vestments were considered to be 'defiled with infinite superstition' (in Beza's words), savouring of popery, and so ordinary dress with a black cloak and white ruff was worn which gradually became distinctive, ending up as the preacher's black gown.

The main duty was preaching, and according to the First Helvetic Confession of 1536, 'to preach penitence and remission of sins through Jesus Christ'. The Second Helvetic Confession of 1566 claimed a very high doctrine of preaching: '. . . when today this word of God is proclaimed in the church by means of preachers lawfully called, we believe that the very word of God is proclaimed'. It is not surprising that architecturally the pulpit became the central feature of the church building, with the font and holy table near it. Preaching, indeed, became *the* sacramental act of nourishment, of which Communion was but a symbol and therefore less direct because it could not be effective unless supported by preaching. Thomas Cartwright, the Puritan divine, attacked the Book of Common Prayer because 'it maintaineth an unpreaching ministry and so consequently an unlawful ministry'.

Ministers also officiated at marriages and funerals, and visited the sick, many dying of the plague in Geneva in 1543–45. In the Great Plague in London in 1665 many ministers who had been deprived by the Act of Uniformity visited the stricken and braved the consequences. Calvin had divided Geneva up into three parishes, and the Presbyterian tradition favoured a territorial ministry, whereas the Congregationalist held to the principle of a gathered congregation.

Ministers exercised their spiritual authority by administering the sacraments and exercising discipline. The former was reserved to ministers because it was indissolubly united to preaching. The most serious disiplinary measure was excommunication, but this was never the verdict of one man but always of a consistory, a kirk session, or a General Assembly – though the Independents claimed the right for a single congregation. (The Genevan consistory consisted of two thirds laymen.)

In reaction against the medieval development of hierarchy, Calvin maintained a parity of ministers. The conflict became acute in Scotland when James VI proposed to make bishops out of reformed ministers. In 1607 James Melville was offered the bishopric of Dunkeld, but his reply was a strong negative. A clean sweep of all hierarchy was made at the Glasgow Assembly of 1638, but earlier there had been 'superintendents' appointed under the *First Book of Discipline* of 1560 to oversee districts roughly corresponding to the old dioceses. They had power to ordain; they were ordained by other ministers; they were under the authority of the General Assembly and also under local control; they had to travel much, doing the duty of a locum while also being parish ministers; and they had no special honour. It is debatable whether the Church of Scotland was originally episcopal.

Calvin, like Luther, was the product of the sixteenth century, and his interpretation of the Bible, like Luther's, suffered from the limitations of contemporary scholarship. His dominant insistence on human sinfulness, to the point of 'total depravity', has led to a major distortion of the gospel. His church organisation owed as much to the republican style of government in Swiss cantons as to the New Testament, but at least it gave an important share of responsibility to lay people, and encouraged close relations between church and state. That this has not always worked to a Christian end may be seen from the support given in South Africa, until 1991, to the policy of *apartheid* by the Dutch Reformed Church. The Calvinist emphasis on preaching led to the formation of numerous colleges where men could be trained for the ministry and also for civic responsibilities.

3. *The Radical Reformers.*

If Luther, Calvin and Zwingli are reckoned as the magisterial reformers, there were others to their far left (or right, as Luther saw it, because he placed the Roman church to his left) for whom the classical reformers had not gone far enough. Indeed they saw in Luther's doctrine of salvation by faith a new indulgence system more grievous than the one which he had attacked; they preferred 'regeneration' to 'sanctification'; they opposed any doctrine of predestination which undercut the personal and corporate discipline by which they strove to reproduce the apostolic life; and in particular they insisted on believer's baptism, and since infant baptism could be of no effect they demanded re-baptism (whence the name Anabaptist) and certain manifest gifts of the Spirit. The radicals set out to re-create the true Church, a *restitutio* rather than *reformatio*, dispensing with magistrates and prelates alike.

They had their problems about church order. Many of the magisterial reformers, such as Zwingli and perhaps Calvin, had been ordained as Catholics and declined to be re-ordained as Protestants. In contrast, among the radicals there were several, like Menno Simons, who felt the need for a new commissioning. Many, however, were laymen who were never formally ordained because their credentials were more moral and charismatic than regular. A fundamental debate arose over the need for formal university theological education on the one hand and prophetic, inspired, vocation on the other.

Akin to the prominence of lay people among the radicals was the elevation of women to a status of almost complete equality with men in the central task of the fellowship of the reborn. We meet several prophetesses, at least two women apostles and one redemptress along with numerous patronesses and protectresses.

The radical reformation was, by it very nature, not a unified movement but rather a loose network of local or regional groups often centring on one or two charismatic figures. It led directly to the establishment of no large church body, although indirectly the Baptists are its heirs. The Restorationist or House Church Movement is a modern spiritual descendant. The main characteristics of the radical reformers are best considered under eight regional groupings.

As early as 1521 Luther had had trouble with the 'prophets' at Zwickau. They were a triumvirate led by Nicholas Storch, a weaver, with Marcus Stübner, who had been educated at Wittenberg University. In that year they sought the help of Philip Melanchthon, Luther's lieutenant, who was impressed by their Biblical knowledge.

Their most important convert was Thomas Münzer who at St Mary's, Zwickau, became an eloquent interpreter of the reformation in a socially radical way, denouncing, among others, the opulent Franciscans. He came to think of himself as a chosen messenger of God. He had to leave Zwickau and fled to Prague where he preached the imminent ingathering of God's chosen people, with vision, dream and ecstatic utterance. His message did not produce the uprising he hoped for. In 1524, however, the peasants declared war on the nobility, and the following year in Mulhausen Münzer identified himself with the revolutionary classes. The landgrave Philip of Hesse moved against them and the peasants were defeated at

Frankenhausen. The rebel leaders were captured, tried, and beheaded, but many people followed the Anabaptists.

In 1524 Zwingli was seeking the reformation of the Church in Switzerland, but the radicals wanted the restoration of a righteous remnant with a mobile fellowship of conventicles. The radicals were certain that Zwingli was wrong in equating baptism in the new covenant with circumcision in the old, and so they broke with him and became a new sect. The birthday of the Swiss Brethren is held to be 21 January 1525 when George Blaurock, a priest and canon, accepted believer's baptism at the hand of a layman in the home of Felix Mantz in Zurich. Eight days later Blaurock entered the village church of Zollikon and interrupted the Zwinglian pastor with the words 'Not thou but I have been called to preach'. He caused such a commotion that the magistrate threatened to lock him up. Some of the Anabaptists were characterised by a stubborn legalism, with the practice of daily excommunication for anyone who transgressed their strict standards, but others fell into a frenzied antinomianism which was enough to bring their whole movement into disrepute. In 1526 the Zurich town council passed a new law attaching the death penalty to re-baptism and attendance at Anabaptist preaching. Mantz and Blaurock were arrested and in January 1527 were sentenced: that Mantz should die by drowning, and that Blaurock should be whipped through the town into perpetual banishment. So died the first Protestant martyr at the hand of Protestants.

Melchior Hoffmann, a furrier by trade, had been Luther's fiery apostle to Livonia (on the Baltic) before becoming an itinerant evangelist and popular preacher. In 1523 he came to consider himself a prophet, perhaps Enoch or Elijah, ordained to usher in the end-time, and he antagonised the settled clergy. In order to produce some ecclesiastical law and order against this religious anarchy, a synod was held in Strasbourg in 1533 under the leadership of Martin Bucer, to which Hoffman and other Anabaptist leaders were invited. In the event he was sentenced to life imprisonment and died ten years later. Other leaders, however, took over, and the final act of this apocalyptic nightmare took place in Münster, a considerable city in north-west Germany. The Anabaptists seized power, threatening to kill all who had not been re-baptised, and the troops of the prince-bishop sealed off the city. Within, strict martial law was declared, suitable to the Lord's army, with common ownership of money, food, houses, and, strangely, wives (this last out of emulation of the Old Testament patriarchs). On 13 October 1534 a great meal was shared in the town square, a veritable Messianic banquet. In June the following year after a fearful battle the city was taken and almost all the inhabitants slaughtered. The three surviving principal actors were tried, condemned, and tortured to death in January 1536. But the Melchiorite gospel was far from silenced.

In England Anabaptists of Dutch and Flemish origin were present in some strength before 1536, following the wool and textile trade to the east coast. Already in 1528 Thomas More was corresponding with Erasmus about the *Anabaptistarum Haeresis*, and in 1538 king Henry VIII received a letter from Philip, landgrave of Hesse, warning him to beware of 'the Anabaptist pest'. He issued two proclamations prohibiting the printing and importing of their books, and ordering all re-baptised persons to leave England immediately. Some did not, and three died at the stake for their beliefs. In 1560 Elizabeth I decreed that all Anabaptists must conform to her establishment or leave the country, but many were flocking here following persecution. Men and women were arrested; some recanted; some were shipped back to Holland; and some were burned at the stake.

Anabaptist refugees from Switzerland penetrated into Bohemia and Moravia (most of modern Czechoslovakia) and found ready acceptance. In 1467 the *Unitas Fratrum* was founded as a socially egalitarian and pacifist fellowship. They selected by lot three of their number to be priests and one of them their bishop. Ordination was secured from a local Waldensian elder. In 1519 Jacob Hutter became the chief pastor of the Tyrolese Anabaptists and later became convinced that he was called of God in a unique way to guide these federated groups in the way of the Lord. The Hutterites maintained that God from the beginning had commanded the communitarian way of life, and salvation is only to be found in this community. Brotherly love went hand in hand with absolute obedience towards God and the eldership. Living co-operatively was the Hutterite answer to the poverty of the Franciscans.

Caspar Schwenckfeld was a devout landed nobleman from Silesia (modern western Poland), a knight of the Teutonic order. He was converted to Lutheranism in 1518, but eight years later came to believe that the eucharist must be suspended in favour of an inward and spiritual feeding on the 'celestial flesh' of Christ. Similarly, outward baptism became unimportant; what mattered was baptism by the Holy Spirit. He did not see his prayer-meetings as a substitute for the established church, but he looked forward to a church of the Spirit which would manifest the unity, purity and gifts of the apostolic church. In 1529 he moved from Silesia into voluntary exile, leaving behind many Anabaptist followers identifiable by their insistence on baptism by total immersion and community of goods. In 1558 all Anabaptists were banished by royal decree.

The Polish Minor Church was anti-Trinitarian and largely Anabaptist, and it was transformed into the Socinian movement by Socinus, born in Siena, Italy, in 1539. In 1574 he settled in Basle and worked out a theological system denying Christ's essential deity, denying that the atonement should be seen in terms of penal satisfaction, and denying that the effects of Christ's obedience could be transferred to others. His system, in all its clarity, highlights the divergence of the radicals from the magisterial reformers. The radical reformers, in loosening the conception of the solidarity of mankind in Adam's sin, dismantled the conception of a universal church with the Second Adam as its head. In stressing God's love rather than his justice, they located the response rather in the self-disciplined conventicle separated from the state than in the intermingled body of saints and sinners in a coercive territorial or papal church.

At the end of the sixteenth century a large body of the Polish

Brethren sought refuge in Holland and introduced among the Mennonites there the practice of baptism by immersion. About 1608 an English Puritan preacher with the very English name of John Smith led a company of exiles to Amsterdam and the next year established there the first modern Baptist church. He died there in 1612, having been much influenced by the Mennonites, and in that year a company of his associates returned to London to establish the first Baptist Church in Great Britain. It was destined to become over the next three and a half centuries, one of the largest world-wide Protestant communions.

The Radical Reformation was a gallant attempt to re-establish the spiritual and prophetic dimension in a church which, it seemed, had become hopelessly legalistic. It attempted to recover the quality of life of the apostolic church pictured in the New Testament, and was prepared to maintain a high moral standard by strict discipline. It was prepared to venture into new ethical realms with its pacifism and experiments in community life. Its proponents were prepared to make amazing sacrifices of money, property, comfort, status, and often of life itself for what they were sure was a divine calling.

In retrospect, however, it shows all too clearly the weakness of a 'spiritual' interpretation of the church divorced from, on the one hand, matter, and, on the other, the church's wider corporate tradition. With matter derogated, there is little place for the sacraments. With a narrow understanding of tradition, there are all the dangers of eccentricity in charismatic leaders. With a narrow interpretation of the Bible, the view can be blocked by apocalyptic expectations of a second coming; and the loss of a sense of human solidarity both in sin and in redemption, leads to a multitude of small, separated, and often contending communities. It is not surprising, therefore, that the Radical Reformers, on the whole, had a low estimate of ordination and of training for holy orders.

4. *The Counter-Reformers.*

There had been considerable movement for reform within the Roman Catholic Church long before Luther released his avalanche in 1520. In the previous century the attempts to replace the authority of the popes by that of General Councils was killed by the papacy at the Council of Basle in 1449. At the end of the century a new crisis loomed when the heirs of Marsilio and Wycliffe met in Germany in 1510 at the Diet of Augsburg accompanied by a stream of books and pamphlets challenging the whole ecclesiastical structure. There had been a spate of university foundations between 1450 and 1500 together with a proliferation of printing presses, and in the critical 1520s the output of Protestant books vastly exceeded the Catholic defence.

Cardinal Ximenes, the High Chancellor of Castille, reformed his own Franciscan order, and founded the University of Alcala (Complutum) for the better education of clerics, with a humanistic approach to biblical studies. In Paris Jean Standonck reorganised the Collège de Montaigu for the formation of priests, to be brought up on a classical education, who 'will be taught to embrace mortification and virtue together with knowledge.' In Italy the most influential reformer was Gian Matteo Giberti, bishop of Verona from 1524 to 1543. He toured his parishes, expelled ignorant priests from their benefices, forced non-residents to return, questioned the laity about the needs of their churches, relieved the distress of peasants, and founded orphanages and almshouses. Above all he laid stress on parish worship and the sense of congregational brotherhood. He promoted able preachers, and removed all women from presbyteries. Few matched his heroic efforts or his own example.

A product of the new age was the creation of a number of religious orders designed to strengthen and develop the spiritual life of the clergy. The Theatines were founded in Rome in 1524 by Cajetan Thiene and Pietro Caraffa, intended for secular clerics working in the world but bound to a rule, and it proved to be a school for future reforming bishops. Greatest of all the new orders was the Society of Jesus, the conversion of whose founder, Ignatius Loyola, from a military to a spiritual knight-errantry was comparable with Luther's. His visions of God led him to preach in the streets and consequently landed him in prison at the hands of the Spanish Inquisition. The cosmopolitan university of Paris liberated him from the narrowness of his Basque background, and for seven years he studied at the Collège de Montaigu – from which Calvin had just departed. Between 1546 and 1554 the order founded five colleges in Italy, seven in Spain, one in France and two in Germany, but progress in England was slow. One of the most remarkable missionary undertakings of the Jesuits was Francis Xavier's foundation of Christianity in Japan in 1549. He died in December 1552, hungry and half-frozen, on an island just off Hong Kong at the gateway to his final objective, China.

The popes were remarkably slow to respond to increasing agitation for reform, but eventually foundations for renewal were laid by Paul III, pope from 1534 to 1549. He called the Council of Trent in 1545 (and in the same year appointed Michelangelo chief architect of St Peter's). Eight years before, a report had been published by a commission making radical proposals about the clergy. (It was printed in 1538 without authorisation and was widely used by Luther as a weapon against Rome.) It traced the fount of evils to papal despotism and recommended better selection and education of ordinands, the denial of foreign benefices to Italians, the abolition of the sale of benefices and ending of non-residence of bishops and priests, along with sweeping reforms of the monastic orders. It also advocated a harder policy about liberal education – by those who had enjoyed its benefits. Whereas Luther diminished the importance of clergy, this programme concentrated on the clergy as the key to improvement.

The last significant effort for a negotiated settlement with Luther was the Colloquy of Regensburg (Ratisbon) in 1541 under the cardinal legate Contarini, with Melanchthon and Bucer (and the young Calvin sitting in the wings) which did reach a compromise formula on the subject of justification but finally foundered on transubstantiation.

In 1545 the Council was summoned to Trent (Tridentum) as the nearest imperial city to the Tyrol because of local wars which restricted the opening session to thirty-one bishops. Of the 270 bishops who ever attended, 187 were Italian, but there was a capacity for self-criticism and a passionate desire to rescue the Holy Catholic Church. Dogma and discipline were debated side by side.

The Council set out on a headlong collision course with Lutheranism by putting scripture and tradition on an apparent level:

> It [the Council] also clearly perceives that this truth and this discipline are contained in the written books and in the unwritten traditions which, received by the apostles from the mouth of Christ himself, or from the apostles themselves, the Holy Spirit dictating, have come down to us, transmitted as it were from hand to hand.
>
> *(Fourth Session.)*

The iron fist of doctrinal conservatism was banged loudly on the table with the declaration of the absolute authenticity of the 'old Latin Vulgate Edition' of the Bible, and that 'no one dare or presume under any pretext whatsoever to reject it'.

> Furthermore, to check unbridled spirits, it decrees that no one relying on his own judgement shall, in matters of faith and morals . . . presume to interpret them [the Holy Scriptures] contrary to that sense which holy mother Church, to whom it belongs to judge of their true sense and interpretation, has held and holds . . .
>
> *(Fourth Session, 2nd Decree).*

The same decree required any book on sacred doctrinal matters to carry an *Imprimatur* of official approval, a rule quietly rescinded only in the middle of the twentieth century.

This same year saw another conservative victory, that of scholasticism over biblical humanism, and attempts were quashed to encourage the laity to read the scriptures and to prepare for the laity a scripture-oriented catechism, for this would be playing into the hands of Protestantism. When seventeen years later, the Council decreed seminaries, human-ism was out.

The second period of the Council was a short one, from 1551 to 1552. It dealt mainly with the eucharist by reiterating the formula of transubstantiation but in a crudely materialistic way without regard for the philosophical subtlety which lay behind the word 'substance'. Consideration of the mass con-tinued in the third session from 1562 to 1564, with canons aimed at aspects of the reformers' teaching which criticised the medieval teaching about the 'true and only sacrifice'. It is noteworthy, however, that this exposition is careful to speak of the 'representation' and 'commemoration' of Christ's sacri-fice on the cross, and it does not state that in any subsequent celebration anything is added to the original offering (*Twenty Second Session, Chapter 1*). The weakness of this kind of sacrificial imagery, however, is clearly shown in the next chapter when it is declared that 'appeased by this sacrifice, the Lord grants the grace and gift of penitence and pardons even the gravest crimes and sins'. That sacrifice is basic to the gospel is unde-niable; that sacrifice is primarily to be understood in terms of propitiation must be denied.

Chapter 6 underlines the propriety of the private mass against which Luther had fulminated, and *Chapter 8* insists on keeping Latin as the language of the mass.

Holy orders came to be debated in the closing months of the Council. Priesthood is defined in terms of eucharist, as eucharist is defined in terms of sacrifice. The priesthood of the New Testament is to be understood in terms of the priesthood of the Old:

> Since therefore in the New Testament the Catholic Church has received from the institution of Christ the holy, visible sacrifice of the eucharist, it must also be confessed that there is in that Church a new, visible and external priesthood, into which the old has been translated.

The indelibility of ordination is asserted; bishops are declared to be, as successors of the apostles, rulers of the church and ministers of confirmation and ordination, and for ordination the consent of people or magistrate is not vital. There could be no reconciliation with Luther or Calvin along such lines.

One practical provision which did have a lasting effect was the requirement that every diocese should set up a seminary for boys 'whose character and inclination justify the hope that they will dedicate themselves for ever to the ecclesiastical ministry'. The pattern of education was dictated by the medieval shoolmen led by Aquinas, and the image of a priest, with an appropriate spirituality, was largely shaped by the Flemish theologian, Josse van Clichtove. It was dominated by the idea of the priest's being removed from the world, even from his parishioners, essentially a cultic and not a pastoral figure. The only adequate sign of this 'set-apartness' is celibacy, which Clichtove maintained is warranted by 'divine law' and so not even the pope can dispense anyone from it. Priesthood is based on the sacred power of offering sacrifice, and on the basis of this power the priest is mediator between God and the faithful. This pattern remained substantially unchanged until Vatican II.

The Council of Trent did indeed pull the Roman church together, but at a high price. It delivered the church over to a papal monarchy, with no further Council for three centuries. It delivered the church over to a clerical hierarchy which demoted the laity to a level of total subservience. It delivered the church over to an antique method of Biblical interpretation just as literary criticism was beginning to burgeon with the Enlightenment. Above all it constricted the church to a narrow sphere of thinking about God, man, and the universe as Europe stood on the threshold of vast new discoveries in the sciences. Beyond the authoritarianism of Rome loomed the menacing figure of Voltaire, and beyond the clericalism of Rome loomed the anti-clericalism of the French Revolution.

10

The Middle Way –
Ecclesia Anglicana

'FOR my part, Sir, I think all Christians, whether Papists or Protestants, agree in the essential articles, and that their differences are trivial, and rather political than religious'. This judgement made by the doughty high-churchman Samuel Johnson seems well founded now, two hundred years later, when a plethora of ecumenical documents indicates a surprising doctrinal agreement, but the churches concerned show marked reluctance to alter their polities.

The Church of England emerged from years of turmoil in the reign of Elizabeth I (1558–1603) to present to the world the unique spectacle of a church at once catholic and reformed. Its principal vindicator was Richard Hooker in his *Laws of Ecclesiastical Polity*, the first four books of which were published in 1594. The fifth, published three years later, acknowledges in its dedication that church's debt to the Queen: 'By the goodness of almighty God and his servant Elizabeth we are.'

This was no conventional politeness but reflects a deeply held conviction of the theological importance of the 'godly prince', as significant for Lutherans, Calvinists and Anglicans then as it seems curious to many now. The doctrine was rediscovered from the historical books of the Old Testament, and the precedent set forth so clearly there could not be contradicted by the New. John Whitgift, Elizabeth I's Archbishop of Canterbury from 1583 to 1604, declared

> The archbishop doth exercise his jurisdiction under the prince and by the prince's authority; for the prince having the supreme government of the realm, in all causes

and over all persons, as she doth exercise the one by the Lord Chancellor, so doth she the other by the archbishops.

(Works, 2.246.)

The only limiting factor was that 'nothing be done contrary to the word of God'. John Jewel, bishop of Salisbury, in his celebrated *Apologia Ecclesiae Anglicanae* of 1562, emphasises that the scriptures are the foundation of the Church and that the truth is more important than unity:

> Of a truth unity and concord doth best become religion; yet is not unity the sure and certain mark whereby to know the church of God . . . The catholic church of God standeth not in multitude of persons, but in weight of truth.

(Works, 3.360 and 268.)

Neither Whitgift nor Jewel said anything about a particular form of ministry being essential to the church, though Article 36 of *The Thirty-nine Articles* affirms the Ordinal in whose Preface the Church of England's polity is set out:

> It is evident unto all men diligently reading holy Scripture and ancient Authors, that from the Apostles' time there have been these Orders of Ministers in Christ's Church; Bishops, Priests, and Deacons . . .

and the Article goes on to require that every man shall be 'called, tried, examined, and admitted thereunto, according to the form hereafter following'.

So from the beginning of its reformation the Church of England maintained the episcopal succession, holding the 'godly bishop' next in importance to the 'godly prince', in contrast to the corrupt prelacy of the later middle ages. Jewel interpreted this succession as one of doctrine, not of sees. Of former bishops of Salisbury, he observed that 'we succeed them in place, but not in error'. Whitgift and Hooker never abandoned their position that *no* form of polity is exclusively prescribed in scripture, a fact noted regretfully by Keble (in the Introduction to his edition of the *Works* of Hooker).

93

Hooker made precisely the same distinction between matters like faith which are *necessary* to salvation, and matters like ceremonies, order, and the kind of church government, which are accessory (*Eccesiastical Polity* 3.4). In his later writings (whose authenticity have been questioned) there is clear evidence of a movement towards a higher view of bishops, but even then he claims for it only apostolic, not dominical, authority. The institution of bishops may even have been of God (5.10), but then for Hooker all good forms of polity, both civil and ecclesiastical, are established by God.

It is generally agreed that the first reformers, Calvinist as well as Lutheran, had no objection to episcopacy in principle. The Augsburg Confession of 1530 uses very moderate language about the episcopate, stating that the purpose of jurisdiction of bishops, even by divine right, is to reject doctrine inconsistent with the Gospel. So too the Schmalkaldic Articles of 1537 allowed episcopacy 'if the bishops were real bishops who served the Church and the Gospel'. Luther, like Jewel, interpreted apostolic succession as a succession of doctrine, not of office (*Evangelium soll die Successio sein*). He did in fact have to appoint overseers or superintendents to exercise the jurisdiction traditionally associated with the episcopate, and the accidents of history have determined that Lutherans in Sweden and Finland still have bishops who alone have the power of ordaining.

From this could have emerged a mixed polity, embracing elements episcopal, presbyteral and lay. Even names of office-holders were up for review. If 'bishops' could become 'superintendents', 'priests' might become 'presbyters', particularly to remove the odium of sacrificial connotations. Whitgift preferred to keep the word 'priest', explaining that it was only the English form of the word 'presbyter' and claiming that meanings can be changed. 'It is mere vanity to contend for the name, when we agree of the thing.' (*Works*, 3.351.) Hooker had less time for the old name and preferred 'presbyter':

> . . . whether we call it a Priesthood, a Presbytership, or
> a Ministry, it skilleth not. Although in truth the word

Presbyter doth seem more fit, and in propriety of speech more agreeable than *Priest* with the drift of the whole gospel of Jesus Christ.

(Ecclesiastical Polity, 5.78, 2–3.)

In the first fifteen years of Elizabeth I, until 1573, prospects for close cooperation between the Churches of England and Scotland were bright. For its first twenty years the Church of Scotland enjoyed a mixed polity of episcopal and presbyteral authority, strengthened in 1572 by the Convention of Leith. So John Douglas was instituted, with the laying-on of hands, as 'Archbishop of St Andrew's and Superintendent of Fyfe'

At this moment there began in England a movement which was to come near to overthrowing episcopacy in the Church of England. Its leader was the Puritan divine, Thomas Cartwright, then a professor of divinity at Cambridge (though he was deposed after twelve months in 1570). In 1572 these puritans published *Admonitions to Parliament* with strident demands for a 'right reformation', in particular for an 'equality of ministers': the Church must be committed only to ministers, seniors [that is, presbyters], and deacons. Similarly the Book of Common Prayer must go since it was 'an unperfect book, culled and picked out of that popish dunghill, the Mass Book, full of all abominations'. This was, however, too much both for the godly prince (Elizabeth) and the godly bishops, and the royal prerogative was enough to disarm the House of Commons. Not so, however in Scotland, where in 1581 the Assembly of the Kirk dropped the office of superintendent and introduced the new court of the presbytery.

This Presbyterian aggression of Cartwright produced over the next generation a distinct hardening of attitudes among Anglican divines in favour of episcopacy, which continued and developed in the next century. Firmer deductions were drawn from the historical evidence and greater weight placed upon episcopal authority as *divino jure*. Archbishop Laud held firmly that:

bishops might be regulated and limited by human laws in those things which are but incidents to their calling;

> but their calling, as far as it is *divino jure*, by divine right, cannot be taken away.
>
> (*Works*, 4.310–11.)

Not all bishops agreed.

In the course of a century of acute controversy Anglican divines like George Downham, John Whitgift, Lancelot Andrewes, Joseph Hall, John Bramhall, and even William Laud and Jeremy Taylor shrank from unchurching non-episcopal churches. (References are in N. Sykes, pp. 71–81.) Episcopacy, they held, was *divino jure* in the sense that it was of apostolic but not of dominical appointment; it was necessary to the perfection of a church but not to its essence; and on the ground of historic continuance its restoration in foreign non-episcopal churches was much to be desired.

How did these theological principles work out in practice? Were ministers of reformed churches who had been presbyterally ordained admitted to Anglican benefices without episcopal re-ordination? The answer is not absolutely clear, but there is strong evidence that they were. Joseph Hall (bishop of Exeter and then of Norwich) affirmed in the time of Charles I:

> I know those, more than one, that by virtue only of that ordination which they have brought with them from other reformed churches, have enjoyed spiritual promotions and livings . . .
>
> (*Works*, 10.341).

When the Scottish bishops returned home they consecrated other presbyters to share the episcopal office, but they did not re-ordain parochial presbyters.

Throughout the Anglican debate there runs the theme of historical necessity. It was widely agreed that the medieval papacy had brought episcopacy into such discredit that leading reformers had no way of proceeding except by abandoning the episcopal order. The fortunes of the movement depended absolutely on the policy of civil rulers, and only in England and Sweden were rulers and bishops together able to ensure the continuance of episcopacy along with doctrinal and liturgical reform. In England that continuity came very near to perishing. If Mary Tudor had reigned for twenty-five years instead of five, it would have ended: as it was, when Elizabeth I's accession saved the situation, Matthew Parker was the only one of the surviving Roman bishops willing to take the Oath of Supremacy. Again, if Cromwell had lived another decade (and he was only fifty-nine when he died), the episcopal succession would have become all but impossible. Anglicans had good reason to take seriously the argument from historical necessity.

The changes and chances of the seventeenth century exacerbated relations between Anglicanism and Presbyterianism. The alliance of Scottish episcopacy with the Stuart monarchy led to its fall in 1638. English episcopacy fell with the Civil War, and at the restoration of Charles II bishops and the Book of Common Prayer were reinstated in England and reimposed upon Scotland, and in 1662 the Act of Uniformity required, for any incumbent, ordination as priest according to that book. The ways had finally parted.

The turmoil of the times, not surprisingly, wrought havoc among the ordinary clergy. In 1534 Henry VIII ordered a survey of the revenue of every parish, the *Valor Eccesiasticus*, so that the tenth part which had formerly gone to the pope could be diverted to the crown. Many clergy feared a wider expropriation of clerical funds, and this led to a growing uncertainty and to a further decline in the number of ordinands. In 1549 Cranmer's new Prayer Book in English was imposed on all clergy who were obliged to use it on pain of imprisonment, and another followed in 1552, when attendance at church was required by law, again under penalty of imprisonment. Soon after becoming bishop of Gloucester in 1550 John Hooper examined some three hundred clergy in his diocese and discovered that one hundred and eighty-six could not repeat the Ten Commandments, thirty-nine did not know where the Lord's Prayer appeared in the Bible, and thirty-four could not say who was its author.

In 1553 the pendulum swung back to Mary's violent rule

under which eight hundred clergy were deprived of their livings because they had married, and seven bishops went with them. Elizabeth I's moderation was displayed by her choice in 1559 of Matthew Parker as Archbishop, and much of the subsequent ethos of the Church of England is the fruit of his energy and tact. In that year the Second Prayer Book was re-introduced with some important additions and alterations, and two hundred clergy were removed from their parishes for failure to adopt it.

There was a desperate shortage of clergy. In 1559 in the diocese of Canterbury fewer than half the parishes had a resident clergyman, at a time when the requirements for a literate, learned, and articulate ministry were now much greater. The ministry was poorly paid, graduates remained in short supply, and prestige was low.

The appearance and worship of the parish churches had undergone an astonishing change. Walls were whitewashed to hide medieval paintings. The minister now occupied a desk at the top of the nave or just inside the chancel screen where he could be seen and heard. Cranmer's intention for the main Sunday service was Morning Prayer followed by Holy Communion, but he had overestimated the average English person's endurance and underestimated his or her hesitation about frequent communion. In 1611 the King James or Authorised Version of the Bible was published and soon became the standard copy in churches. It was not a translation into 'modern' English, its majestic sonority owing a good deal to the work of Tyndale and Coverdale a century and more before. But it, and the later Book of Common Prayer of 1662, became the twin foundations for Anglican worship at home and abroad for some three hundred years.

The new Church of England emerged from the prolonged and often bitter controversy of a hundred years with a firm doctrine of ministry. It was catholic in highly valuing historic continuity, and it just managed to keep the succession of bishops. It held a high doctrine of episcopacy, though it saw this order as of apostolic and not dominical appointment. It was reformed in that it saw scripture to be basic, and if bishops were not faithful to scripture, then, in extreme circumstances, bishops might have to go. It declined to unchurch other reformed churches. It held truth to be more important than unity. It also took secular government seriously, partly because it had to, but also because it understood the godly prince and godly government to play an important part in the divine ordering of society, a belief still attested by the presence of bishops in the House of Lords.

Amid all the turbulence of the century from 1550 to 1650 many clergy carried out a faithful ministry in their parishes. Two of the most attractive figures who helped to shape the emerging ethos of Anglicanism were George Herbert (1593–1633) and his friend Nicholas Ferrar (1592–1637). The former was descended from the earls of Pembroke, and his education was carefully watched over by his mother, a woman of serenity and devotion and a friend of John Donne. He gave up a promising public career to seek ordination, and in 1630, to everyone's amazement, he became the rector of Fugglestone with Bemerton, near Salisbury, where he soon became a legend. His book, *A Priest to the Temple, or the Country Parson: His Character and Rule of Life* was especially valuable because it was the reflection of his own practice. He recalled the clergy to a life of prayer, and every day he read Morning and Evening Prayer at the hours of ten and four, where he was joined by 'most of his parishioners and many gentlemen of the neighbourhood, while some of the meaner sort would let their plough rest, whenever Mr Herbert's saint's-bell rang to prayers'. (So Izaak Walton in his *Life*.) He also advised his brother-clergy to gain a knowledge of tillage and pasturage, 'because people, by what they understand, are best led to what they understand not', and he stressed a knowledge of medicaments as indispensable to the cure of souls. The end of all was to be achieved 'by making humility lovely in the eyes of all men.' His poetry has been described by a modern poet (R. S. Thomas) as 'proof of the eternal beauty of holiness'. He died of tuberculosis after only three years of ministry. He remained very much a gentleman, and at his death his household contained six servants and two curates – for a parish of three hundred souls.

Nicholas Ferrar (to whom Herbert bequeathed his collection of poems) was a Londoner who enjoyed a brilliant career at Cambridge, and in 1624 was elected to Parliament. He also threw up the prospect of a distinguished future and settled the next year on a country estate at Little Gidding in Huntingdonshire. There he was joined by his brother and brother-in-law with their families to form a community whose life would embody the spirit of the Church of England. In 1626 he was ordained deacon by William Laud, and directed this household of some thirty persons in a life of prayer and work under a strict rule. He remained a deacon all his life. The community visited and relieved the poor and sick of the neighbourhood and taught the children the Psalms. They were also skilled in book-binding. A study-circle met frequently to tell and discuss stories illustrating events in the Church's year and Christian virtues.

This attempt to devise a monastic style of life appropriate to married people with families incurred the hostility of the Puritans who raided the house in 1646, nine years after Ferrar's death, destroying the building along with most of his manuscripts. It brought the community to an end, though in recent years a new community has been formed at Little Gidding, again centring its life on worship in the little church where prayer has been valid and whose fame is now assured by the poem bearing its name in T. S. Eliot's *Four Quartets*.

11
Modern Movements

PRESENT-DAY ministry (not only in the Church of England) has been largely shaped by three nineteenth-century movements, the Evangelical Movement, the Oxford Movement, and Christian Socialism, to which the twentieth century has added the Ecumenical Movement and the Charismatic Movement.

The Evangelical Movement

The term 'Evangelicalism' dates from the nineteenth-century Revival, with Wycliffe and Cranmer as its heroes. Evangelicals look to the Book of Common Prayer for their doctrine, but many are not happy with Cranmer's clear insistence that in baptism an infant is born again. John Wesley, that redoubtable Anglican priest, is another hero, but they tend to forget that he was a high-church Arminian (believing that everyone is potentially redeemed), a strong sacramentalist and believed in prayers for the dead. They value particularly the pietism which he learned from the Moravians and the heart-warming experience he had in Aldersgate Street in 1738, though historians now decline to see this as his conversion.

The Revival was in part a reaction to the dry Deism of the eighteenth century and the rationality of the Latitudinarians. It offered an approach to religion which was vibrant and experiential. Anglican evangelicals were, on the whole, strict churchmen and disapproved of the growing lay leadership among Wesley's followers and of wandering clergy preaching outside their parish boundaries. The effective breach with the Methodists came in 1784 when Wesley ordained two lay-preachers and set apart Dr Coke as Superintendent for Methodist work in America. Before 1800 there were only a few pockets of Evangelicals in the Church of England, not least in Huddersfield under Henry Venn, Vicar from 1759 to 1771. The parish produced twenty-two ordinands with working-class backgrounds but since they could not gain admittance to Oxford or Cambridge they went to dissenting academies and so were lost to the church. By 1800 there were about 500 Evangelical clergy; by 1830 between 2000 and 3000, nearly a quarter of the total.

Two names stand out, Charles Simeon and William Wilberforce. Simeon was ordained deacon in Cambridge in 1782 and in the same year became perpetual curate of Holy Trinity where he began to proclaim the new-found convictions and met with intense hostility which lasted for ten years. He set his sights on the undergraduates, half of whom were intending ordination though with no theological training provided. In 1792 he started after-church sermon classes, and in 1813 conversation parties on a Friday evening. In order to safeguard the continuation of his work he used money (from the family at first) to buy the patronage of livings. The Simeon Trust thus came to own the appointment of incumbents in more than a hundred parishes. (Cheltenham was bought for £3000.) The movement certainly kindled a new fire of devotion and raised the standard of clerical duty. Preaching became prominent, and the message was based on a dour calvinism: mankind was totally corrupt and deserved only eternal death from which we are rescued by the cross on which Christ died as our substitute. Conversion demands personal holiness which meant no card-playing for the men and no rouge for the women. Hymns and hymn-singing became popular, as also the small group meeting. Scripture was inerrant. No great inroads were made into the working classes; the main success was with the lower-middle class.

William Wilberforce inherited a fortune with which he bought himself a seat in the House of Commons. In 1787 Pitt persuaded him to undertake a campaign for the abolition of slavery which became a titanic struggle against vested interests. The slave trade was abolished in 1807 but slavery was not ended in the Empire until 1833. Wilberforce worked with a small group of influential Evangelicals later known as the Clapham Sect, but they were singularly unconcerned with the sufferings of the industrial poor at home, and had no interest in re-ordering social structures. Wilberforce introduced the bill to strengthen the laws preventing the combining of workmen against their masters which became the detested Combination Act of 1799, and this in order to save the poor from political agitators.

Family piety was encouraged with strict Sunday observance, and education was designed to subjugate rather than sanctify the senses. Casualties among the sensitive and the intellectual were high, including the Bronte sisters, George Eliot, Charles Kingsley, Ruskin, Macaulay, Peel, Gladstone, Pusey, Manning and Newman. Against the challenges of Darwin's *Origin of Species* in 1859, of *Essays and Reviews* in 1860, and the *Commentaries* of Bishop Colenso of Natal on Romans and the Pentateuch in 1861–2, the Evangelicals had not the equipment to contend and could only retreat into a fortress of reaction, bastions of which were the 'sound' theological colleges, in 1863 Peache's College, 'a Protestant, Evangelical and Truly Church of England College', followed by Wycliffe Hall at Oxford in 1877 and Ridley Hall at Cambridge in 1881.

The arrival of Biblical criticism threatened their basic tenet of the inerrancy of scripture, as also of the substitutionary theory of the atonement, and major splits became inevitable: in 1910 the Cambridge Inter-Collegiate Christian Union opted out of the Student Christian Movement and in 1922 the Bible Churchmen's Missionary Society was formed out of the Church Missionary Society. After the Second World War a measure of revival came from the missions of the American Baptist Billy Graham, and this enhanced the ambiguity of the Evangelical claim to be the true Church of England. In the early 1970s a prominent Evangelical, James Packer, described their wider image as one of 'archaic theology, spiritual conceit, ecclesiastical isolationism, social unconcern, pessimism about the world and the Church, an old-fashioned life-style, and a cultural Philistinism' (in *Evangelicals Today*, ed. King, p. 61). The arrival of the Alternative Service Book in 1980 and the parish communion, with new translations of the Bible, new hymn-books, the ordination of women, and frequent official restatements of doctrine and morality have all caused the 1980s to be, in the words of one Eclectic, 'a period of anomic disorientation'.

The Oxford Movement

It is often thought that the Oxford Movement was primarily concerned with forms of worship. In origin it was not. On 14 July 1833 John Keble, the Professor of Poetry at Oxford, preached a sermon on 'National Apostasy' in defence of the Church which was threatened by the government's proposal to suppress ten Irish bishoprics (though the Ecclesiastical Commissioners) and re-allocate their revenues. He then co-operated with John Newman, Vicar of St Mary's Oxford, in publishing *Tracts for the Times*, ninety of which were issued between 1833 and 1841, four years before Newman's departure to the Church of Rome. The first was addressed to the clergy:

> Should the Government and Country so far forget their GOD as to cast off the Church, to deprive it of its temporal honours and substance, *on what* will you rest the claim of respect and attention which you make upon your flocks? Hitherto you have been upheld by your birth, your education, your wealth, your connexions . . .

Newman's answer was 'the apostolical succession'. 'The Lord Jesus Christ gave His Spirit to His Apostles; they in turn laid their hands on those who should succeed them; and these again on others; and so the sacred gift has been handed down to our present Bishops . . .'; from which he drew the corollary that 'we must necessarily consider none to be *really* ordained who have not *thus* been ordained.'

Only ten of the *Tracts* concerned liturgical matters, and in *Tract No 3* Newman resisted any alterations. He had a high, not to say providential, view of the Book of Common Prayer, and Keble and he preached in black gowns and presided at communion in surplice and hood at the north end of the altar. It was their doctrine of the eucharist and of 'the real presence' which encouraged candles, vestments and genuflexion, powerfully reinforced by the Camden Society, formed at Cambridge in 1839. As the theologians went back to a golden age of the Fathers, so the aesthetes went back to the golden age of Gothic, as innumerable red-brick Victorian churches bear witness.

It is alleged that the first fully sung service of Holy Communion took place in London at Margaret Street Chapel in 1847, and it was not long before Anglo-Catholic priests were teaching that communion must be received fasting, and so a new pattern emerged of an early mass before breakfast and then a High Mass at 10.30 or 11.0 with no lay communicants. The first Tractarian to advocate this in writing was Robert Wilberforce in his *Doctrine of the Holy Eucharist* in 1853, and many Anglo-Catholics only considered themselves absolved from the duty of fasting before communion by the Roman *Christus Dominus* published exactly one hundred years later. Even Evangelicals came to accept the 'early service' at eight o'clock as the norm. By the end of the nineteenth century a bewildering array of forms and styles of worship proclaimed a state of liturgical anarchy.

The period 1890–1914 was judged by C. G. Lang to have been the Golden Age of parochial work, yet the first World War provided a sobering shock. An extensive interdenominational investigation revealed, in *The Army and Religion*, that the Churches had failed to attract four-fifths of the country's young men, and an Archbishops' Committee of Enquiry (in *The Worship of the Church* in 1918) concluded that the Communion service ought to be restored to its primary place in church order. It also concluded that 'only by removal of the worst features of our social and industrial system, or even by a radical change in the system itself, will the way be made clear for the return of the people to the public worship of the Church.'

The seeds of what came to be called the Parish Communion were sown by W. H. Frere as curate-in-charge of St Faith's Stepney between 1890 and 1892 when he suggested the unknown hour of 9.30 to give the family a chance of worshipping together and going home to prepare the Sunday lunch. In 1904 C. G. Lang, then Bishop of Stepney, advocated 'one great parish communion every Sunday . . . of the Household of God at 9.0, 9.15 or 9.30.' and in 1931 William Temple in his Primary Visitation as Archbishop of York stated, 'In many places admirable results have followed the custom of holding a parochial Communion at 9.00 or 9.30.' and discouraged, as a normal practice, attendance at two Communions on one morning. He also declined to make fasting obligatory. It was quite clear by now that the movement was breaking the mould of the Book of Common Prayer. A revised Prayer Book was rejected by the House of Commons in 1927 and again, with further revision, in 1928, and perhaps this was no bad thing (though many were scandalised at the time) because it opened the way for a much more thorough process which resulted in the Alternative Service Book of 1980.

The revised Prayer Book of 1928 made no provision for greater vocal participation by the congregation, and laid no greater emphasis on the social implications of Christian worship. It is significant that the early protagonists of the Parish Communion insisted also on the weekly Parish Meeting as its secular counterpart, but this has never become a regular feature of the scene. A few parish priests kept to it, like Alan Ecclestone in Sheffield, where the Meeting would consider everything from the latest novel of note to the state of the local drains.

By 1920 the vestments battle had been won and that decade was the great age of Kelham and Mirfield, the Anglo-Catholic Congresses and Summer Schools of Sociology. The standard of Anglican liturgical practice went up steadily until a moderate Anglo-Catholicism became almost a clerical norm. By the 1960's at the moment of its greatest victory the movement was devastated, in part by the revolution of Vatican II and in part by the chill winds of secularism. Half of its goals had by now been accepted and half were seen to be absurd. Celibacy became suspect when some of its protagonists were found to be practising homosexuals. Even its doctrinal foundations seemed unsure when Rowan Williams asserted that Christian orthodoxy subverts its own existence: all formulations are inadequate for the truths to which they refer, and therefore any formulation of orthodoxy must be provisional. (Leech and Williams, 1983, pp.21–2) By 1990 the movement was split into a conservative rump with a record of opposition to change, particularly over the ordination of women to the priesthood, and a body of would-be radicals searching for an identity.

Christian Socialism

The third considerable influence on the nineteenth and into the twentieth century was not a movement as such, but a group of people centred on F. D. Maurice and a visible line of succession of Anglican clergy which M. B. Reckitt has traced in his *Maurice to Temple*. The word 'socialist' appeared for the first time in *The Co-operative Magazine* in November 1827 and was suspect to organised Christianity. Had not W. Wilberforce written in 1797 that Christianity renders 'the inequalities of social state less galling to the lower orders whose lowly path has been allotted to them by the hand of God'? The Methodist movement was no more favourably inclined. S. T. Coleridge was, perhaps, the first voice of Christian Socialism in England, and he had a great influence on Maurice. Maurice, born in 1805, and brought up a Unitarian, was baptised in 1831 and ordained in 1834. In 1838 he wrote his most enduring book, *The Kingdom of Christ*, addressed to a Quaker. His other great influence was J. M. Ludlow, a young barrister whom he met as Chaplain of Lincoln's Inn, and who had studied at first hand Lutheran work among the poor in Paris. 1837 saw the virtual collapse of the trade-union movement and the publication of the People's Charter the next year. 1847 was a year of deep economic crisis following a series of crop failures. 1848 saw in February a revolution in France and in April the abortive Chartist demonstration on Kennington Common. Four years earlier Maurice had met Charles Kingsley, and those two, with Ludlow, published a series of seventeen weekly tracts, *Politics for the People* during the summer of 1848.

The theme was that religion and politics could not be separated: the Christian dynamic must be infused into Socialism, otherwise it would be the worse for both. The problem was how to supply this dynamic through a Church where the Evangelicals were concerned with individual salvation and the Tractarians were absorbed in the early Fathers. Reformation required a new emphasis on the social implications of Christianity based on God's intentions for mankind. The journal made little impression, but a small brotherhood of men grew up, though Maurice wished to avoid the implications of a party with a programme. The problem was how to make the workers understand themselves as spiritual beings belonging to the Divine Order, since 'the truth is that every man is in Christ; the condemnation of every man is, that he will not own the truth' (*Life*, 1.155). He saw his own task as a Professor at King's College, London, the training of a new generation of priests fired with a vision of all men as God's family. Maurice would not support the Owenite Home Colonies because he would not countenance the abolition of private property (which for him was holy), and in any case 'the Communist principle' (Maurice's own phrase) was already a living reality in the Church as a universal fellowship. (*Life*, 2.8). He had warned in *The Kingdom of Christ* (1.20. 7–8) that without the recognition of the true religious foundation of the social order the state would begin to assume the appearance and perform the duties of a universal spiritual society – and then there could be real danger to individual liberty. In 1848 he founded The Society for Promoting Working Men's Associations, and these associations were the forerunners of the legislation of organised labour.

In 1853 he was expelled from his chair at King's because he denied the doctrine of eternal punishment, and the following year he founded the Working Men's College in London and became its Principal. He had high hopes of education for the urban proletariat, and persuaded many eminent people to teach there.

The first phase of the 'movement', ended in 1854, but the seed was sown, not least among the Puseyites, and there followed a succession of high-church priests who did heroic work in the slums of England's industrial cities, from the London Docks to Miles Platting in Manchester. The Guild of St Matthew, the first example of 'sacramental socialism', was founded in 1877 by Stewart Headlam when he was a curate at Bethnal Green. He mixed in theatrical and artistic circles, and was banned from preaching by Frederick Temple, Bishop of London, as having 'a tendency to encourage young men and women to be frequent spectators of ballet dancing.' That line of succession led through the League of the Kingdom of God to the Summer Schools of Sociology in the 1920s. It was Francis Underhill's judgment at the first of these in 1925 that a large section of the Oxford Movement had been permeated by Christian Socialism.

As Maurice had a high doctrine of the Church, so he had a high doctrine of the ministry. He began with the fact that the existence of a permanent ordained ministry is a sign that there is a constitution and order for mankind, based on the principle that in Christ's kingdom the chief of all is servant of all (see for this section *The Kingdom of Christ* ch. 4, sec.5). The original and characteristic ministry in the kingdom of Christ was the apostolate, and Maurice was not unduly concerned about the details of how the three orders of ministry emerged. The episcopate is the main constituent of church policy, witnessing to the permanent and universal episcopacy of the invisible Head of the Church; it is 'one of the appointed and indispensable signs of a spiritual and universal society.' He spoke of 'the necessity for Apostolic Succession and Episcopal Ordination', but did not wish to unchurch those Christians who did not share it, as Newman did.

Similarly, the presbyteral office witnesses to the Elder-brotherhood and Priesthood of Christ, where *presbuteros* includes *hiereus*. The priest feeds his people with the sacrifice of Christ's self-offering, the pledge of a communion already consummated. It was, for Maurice, of supreme importance to remember that the Christian ministry is *representative* and not *vicarial*. The priest is not a kind of machine for doing the work of one who is absent. 'By the word representative I mean to express the truth that the minister sets forth Christ to men as present in His Church at all times.' It seemed to Maurice that the cardinal error of Romanism was that it treated the ministry as vicarial instead of representative, and a system which regarded the Pope as Vicar of Christ and substitute for him was the deadly opposite of the Catholic Church. When the high-church Professor R. C. Moberly wrote his *Ministerial Priesthood* in 1897, he echoed most of Maurice's main themes, though with differing emphases. So thoroughly had Maurice penetrated the Oxford Movement.

The Ecumenical Movement

The great new fact of the twentieth century has been the drawing together of Christian churches tragically split for half the history of Christendom. The Ecumenical Movement date from the Edinburgh Missionary Conference of 1910 and reaches to, and beyond, the visit of Pope John Paul II to England in 1982 when he read the Gospel at a great service in Canterbury Cathedral. Repeated failures of reunion attempts by the Church of England, sketched in Chapter 20, may perhaps presage a more comprehensive reconciliation including the Church of Rome.

The Charismatic Movement

The other major development of recent years has been the Charismatic Movement (that name dating from 1963), though its roots go back to the nineteenth century. It shares many features of classical Pentecostalism which originated in the United States in the encounter of the black spirituality of former slaves with a Catholic spirituality whose grandfather was John Wesley, since he translated the writings of French Catholic devotional writers for the use of his lay preachers.

The black spirituality was represented by scores of black hymn-writers and evangelists, notably William Seymour, the son of former slaves, who taught himself to read and write, studied (with difficulty) at a Bible School in Kansas, and began to teach in a Holiness Church in Los Angeles. He affirmed his black heritage by introducing negro spirituals and negro music into his liturgy.

In the revival which followed, white bishops and black workers, men and women, Asians and Mexicans, white professors and black laundrywomen were equal – in 1906. Social pressure soon prompted the Pentecostal bureaucracy to tame the revival and churches were segregated into black and white, but that did not hinder a world-wide spread, mainly to third-world countries where membership now is said to exceed 80 million in non-white indigenous churches.

Charismatic movements are those groupings which have accepted some elements of Pentecostal spirituality within the traditional churches, and the present one began in California in 1959. By 1963 it included several hundred Episcopalians, Presbyterians and Lutherans. In that year a Lutheran minister visited Michael Harper, a curate of John Stott's at All Souls', Langham Place (the very heart of the Evangelical establishment) and opened his eyes, or, perhaps, warmed his heart. In June 1964 Harper resigned his curacy and founded the Fountain Trust as the ecumenical church institution for 'renewal'.

This coincided with (or perhaps was a symptom of) a profound change in society where on every side rules were being broken, boundaries crossed and structures abandoned in a search for warm and intimate communities. It also coincided with strong Roman Catholic hopes of renewal in the wake of the Vatican Council; and what might have been just the latest form of American Protestant revivalism made a major impact on the Catholic world and considerably advanced the ecumenical cause.

The main characteristics of the Charismatic Movement can be briefly sketched. The word *charisma* means 'a gift of grace', and the key texts are 1 Cor. 12. 8–10 with its list of gifts, and Eph. 4.11 with its list of kinds of ministry. The critical experience is 'baptism in the Spirit', though it is unclear how this relates to the sacrament of baptism, nor is there any doctrinal agreement about 'speaking with tongues' being a necessary accompaniment; praise is vibrant with all sorts of new songs and choruses which tend to stress the lordship of Christ; some members claim to hear the Lord speaking to them and so can prophesy to the congregation; some claim gifts of healing which is sometimes exercised in the form of casting out evil spirits; there is a renewed awareness of the last things, with occasional predictions of an imminent End; and resulting from all these gifts and offices, an egalitarian approach which challenges any form of clericalism.

The Fountain Trust in England, dissolved in 1978, helped to prevent Pentecostals hiving off on their own, and by 1980 the movement was fairly domesticated by the Roman and Anglican Churches. At times it looked like a refuge for Christians frightened by the intellectual and institutional problems of their own church bodies, offering a euphoric freedom in ecstatic sounds and actions, but many Christians found in it a recovery of joy and faith and a loosening of prejudice between denominations.

A strong Pentecostal minority did, however, move in the opposite direction with the House Church Movement, especially among converts from the old Free Churches less familiar with a sense of wider church authority. By the late 1970s many 'house churches' had been set up, highly clerical, autocratic, intolerant, conservative, and male-dominated. Members were 'discipled' by pastors in every major decision they had to take. Not surprisingly these small communities provided strong support groups, almost communes, but at a high price. Their ethos was ominously like that of the Unification Church. Their claim is to 'restore' the church to its ideal form as portrayed in the New Testament, but their reading of the New Testament is highly selective and often naive.

Many ordained persons who have been confronted by the Charismatic Movement have been sorely tried in their ministry. They needed a thorough understanding of the Bible and its relevance for today, of the sacraments and particularly baptism, of church history (because this is by no means the first charismatic movement in the Church's experience), of human psychology both of individuals and of groups, and above all a deep spirituality, in order to 'test the spirits to see whether they are of God.' (1 John 4.1). Such an encounter provides a test case for ordination training.

It is clear that the Evangelical and Anglo-Catholic movements within the Church of England have run out of steam since they have largely achieved their purposes, the former to ensure the fundamental status of the Bible, and the latter to witness to a high doctrine of the church and sacraments. To which must be added the Liberals' astringent questioning of all orthodoxies, and the Radicals' insistence on the Church's responsible involvement in the society in which it is set, together with the Charismatics' rediscovery of spiritual joy and confidence. All these movements are now called to bring their separate contributions together into a greater Church.

Every Anglican parish can expect, and should rejoice, to have many or all of these traditions, with their strengths and weaknesses, represented in its congregation. The task of the minister is to make clear the foundations on which these traditions are built, and then, like a skilled conductor of an orchestra, to enable each person to make his or her own contribution to the building up of the church of God in that place.

12
Starting Afresh

THE Christian ministry has been shaped in important respects, for better and for worse, by its social setting. In its early centuries which were normative both for doctrine and for ministry the Church's boundaries were co-extensive with those of the Roman Empire, and if the faith had spread eastwards instead of westwards the story would have been different. It is hard now to conceive the Church without its western dress because most missionaries found it almost impossible to separate the gospel from its western cultural forms. In China, however, events from the end of the Second World War have served to wipe the slate fairly clean, and so it is instructive to study recent developments in that vast country with its population of well over one billion, a quarter of the human race. Visitors to the church in China comment on the astonishing similarity between its quality of life and that described in the earliest years of the church's history, not least its spiritual ebullience in response to the naked preaching of the gospel.

Christianity is no newcomer to China. In AD 635 a Nestorian monk, Alopen, travelled from Baghdad to Xian, capital of China in the Tang dynasty, monasteries were established, and there is known to have been a Nestorian bishop in Tibet in the seventh century. A stone tablet with a cross, set up in 781 and still to be seen in Xian, records that 'monasteries abound in a hundred cities'.

The Mongol, Gengis Khan, attacked China in 1212 and captured Beijing (Peking) three years later. The conquest was completed by 1264 under his grandson Khubilai Khan, and many foreigners flocked to China. The Mongol capital was established in Beijing under the name Khanbaliq, and as early as 1235 there was a Nestorian church and theological school in the city. In 1330 the Archbishop of Soltania reported that there were more than 30,000 Nestorians in Cathay.

The Nestorians were representatives of Eastern Christendom, if heretical ones; in 1289 Pope Nicholas IV having heard favourable reports from Marco Polo, sent John of Montecorvino, a Franciscan, to the court of Khubilai, though by the time he arrived in 1294 that Emperor had died and been succeeded by Timur who received him well. For thirty years he worked there with success: in a letter of 1305 he reported that he had baptised six thousand people, but these probably included few Han Chinese. The Mongol rule declined and was followed by the Ming dynasty which sealed China from foreign influence. In 1369 all Christians were expelled from Khanbaliq.

Two centuries passed before the third attempt to enter China, led by that extraordinary Jesuit missionary Francis Xavier 'apostle of the Indies and of Japan'. He died on China's doorstep in 1552 at the age of forty-six, but his vision was the inspiration of another Jesuit, Matteo Ricci (in Chinese, Li Matou) who arrived in Macao in 1582, and in 1594 received permission from his superiors to don the silk robes of the Chinese literati. His object was the conversion of the Emperor and to that end he travelled to Beijing in 1601 carrying many gifts. The embassy was well received, and he stayed there until his death in 1610. In 1608 he reported that Beijing had 'already more than two thousand Christians, among them many scholars'. By the end of the century there were about seventy-five foreign priests in China, and a native Chinese bishop was consecrated in 1685. There may have been 300,000 Christians in China by then.

These promising beginnings, however, were jeopardised by the 'Rites Controversy' of the eighteenth century between the Jesuits and other missionary orders, notably the Dominicans, over the extent to which the faith should be adjusted to Chinese customs, particularly the veneration of ancestors. In 1742 Pope Innocent XIII decreed against the Jesuits, a decision still cited today by the Catholic Patriotic Association in support of its non-recognition of the Vatican. The Emperor

Kangxi, who wrote a moving poem on the suffering of Christ on the cross, issued an edict banning Christianity in 1721 and some persecution followed. In 1773 Pope Clement XIV suppressed the Jesuit Order, though some stayed on in China as secular priests. Many thousands of Christians continued to worship.

The fourth wave started with the nineteenth century, characterised by Protestant fundamentalism's saving of souls. Robert Morrison of the (predominantly Congregational) London Missionary Society arrived in Guangzhou (Canton) in 1807 and secured his presence as a translator for the East India Company. Thus from the beginning Protestant missions were linked with the merchants and governments of their countries of origin. Further access to the country was secured by the infamous 'Unequal Treaties' of 1843 to 1860 which were forced on China as a result of its defeat by Britain in the Opium Wars. These provided explicitly for the right of foreign missionaries to preach Christianity, and also for foreigners and Christian converts to live under the jurisdiction of a foreign power and so claim immunity from Chinese legal proceedings. Hence the saying, 'One more Christian, one less Chinese'.

By 1889 there were forty-one different Protestant missionary societies active in China, with over 8,000 foreign missionaries in 1926. China's modern educational and medical services were almost entirely created by the missionaries, but results in terms of numbers were small. In 1911 there were fewer than 400,000 baptised Protestants, and by 1949 this figure had not quite doubled. China inherited all the divisions of the west, exacerbated by the fact that the word 'God' was translated by Roman Catholics as *Tianju*, by liberal Protestants as *Shandi*, and by evangelicals as *Shen*. More serious was the reluctance of missionary societies to hand over control to Chinese.

Following Sun Yat-Sen's revolution of 1912, a combination of civil war and Japanese invasion led to over thirty years of appalling chaos and misery. In 1937 the Vatican actually recognised the Japanese puppet state of Manchuguo in North

China. In Beijing on 1 October 1949 Mao Zedong proclaimed the People's Republic of China, and for the first time for a hundred years China came under a strong unifying government. It was a marxist government, committed to land reform and modernisation, and also to the view that religion was an opiate of the oppressed classes which would wither away as communism developed. The Korean war of 1950 put an end to any possibility of accommodation with foreign missionaries from capitalist countries, and during 1951 most were expelled.

Christian churches came under the supervision of the Religious Affairs Bureau which sponsored two associations for national representation one for Protestants and one for Catholics: for the first, the Three-Self Patriotic Movement, (self-government, self-support and self-propagation), and for the second the Catholic Patriotic Association. In the 1950s there was a strong move to consolidate the Three-Self Movement, with a driving underground of independent Christian groups, and it is fairly clear that the move to end denominationalism was more the result of the vision of some Christian leaders than of the pressure of government policy. The Roman Catholic Church fared similarly, though for them a break with Rome was of major doctrinal importance. The Vatican, however, continued to recognise the Nationalist régime in Taiwan, and the apostolic Nuncio in Beijing in 1949 continued to issue anti-communist statements: he was finally deported in 1951. The Chinese Catholics seemed to have no radical thinkers, and nothing emerged at all comparable with the liberation theology of Latin America. The turning point came in 1955 with the arrest in one day of the Bishop of Shanghai with over twenty priests and two hundred lay people, and many Catholics went underground. The break became complete in 1958 when the C.P.A. consecrated two bishops, despite the threat of Roman excommunication. By 1988 ninety-two bishops had been thus consecrated, each elected by the clergy of the diocese.

In 1966 the grotesquely misnamed 'Cultural Revolution' was launched with Mao Zedung calling out his Red Guards to rebel against the Party hierarchy over which he had lost control. All public religious activity ceased, as did virtually all art and academic activity, and Christians suffered alongside thousands of others, particularly intellectuals. Many observers, and many Chinese too, supposed that this marked the end of Christianity in China, but the opposite was the case. Christians gathered in meeting points in homes or out in the open air for worship and prayer and study often at risk of life, and by 1976 when the Revolution declined with the death of Mao, the number of Protestant Christians had greatly increased. ('Protestant' in Chinese terms means 'non-Catholic'.) In 1980 a new church structure emerged out of a National Christian Conference, the China Christian Council, which was to be 'the national organisation in charge of affairs for Chinese Protestant Christianity', and its president was K. H. Ting (Ding Guangxun) who was also chairperson of the Three-Self Movement. He was one of the surviving Anglican bishops (of whom there were six in 1987), and it must be said that Anglicans exercised an influence out of proportion to their numbers. So the Protestant Church in China moved into a new stage, not of unity but of post-denominationalism. The latest figures to the end of 1988, published by the Council, speak for themselves:

1. Churches in use: 6,375, among which 2,683 have been newly built since 1980.
2. Meeting points or home gatherings: 20,602. 15,855 of these are affiliated with Christian Councils and Three-Self Committees at different levels.
3. Number of Christians: 4,551,981. [In 1991 Bishop Ting gave their number as six million.] New converts in 1988 alone: 299,097.
4. Number of clergy: 12,060, which includes 6 bishops, 911 pastors (75 female pastors), 2,009 elders, 5,697 deacons, 3,437 evangelists.
5. Newly ordained clergy in 1988: 51 pastors and 213 elders.
6. Lay leaders: 40,108, including 18,078 leaders of meeting point gatherings.

7. Seminarians currently enrolled: 734.
8. Short term training courses in 1988 run by provincial and municipal level Christian councils: 139, with 2,651 participants. Courses run by county level Christian councils: 630, with 33,298 participants.
9. Clergy and laity who were awarded the title of advanced worker by their units in 1988: 16,556.

The crying need was in the area of ministry and training. Very few people had been ordained for thirty years so that nearly all pastors were in their sixties or older, Ting himself being seventy-five in 1990. So it is not surprising that Ting saw his episcopacy to be largely exercised in the Union Theological Seminary at Nanjing (Nanking). This had been set up in November 1952 out of a merger of eleven colleges, with Ting as Principal where he remained after his consecration as bishop in 1955. The college was closed in the late 1950s and reopened in 1961, and was still functioning in 1964, the only one in China. In the Cultural Revolution the Red Guard used it as their headquarters in Nanjing and burned nine out of every ten of its library books. The beginning of 1979 marked a new departure for the study of religion by communists with the establishment of the Nanjing Centre for Religious Studies under the auspices of Nanjing University, with Ting as its director. In May 1979 the first lecture 'On Christian Theism' was delivered to staff and students of this very secular university. A year later over a thousand students attended a series of lectures on Christianity. A lively debate continued in the 1980s on the Marxist doctrine of religion as 'opium' for the masses.

The seminary reopened its doors in 1981 with an initial intake of forty-seven students, eighteen of them women. Almost seven hundred had applied of whom three hundred and eight had sat an entrance examination. By 1989 twelve other theological colleges had been established, though only that at Nanjing was fully staffed with twenty full-time teachers. The others, which are Bible colleges rather than seminaries, are well off if they have three or four staff, and some have to manage with one or two. In 1987 a national Committee for Theological Education was set up to co-ordinate matters to do with selection, syllabuses, provision of text books, and personal formation. It has not had an easy time.

The difficulties in training are daunting and without parallel (though they are not financial because the communist government is paying back-rent for all the ecclesiastical premises it had seized). Nearly all the staff are well over sixty years of age (in 1990) and most of the students are between eighteen and twenty-five. Most of the students' English is not good enough to cope with theological textbooks, and there are few in Chinese. They come from a wide variety of church traditions stemming from the Reformation, placing great emphasis on the Bible, with many not knowing any set form of liturgy. The policy is to seek the common ground and work at differences, and so worship takes place on Saturday for the Seventh Day Adventists as well as on Sunday with a variety of liturgical forms. There is a strong bias towards a literalist understanding of the Bible, and the college accepts this while also presenting the results of modern criticism. Chinese Christians love hymn-singing and the college has a strong musical tradition. Since art is so fundamental to the Chinese spirit it also has an art department with a full-time teacher.

Ministry is the area of greatest doctrinal delicacy in this post-denominational situation, and in the catechism *One Hundred Questions and Answers on the Christian Faith* of 1983 there is only one reference to ordination, and that concerns baptism: 'The person who administers baptism should be someone who has been officially ordained by the Church as a pastor or an elder'. The polity of the China Christian Council is midway between Presbyterian and Congregational, and 'pastor' is the general designation of an ordained person, though elders, deacons and evangelists may also come under the heading of 'clergy'. Ting is clear that the three-fold ministry in its later development is not appropriate to the Chinese scene, though a demand for an authoritative ministry is arising from congregations who are troubled by inadequate teaching which sometimes moves into heresy. Bishops do not enjoy a good name in China and the Little Flock (a large group of Puritan Protestants descended from the Plymouth Brethren) threatened to break away if bishops were appointed, but in 1988 two were consecrated in Shanghai, Shen Yifan of Episcopalian background and Sun Yanli of Methodist background. In his sermon Ting said,

> We are not adopting the episcopal order; we have only the office of the bishop. In the New Testament there is also the office of bishop. So we have bishops, but not the order of episcopacy . . . Our bishops do not use administrative power, do not suppress, do not run a diocese. They have power, but it is spiritual, theological, moral power . . . In the following areas they should, without resorting to power, set themselves as an example:
> 1) in the construction of theological thinking;
> 2) in the renewal and lifting up of the spirit of worship;
> 3) in protecting the freedom of religion and in normalising the relation between the Church and the State; and
> 4) in unifying church co-workers and in respecting the particular worship practice of believers who are in the minority . . .
> We have to tread a path which others have not trodden before; let us make a new path not only in the Church of China but also in the Universal Church.
> (*China Study Project Journal*, Dec. 1988, p. 69)

The Protestant Church of China has been through the fire and has come out stronger, humbler, more united, and above all, Chinese. It has been thrown back on to first principles and has found them in the Bible, in prayer and worship, and in fellowship, often lay-led, for some groups of devout Chinese have maintained the church without having seen a minister for years. The theology of the leaders is built explicitly on the incarnation, 'the materialising of God in the real world', and on creation and re-creation, centred on the claim that 'in Jesus Christ man is a new creation'. This is their theological response to their perception of a renewed Chinese nation.

It is sad, though understandable, that there has been little converse between Protestants and Catholics. The latter, so far from experiencing their separation from Rome as an opportunity for bold experiment, have retreated to an ultra-traditional position, clinging to the Latin mass, at enormous cost to their theological students. Only in 1990 was the possibility of abandoning Latin being discussed. Each church has much to learn from the other, and the contributions of both are needed for a full presentation of the gospel in the church to China.

The story of the Church in China recapitulates many aspects of the history of the whole Church and its ministry sketched in previous chapters, and highlights key issues.

During the difficult years after 1950 the ministry has certainly belonged to the whole People of God, and in many places lay people have kept church communities alive and growing. No doubt some of their sacraments have been irregular, but now, in easier times, this is being remedied. It is noteworthy that the demand for authoritative teaching has come from the local level, and with it the perceived need for properly trained pastors.

China has experienced a multiplicity of western styles of church ministries and government, and the China Christian Council has opted for one of a Reformed pattern, though now incorporating an episcopal element (see Appendix 3, pp. 273f.). The Catholics are experiencing major problems and a deep division about loyalty to Rome. From 1840 to 1950 China suffered the worst effects of western imperialism to which the Christian missionaries were closely tied, and it has needed a communist revolution to sever these ties and allow the growth of a genuinely Chinese church.

Chinese Christians, through persecution and deprivation, have been forced back to first principles, that is to say the scriptures, and have there discovered, or re-discovered, a cosmic Christ who is concerned with justice in society and art in culture, though without any illusions that the kingdom of God has arrived. In K. H. Ting's words (in an address of 1991),

That Christ is cosmic gives us the assurance that God is the cosmic lover, not any cosmic tyrant or punisher. He works by education and persuasion rather than coercion and forced obedience. He lures and invites and waits for free response . . .

That reflects a fully trinitarian doctrine of God, the only sound basis for the organisation of ministry.

PART IV – ORDERS OF MINISTRY

13

Deacons

'IT is evident unto all men diligently reading Holy Scripture and ancient Authors, that from the Apostles' time there have been these Orders of Ministers in Christ's Church; Bishops, Priests and Deacons.' Such is the confident assertion in the Preface to the Ordinal of the Book of Common Prayer, but the language is anachronistic. That there were bishops, presbyters and deacons in the apostles' time is undoubted; that some progress towards an 'order' of deacons may be detected in the New Testament is clear; but it is not until the end of the second century that we first have evidence, in Tertullian, of the use of the word *ordo* with its overtones of Roman class distinction (see p. 57).

The subsequent history of the ministry has served to obscure the fact that these ordained ministers are still members of the *laos* or people of God, with the result that, for example, nowadays all Anglican synods are divided into houses of bishops, clergy and laity. The Second Vatican Council went some way to repair the damage with its emphasis on the Church as the People of God. A footnote to *Lumen Gentium* (2.9) reminds readers that:

> While everything said about the People of God as a whole is applicable to the laity, it should not be forgotten that the term 'People of God' refers to the whole community of the Church, including the pastors as well as the other faithful.

The Church of Rome has not, however, found it easy to give expression to that concept in the matter of shared church government.

Perhaps the confusion about holy 'orders' is greatest in the area of deacons, and so there we must start.

The term *diakonia*, translated as 'ministry' or 'service', has become something of a key-word for interpreting the whole of Christian ministry, based on the passage, Mark 10. 35–45, where Jesus reverses the order of social precedence, 'For the Son of Man came not to be served (*diakonēthēnai*) but to serve (*diakonēsai*) . . .' The lesson was powerfully reinforced by the foot-washing at the Last Supper as narrated by John (13. 16–17). It needs, however, more than one or two passages from scripture to form a doctrine of ministry, and the matter needs to be considered in detail.

The original derivation of the Greek word *diakonos* and its cognates is obscure, but its basic meaning is 'servant', 'attendant', or 'agent'. Service might include waiting at table, but could extend to many other duties in the house or in the management of an estate. In particular, *diakonos* is often used of a confidential messenger or go-between. He or she was normally a free person, unlike a *doulos*.

Careful examination of the New Testament evidence shows that the Christian use of the term is not to do with humble activity or being at the service of one's fellow men, but with being a spokesman or messenger on an assignment from God or from Christ.

In his Corinthian correspondence, for example, Paul is concerned about who could claim apostolic rights in that community. At the beginning of the First Letter he expresses his distress about the existence of parties loyal to Paul or Apollos or Cephas or (even) Christ. 'What then is Apollos?', he asks them in 3.5, 'What is Paul? Servants (*diakonoi*) through whom you believed . . .'. The use of the term here as a messenger of the Lord is entirely in keeping with common Hellenistic usage.

Again, in 2 Cor. 3.6 Paul is concerned with rival preachers and admits that he carries no letter of recommendation as they do, for the Corinthians themselves 'are a letter from Christ delivered by us' (3.2). His sufficiency is from God 'who has qualified us to be ministers (*diakonous*) of a new covenant, not in a written code but in the Spirit' (3.6). He goes on to argue

that the spiritual dimension of the new covenan'
own authority; it is this ministry (*diakonian*) of r.
which has been given to them by God (5.18); and 'we ...
given no offence to anybody, that the ministry (*diakonia*) be
not blamed, but have in every respect, as ministers (*diakonoi*)
of God, proved ouselves . . .' – and he goes on to give a long
list of the hardships he has undergone. A similar catalogue of
labours appears in 2 Cor. 11 as proof of his ministry over
against those who claim to be ministers (*diakonoi*) of Christ
(11.23). Thus the term diakonos in these passages portrays an
authoritative spokesman for God.

J. N. Collins (*Diakonia*, 1990) has examined and assessed
all the available evidence both inside and outside the Bible,
and concludes that in the New Testament the term refers
primarily to the Christian mission, and *diakonos* to an authorised emissary either of God or of Christ or of the Christian
community. The same usage is found in the *Letters* of
Ignatius where *diakonos* may mean either a godly courier
who travels for the church (e.g. *To the Philadelphians* 10. 1–
2) or something much nearer one who is a member of an
'order' of deacons.

What, then, of such an order? Early indications are found
in Paul's Letter to the Philippians which is addressed 'to all
the saints in Christ Jesus who are at the church of Philippi,
with the bishops (*episkopoi*) and deacons (*diakonoi*)'. The origin
of the order used to be traced to the appointment in Acts 6 of
'the seven' to help with charitable aid for widows by serving
(*diakonein*) at table. What we know later, however, about two
of the seven, Stephen and Philip, indicates a ministry primarily of preaching and teaching with healing, and this need cause
no surprise seen against the fuller picture of *diakonos*.

In I Tim 3. 8–13 deacons are treated as a group after
bishops, and certain moral and practical qualities are formulated by which they can be tested for suitability. The language
is similar to that of Polycarp and Ignatius, bishops in the first
decade of the second century (and the date may be similar,
too). The former writes to the Philippians (5.2):

Deacons should be irreproachable in the face of God's justice, as the servants (*diakonoi*) of God and Christ and not of men. They should not be slanderous, not double-tongued, no lovers of money.

The latter exhorts the Magnesians (6.1):

I bid you do everything in godly concord, with the bishop presiding in the likeness of God, with the presbyters in the likeness of the council of the apostles, while the deacons who are so dear to me have been entrusted with the ministry of Christ.

Thus for Ignatius the essence of Christian ministry is located in the diaconate.

The earliest non-Christian reference to the diaconate concerns women. Around the year 112 Pliny, the Roman governor of Bithynia, writes to the Emperor Trajan seeking his advice on what to do with a puzzling group of people called Christians, some of whom he has put to death for their obstinacy since he could find no crime that they had committed. In the course of his investigations:

I thought it the more necessary, therefore, to find out what truth there was in this by applying torture to two maidservants who were called deaconesses (*ministrae*). But I found nothing.

(*Letters*, 10.97.)

The Latin word *ministra* probably translates the Greek *diakonos* which has no feminine form, being used, for example, of Phoebe, deacon(ess) of the church at Cenchreae (Rom 16.1); the word *diakonissa* does not appear until the fourth century and then only in the east.

Justin, around 150, in describing the eucharistic celebration says,

When the president has given thanks and all the people have assented, those who are called deacons with us give to those present a portion of the eucharistic bread and wine and water, and carry it away to those who are absent.

(Apology 1.65)

The *Didachē* (Teaching of the Twelve Apostles) of about the same date, esteems deacons highly:

> Appoint for yourselves, therefore, bishops and deacons worthy of the Lord, men who are meek and not lovers of money, and true and approved; for unto you they also perform the service (*leitourgian*) of the prophets and teachers. Therefore despise them not; for they are your honourable men along with the prophets and teachers.
>
> *(Didachē,* 15)

The first full account appears in the *Teaching of the Apostles* (*Didascalia Apostolorum*), coming from Syria or Palestine in the first half of the third century. Here again the deacon stands in the place of Christ, and as God is to be approached through Christ, so the bishop is to be approached through the deacon. He has become the bishop's ear. He also does some social and welfare work and visits the sick. Liturgically, he is responsible for keeping order in the congregation and keeping heretics away, making announcements and giving instructions during the service. *The Apostolic Tradition* of the same date adds to his duties preparing the eucharistic gifts, and proclaiming the gospel and also the *Exultet* at Easter. Cyprian in his 18th letter allows for the deacon to pronounce absolution in extreme urgency. 'The deacon' says Hippolytus, is not ordained for the priesthood but for the service of the bishop to do the things commanded by him.' (*Apostolic Tradition,* 9).

In the third century as the church expanded and increased its ownership of property, administrative tasks grew accordingly. In about 200 Callistus the deacon was put in charge of 'the catacomb' by Pope Zephyrinus. The Church of Rome was governed for fifteen months by presbyters and deacons between the execution of Pope Fabian and the election of his successor Cornelius. The latter no doubt needed his seven deacons and seven sub-deacons to assist with the 1500 widows and other poor persons on the church's roll. The title 'archdeacon' first appears in Rome carried by Stephen in the time of Pope Cornelius (251–3) whom he succeeded. (*Liber Pontificalis*, 1.153), and by the end of the century the senior deacon at Carthage was '*archidiaconus*' (Optatus, *De Schismate Donatistarum*, 1.16). In 311 after Bishop Mensurius' death, archdeacon Caecilian outwitted the presbyters and secured the succession at the cost of precipitating the Donatist schism. A few years later, Athanasius, the champion of orthodoxy against Arius, was deacon and secretary to Alexander, bishop of Alexandria, attending him at the Council of Nicaea in 325 (still in his late twenties) and succeeding him as bishop in 328. At Chalcedon in 451 Actius, archdeacon of Constantinople, was responsible for much of the organisation of the Council. By the end of the sixth century the papal estates had grown to vast proportions and Pope Gregory I organised a huge clerical civil service to administer them, with a staff of archdeacons, deacons and subdeacons. The Roman subdeacon Peter as rector of the papal estates in Sicily had a staff of four hundred bailiffs at his call. The archdeacon Laurentius was summoned to Rome in 591 and dismissed for arrogance: he may have been a rival for the papacy the previous year.

So the diaconate slipped into becoming the third 'order' of clergy, with little clear definition of its status or functions and heavily influenced by the social setting of particular churches at particular times. Cyprian regularly refers to 'bishops, priests and deacons', as in his *80th Letter*, where he puts them alongside senators, men of rank, and Roman knights, which were the Roman *ordines*. Pope Siricius (384–399) laid down that the minimum age limit for ordination as deacon should be 30, as presbyter 40, and bishop 50, but in 393 the African Council of Hippo reduced the first to 25.

The task of charitable work and organisation developed and expanded as the Church grew; there was a strong emphasis on the deacon as the bishop's right-hand man; and the deacon had appropriate liturgical responsibilities next to his bishop. Some deacons became bishops without proceeding through priest's orders, giving the impression that in some respects the diaconate ranked alongside the presbyterate, though the tradition of a senior 'career' diaconate also continued.

The medieval Schoolmen codified the matter, with particular reference to the eucharist, requiring celibacy for all three orders because those who touch holy things must be pure and holy (*Summa Theologiae* 3, Sup. Q. 37. a.3). The priest may alone handle the consecrated elements, the deacon may administer the chalice, and the sub-deacon may wash the vessels. The deacon received the people's offerings, gave the cup at Communion, sometimes read the Gospel, led the people's prayers, and with the bishop's permission might preach, baptise, and even reconcile penitents.

The theological confusion surrounding the diaconate was magnified at the Reformation. Luther was concerned with more important things and so deacons were either abolished or reduced to lay function as parish clerks or vergers, though today the term is used of assistant ministers in full Lutheran orders. In Geneva Calvin endeavoured to build a four-fold ministry purely on scripture, and in his *Institutes* (4.3.9) he advises 'two kinds of deacons, of which the first are to serve the church itself by organising the alms of the poor, the second by attending to the sick and the other poor'. This remains the Presbyterian pattern where there is also provision for a deacons' court responsible to the presbytery for the proper distribution of church goods, though these functions may be performed by elders. In the Congregational, and also the Baptist, traditions more definitely spiritual functions belong to the deacons who assist the pastor, and distribute the elements at Communion.

The Anglican Ordinal of 1549 accepted broadly the medieval pattern, though with some movement in a Reformed direction. Candidates must be 'of vertuous conversation . . . and . . . learned in the Latyne tongue, and sufficiently instructed in holye Scripture'. Their duties are to assist the priest in divine service, especially in the distribution of the holy communion, to read holy scriptures in the congregation and to instruct the youth in the catechism; to preach and to baptise with the bishop's authorisation. In addition they are 'to search for the sick, poor, and impotent people of the parish' so that they may be relieved. The concluding rubric assumes that normally such deacons will be admitted to the order of priesthood after a year. A deacon must be at least twenty-one and a priest at least twenty-three years old. The description of the office has not changed substantially to the present.

The confusion, however, has become most pronounced in the matter of women. Deaconesses had been active in both east and west until the eleventh century but their role passed to the religious orders. In 1861 Elizabeth Ferard founded the Community of St Andrew with the support of Bishop Tait of London. Its members were to be both religious and deaconesses, to work within parochial and diocesan systems, particularly amid the slums which were the squalid aftermath of the Industrial Revolution. A potent influence on this foundation was the Kaiserwerth Institution begun in 1836 by Pastor Fliedmer in Germany which by 1861 had 220 deaconesses devoted to the care of the sick and poor, for teaching neglected children and for parish work.

The Order of Deaconesses was revived in the Church of England in 1862 when Bishop Tait ordained Elizabeth Ferard as a deaconess, an act recognised by the Lambeth Conference of 1897 and the Convocations in 1923 and 1925. The order passed into Canon Law in 1964 but there have been no further admissions to the order since 1986. The precise status of the deaconesses has been a matter of dispute. A preparatory commission for the 1920 Lambeth Conference judged that the ordination of a deaconess conferred Holy Orders on her, though the Conference Resolutions did not state this. It was denied by a special committee of the 1930 Lambeth Conference, but affirmed by the Archbishops' Commission on the Ministry of Women in 1935. The extraordinary position arose before 1987 that men and women took part in the same service, with the same liturgical words (gender apart) and acts, at the end of which the men were in holy orders as deacons, and the women as deaconesses were not. In 1987 a majority of deaconesses were ordained deacons and are now officially clergy with the rights pertaining, except (at present) that of passing on to the order of priesthood.

In recent years there has been a movement to strengthen the order of deacons, not least in the Anglican Communion and in the Roman Catholic Church, with the emphasis in America more on charitable and social ministry, but in England more on liturgical function.

What, then, is to become of the diaconate, at least in the broad catholic tradition of which Anglicanism is a part? There are three possibilities: either that it is consolidated into a 'permanent' or 'distinctive' order; or that it is abolished; or that it continues as an apprenticeship for the priesthood.

Neither 'permanent' nor 'distinctive' are happy titles for a strengthened order because all diaconate remains permanent, both for priests and for bishops. To label it 'distinctive' is to seek to separate off into one order what ought also to be characteristic of each order. Its protagonists argue: 'We need ministers whose life is spent in the environment of every day life in our society in order to galvanise and coordinate on behalf of the Church the overall ministry of the Church to the world.' This is certainly one of the objects of non-stipendary ministry (see Chapter 23), and it begs the large question of the responsibility of the laity (which will be considered more fully in that connection). Many lay people would see their ministry to the world worked out in their daily occupation, like the baker who, when asked what he did for the Church, replied, 'I bake.' As for the care of the sick and needy, in Britain basic needs are met by the state. Many Christians are involved in this provision, and many Christians would be happy to see God's work being done by those who would not see it that way themselves. The Church still has much to do in supplementing basic services and in monitoring government provision, but that is too great a task for one ministerial 'order'.

In a more ecclesiastical direction, if all worthy church servants were to be included in an order of deacons, where would the limit be? All organists, churchwardens, church council secretaries? And would diocesan secretaries and general synod secretaries be archdeacons? The prospect is staggering. Nor is the argument convincing of *pars pro toto*, that there should be a small diaconal order as an example of what service should be. All Christians are called to that task, to be a light to the world and salt as a preservative of society, and all ordained ministry exists to help them to be that. As for liturgical functions, all of these, like preaching, distributing communion, reading lessons and leading prayers are now also performed by lay people, sometimes with episcopal authorisation. It would be impossible either to restrict these functions to a small 'order' or to extend the 'order' to embrace all these people. The Roman Catholic bishops, at least in England, are divided on the issue of a 'permanent diaconate': some see it as a reinforcement for a much diminished priesthood (and it does, of course, allow an ordained ministry for married men); others see it as too permanent and too ecclesiastical and prefer to train responsible laity as pastoral helpers, with such duties as reading lessons in Church and taking communion to the sick.

The second choice for the diaconate is to abolish it. This was the conclusion of the Anglican Advisory Council's Working Party in their report *Deacons in the Church* of 1974, but it was not ratified by the General Synod. The report agreed that deacons are not essential, not being intrinsic to the Church in the exercise of any of her principal functions, and was not in favour of enlarging this order to form an *omnium gatherum* diaconate. There are, however, severe practical difficulties about such a recommendation in terms of the Anglican communion and also the many ecumenical conversations at present taking place. Anglicanism, however, is not absolutely committed to the three-fold ministry because the *Lambeth Quadrilateral* of 1888 in setting forth four articles as the Anglican essentials for a reunited church mentions, concerning the ministry, only 'The Historic Episcopate, locally adapted . . .' (The document is given in Appendix 1 p. 269.)

A third choice remains, that of keeping the present practice of the diaconate as, more or less, an apprenticeship period for the priesthood. There is, perhaps, more to be said for this than is often supposed. A person's training is not complete at the end of his or her college or course; it remains to be continued in the first parish. There a deacon is able to experience at first hand how *diakonia* actually works, or should work, in the case of an experienced priest as he exercises his authoritative ministry as a servant. This is a task of complex and subtle difficulty, not to be learned simply by books or lectures or even by group dynamics, but most effectively by personal discipleship.

Concerning training for the diaconate it is impossible to be specific since there is so little clarity about the order's nature and practice. In the case of the third choice above, training will be as for the priesthood, to be considered in chapter 26. Much of what follows in chapter 14 about priests applies equally to the role of deacons.

14

Priests or Presbyters

Priests or presbyters (and their equivalents in other traditions) are, by their ordination, normally given authority to preside over a particular Christian congregation. As priests (to use the word as a convenience) they are also deacons: their presidency must be imbued with a spirit of service; it can never be tyrannical.

The best antidote to tyranny is a comprehensive sense of proportion, and that, in New Testament terms, means seeing the church itself as servant of God's kingdom. So ministers are ministers of the kingdom before they are ministers of the church. The church is a sign and agent of the kingdom, of the universal lordship of God in Christ. The primary ministry is to proclaim that lordship by word and deed, and to nurture the local church as it seeks to acknowledge and respond to it.

The term 'servant' is widely used to describe both Church and ministry, but it needs careful qualification. Jesus specifically declined to use it of his disciples. 'No longer do I call you servants (*doulous*), for the servant does not know what his master is doing; but I have called you friends, for all that I have heard from my Father I have made known to you.' (Jn 15.15). There is nothing servile about the ministry; on the contrary, there is a proper confidence, not to say boldness. The 'serving' aspect of ministry is, or ought to be, most clearly seen in the openness and honesty with which a minister sets about helping and enabling those for whom he is responsible to see themselves as, and work out the consequences of being, the people of God. (The masculine gender is used purely for convenience.) Authority he has, but he is called to be authoritative, not authoritarian. It is to be exercised in at least four areas.

First, he is responsible for corporate worship, to see that in a service all may make their proper contribution. It is sometimes supposed, for instance in debates about lay presidency, that leading worship is simply the individual performance of a rite. In fact it is anything but that, and if it is that, the result is likely to be dead and deadening. Leading an act of corporate worship is more like conducting an orchestra. The stage has to be set, and often the church building itself poses grave obstacles to the performance. Furniture may need to be rearranged and the decoration of the building should provide a harmonious and purposeful background. The programme has to be chosen from a wide variety of rites, variations, and times. Music has to be chosen and performed to the best ability of players and singers: is the organ mandatory when the local school has an excellent young people's orchestra? Which of the many new hymnals is to be invested in? On what grounds? Those who lead spoken prayer will need help in its formulation, as those who read the Scriptures will need speech training. And what part are women and children to play in a scene which has long been dominated by men? Why should the choir dress up like clergy and expect to receive communion first if they are the musical servants of the congregation? If a service is to be spiritually alive and vibrant for everyone participating, all these matters, and many others, will have had to be worked through with as much participation as possible, and that is a difficult and never-ending task, calling for considerable liturgical knowledge and skill on the one hand, and on the other, equal skill in dealing with people in matters which touch them deeply.

As the result of the Liturgical Movement, particularly over the last fifty years in Britain, the eucharist has increasingly become the main service on a Sunday morning. This has certainly restored the balance between word and sacrament and has encouraged a more active sense of participation by worshippers. It has been at some cost. There is a risk of domesticating so great and solemn an occasion; it does raise barriers for the uninstructed; and, perhaps most serious, it has restricted the reading of Scripture to the set lections and has limited expository preaching. In Anglican ministerial terms it has raised questions about the place of the licensed reader whose duty was originally conceived in terms of Morning and Evening Prayer rather than of the eucharist, though he or she may preach at the latter and administer the chalice.

There has been quite a considerable movement for lay presidency at the eucharist, argued, for example, by A. E. Harvey (1974, p. 48), and urged by a significant group of Anglican bishops at the 1978 Lambeth Conference, though without success (*Report*, p. 83). Behind this argument seems to lie a view of the eucharist and of the ministry which is unduly restricted to the local scene. There is no practical reason why an intelligent lay person in good standing could not be taught in a couple of hours how to go through the motions of presiding. The eucharist, however, is not just a local celebration and the minister is not just a local minister. Both service and minister are local manifestations of something, or someone, much greater, spanning the centuries and the continents. Vestments, if they are worn, speak of this universality. The person presiding stands as representative of a tradition much wider than himself or herself, and it is out of that tradition and on behalf of that tradition that he or she speaks and acts. Such a 'catholic' view of presiding is in fact characteristic also of most of the main-stream tradition of non-conformity, even if some of them, like the Methodist, allow for occasional exceptions in emergency.

It is often assumed that the eucharist is the primary sacrament. In fact, baptism is. It is worth recalling that lay people may, in emergencies, administer that sacrament, as do many nurses frequently in maternity wards. The Church of England badly needs to recapture the solemnity of this service since, as the national church, it receives far more candidates than any other. In large town parishes the burden on the clergy is heavy, and the proper answer is that it should be shared with the laity. It is perfectly possible for a 'clinic' to be set up where enquiring parents are hospitably met by lay people (properly prepared) and are given a short account of what the church has to offer. They are asked to accept a 'sponsor' from the congregation who will visit them in their home to carry forward the preparation, who will be present at the service, and will maintain contact afterwards. There could be no better example of shared Christian ministry.

As a standing reminder of the importance of regular common prayer, it is required of all parish clergy of the Church of England by Canon Law (B.11.3) that on weekdays they 'shall resort to the church morning and evening, and, warning being given to the people by the tolling of the bell, say or sing the Common Prayers and on the appointed days the Litany.' One suspects that this rule is more honoured in the breach than in the observance.

The minister's second area of responsibility is for the preaching of the gospel. The word 'preaching' has acquired an unpleasant flavour (reflected in the dictionary definition 'to give advice in an offensive, tedious, or obtrusive manner') far from the original meaning of *kērussein* which was the town-crier's proclamation of news good or bad. The gospel is emphatically good news (and not good advice), which is exactly the meaning of the original term *euaggelion*. It is the good news of what God has done, is doing, and will do, in Jesus Christ through the Spirit. The preaching tense is indicative, not imperative.

The purpose of preaching, like the purpose of the eucharist, is to feed people with the bread of life. The two ministries are complementary, are indeed two aspects of one ministry. As common bread is taken and transformed through the blessing and the breaking and the sharing, so commonplace words are taken and transformed through the speaking and listening. The good news is that everyone's vocation is to be human, and that the way to be human is to be a Christian. To believe this is to repent, and to discover freedom. The gospel makes people free, but often slavery seems a more reasonable and happier way. To repent is to hear and answer the call of God's creative activity, which may set us against our family and friends and neighbours.

Lord, how can *man* preach thy eternal word?
He is a brittle crazie glasse;
Yet in thy temple thou dost him afford
This glorious and transcendent place,
To be a window, through they grace.

(George Herbert, *The Windows*)

In a sense, the sermon does not matter. What matters is the ineffable thing that comes through, the expression of the ceaseless creative activity of God, the sudden illumination of human experience. Unlike an advertisement, a sermon, like a poem or any other work of art, does not try to impose something on those who pay attention. The preacher does not seek to possess or dominate others, but hopes that his hearers may come to possess their own true selves and resolve to pursue their own right way. The preacher will not tell people *what* to think, but *how* to think. He will show his listeners that life is important and that doctrine illuminates it, not that doctrine matters and that life must be adjusted to fit it.

He can only do this if he is steeped in doctrine, the living faith of the dead, and also deeply immersed in the life of his own community. After the year-long coal-miners' strike in 1984–1985 the diocese of Sheffield, which was deeply affected by it, set up a working-party to assess how the church had coped. Its report, *The Church in the Mining Communities* (1988), after a year's close investigation, concluded that the churches had dealt well with welfare needs but had failed to address the issues:

> Close identification with the community as a participant, not just an onlooker, permits a wider teaching ministry than is possible through an over-cautious, carefully neutral approach. Where the vicar felt he could not preach on questions raised by the dispute, it could convey the message that the strike was not of any great concern to the church. The price paid for the 'island of peace' was that the congregations received no training or support as they tried to make up their minds about their individual attitude towards the strike and the strikers.

Thus the third area of the minister's responsibility is teaching. It is not the same as preaching, but must precede and follow it. In the New Testament it has its own word *didachē*, where a regular pattern appears to have been drawn up concerning relationships: of everyone to civic authorities, of slaves to masters, of wives to husbands, of children to parents, of younger people to elders, most of which are reciprocal. (A summary can be found in E. G. Selwyn's commentary on 1 Peter, p. 423) This New Testament approach to adult Christian education (or training, or development, or formation: it is hard to find the right term) offers three important clues about the process: it starts where people are; it is concerned with personal relationships; and it has important implications for wider society beyond the church.

Its purpose is to equip God's people to be God's people, participating in God's mission to the world, meeting the world at its strong, as well as its weak, points. This requires a sensitive awareness of the constant activity of the living God, which is nurtured by prayer and worship. The congregation's part in the mission is to disclose the presence of God: there can be no question of taking God to where he is not.

Training will be centred on the local situation. This may be the parish, but it may also be a working unit like a group of factories or farms, a professional group like doctors, town-planners or artists, an inter-professional group like those involved in questions of law and order, or those concerned with special need in society like the suicidal or AIDS sufferers.

As for method, Christians must first find the facts, and for that they should be glad to receive help from experts who know the field. Then the findings must be assessed in the light of the whole Christian tradition, including Bible, doctrine, ethics and prayer. A Christian group will avoid partisan approaches and will discuss the matter with a deep openness to each other and to God. There are no ready-made Christian answers. The Christian's task is to create, or discover, a spiritual dimension for common problems. Any problem dealing with people or people's use of things admits of spiritual treatment because at root lie the questions, What is good for people? Who are we? What is good for society? What sort of society do we want? What is our responsibility for the whole of God's creation? The task of the clergy is to sit with such groups, not leading them but learning the facts with them, and then to know how to bring to bear the relevant insights from the whole breadth of the Christian tradition.

The parish will be one Christian unit, but only one among many and not necessarily the most important. Any group will be a eucharistic one with priest and people but that does not necessarily require a church building; much in the way of our ecclesiastical tradition is foreign to working people. In a city or heavily urbanised area the parish church should serve to hold together different working units, and the provision of non-parochial clergy to serve these units must be seriously considered.

This engagement of the laity in the world's problems *is* evangelism, not a preparation for evangelism. Witness starts not with speaking about God, which can be misunderstood, but with individual and collective lives lived to God in the secular world. Talking comes after Christians have been asked questions. *The Church in the Mining Communities* finishes with these words:

> In these parishes, the giving and receiving of help was indeed a deepening of their faith in the living God, and this was often apparent to those outside the church. 'It's the way the church did it during the strike, and talking on the line with the lads, that made me turn my head towards the church. I decided to come in.'

The Church of England has also been giving serious thought to the nurture of its children, and has suggested new directions in the report *Children in the Way* (1988). It builds on an observation in an earlier report, *The Child in the Church*.

> The Church that does not accept children unconditionally into its fellowship is depriving those children of what is rightfully theirs, but the deprivation such as the Church itself will suffer is far more grave.

It follows from this that adults are fellow-learners and have much to learn from the growing faith of the young. As one eleven year old boy remarked 'I think Jesus finds it very sad when adults lose the faith that children have.' Adults must talk with children about their own growth in faith, and parishes need to provide opportunities for this talk together, whether it is in a shared making of a collage or the opportunity for children to knead and bake rolls which are later brought up, still hot, in the offertory procession for use in communion. This will raise hard questions if the children are then excluded from receiving communion themselves.

The report suggests that every parish should have an education committee and a spokesperson for children on the church council. The incumbent and council are jointly responsible for the nurture of the church's children and for reaching those outside, and if the incumbent himself is not 'good with children' he can certainly find those with many talents in that direction to share this vital ministry.

The fourth area for which the minister is responsible is that of pastoral care. The word 'pastoral' is a word carrying approval in ecclesiastical circles. 'He has a good pastoral sense' means that he is 'good with people', is warm, understanding and sympathetic when life is difficult, is available, and mixes freely with all sorts; he is a caring person. There is nothing specifically clerical about such a description because it is true of many lay people. Indeed there is nothing specifically religious about it because it describes some, at least, of today's secular carers, the doctors, solicitors, bank managers, Samaritans, marriage guidance counsellors and the personnel social workers, of citizens' advice bureaux, to whom the great majority of people resort with their severer crises.

What then is 'pastoral care' for the ordained minister? Sadly it has come to be all but identified with 'pastoral counselling', understood as a private consultation in the parsonage when the troubled parishioner can talk through his or her problem in a 'non-directive' atmosphere, and thus be helped to arrive at his or her own answer. Many people have in fact been greatly helped by such a process, but it is gravely deficient theologically as a total understanding of pastoral care.

Its weakness was clearly analysed by R. A. Lambourne as long ago as 1970 after a visit to America in a paper entitled *With Love to the USA* (in *Religion and Medicine*, Vol.I, ed. M. A. H. Melinsky). He had noticed the flood of literature on pastoral psychology and the trickle of writing on the theology of pastoral care during the preceding twenty years. It seemed to him that what was emerging was a 'virulent psychological pietism' which never said anything radical about the central concepts and structures of medicine, though it provided the framework for training hospital chaplains and other ministers. The claimed dialogue of theology with medicine had not begun and the much-hailed dialogue with psychiatry was a psychiatric monologue. On the other hand there were those who taught pastoral care by immersion in depressed urban situations. They relied heavily, if not entirely, on sociology, accompanied by a selected exposure to cultural shock, with the resultant danger of a personally insensitive activism. (It was in the same 1950s and '60s in Britain that the Student Christian Movement withdrew from specifically Christian commitment, opting enthusiastically for secular action, so that by the late 1960s it was left almost without message, constituency or even material resources.) Lambourne called the dialogue between theology and psychology 'tribalistic', concealing important value judgments in the ghetto-like isolation of the consulting room, removed from the realities of cultural relativity, poverty, stupidity, unemployment, poor housing, and physical coercion. In this tradition, as also in the Rogerian school of non-directive counselling, problems of justice and power were either secondary or irrelevant. So the theory and art of loving and acceptance were separated from the theory and art of justice and judgement.

Another Christian psychiatrist, J. R. Mathers (in *Religion and Medicine*, Vol. II, ed. M. A. H. Melinsky, 1973) is cautious about the over-easy use of the model of shepherd and sheep. Most Christians do not take kindly to being thought of as sheep, and, in any case, sheep have the regrettable habit of following the shepherd whether he knows where he is going or not. The pastoral model does tend to emphasise people as weak and dependent. It is true that one part of the shepherd's task is caring for the lost and damaged, but the more important one is leading the flock to good pasturage, because without that they will die. Moses was a great pastor because he knew where he was going and managed, with difficulty, to take his flock with him. But few of them would have regarded him as a kindly pastor.

James Mathers, as an army psychiatrist in the Second World War, was commissioned to discover why the rate of sickness varied very much in different units. He investigated carefully and concluded that the sickness rate went down as morale went up; and morale depended on the soldiers being given clear aims of what they were expected to do and clear instructions about how to do it. When he finally reported to the general that health depended more on the commanding officer than on the medical officer he was dismissed for his pains. His work has been substantially confirmed.

It is of the highest importance, therefore, to try to ensure that (in Dr Lambourne's words) 'pastoral training is motivated as much by a struggle for corporate excellence as a struggle against defects'. When a compassionate pastor or doctor is faced with another human being in distress he experiences distress himself and so resorts to unconscious defences for self-protection. One defence is to find some partial or external object to point to as the cause of the person's badness or ill-feeling. Psychologically it does not matter whether *it* is a witch to be burned, a demon to be exorcised, an ulcer to be removed, or a mosquito to be sprayed with DDT. This analytic method, fundamental to all science, is divisive and atomising. The other main defence is detachment, symbolised by the surgeon's face-mask or the general practitioner's desk. But pastoral work is not entirely 'scientific': it requires controlled involvement, and that raises the deepest questions: not only What is man?, but also Who am I?, and Who do men say that I am?

The healthy man is called upon to die a little death

repeatedly and continually, to lose each successive self in order that a more mature and comprehensive self may be born. The gospel injunction about losing one's real self to find it is not a sudden once-for-all commandment but a statement of the law of healthy growth of personality. The pastor stands alongside men and women at the extremities of pain and tension and life itself with this message. It is a demanding task.

Michael Wilson has explored the role of the pastor in a hospital setting, but this description of the hospital chaplain is a profound summary of the Christian minister as pastor:

> The role of the hospital chaplain, like that of his master, is an enigma. Essentially an adventurer, he explores the dangerous territory of man's making and breaking; where every meeting is new and no situation is ever repeated.
>
> He is one who is called to communicate in the language of the other. Quick to turn from work to prayer and prayer to work giving full attention to each: to turn swiftly from weeping with the mother who has lost her baby, to laughing with the mother who is suckling her first-born son.
>
> A man for others by calling; formal or informal, authoritative yet servant, powerful yet vulnerable, at the disposal of all but at the mercy of none. At ease with all men and women, young or old, consultant or domestic, because at ease with himself. Friend of all but concerned for the greatest good of each even to wounding. A peacemaker, but not through escape.
>
> In an institution whose tasks include the cure of illness and the care of sick people, he is as interested in the healthy as the sick, and primarily in people who happen to be patients, not patients who happen to be people. He is concerned with health in terms of quality of life not quantity; but is ready to sacrifice his own by giving his life to something more valuable than health. Death for him is not the worst thing than can happen to a man.
>
> But above all he is a man: strong and weak: subject to

temptation and doubt, misrepresentation and weariness, as well as joy, hope and encouragement.

He is one of the most public of men, yet his basic work is done in privacy as well as community: he is a man of God, with God and for God, which marks him out as intensely human, able to quicken the humanity of others.

(Michael Wilson, 1971. p. 104)

15
Bishops

WHAT is a bishop? What is a bishop for? How does one set about answering the question? One can appeal to Scripture, where the answer is ambiguous because on a superficial reading it would appear that *episkopoi* and *presbuteroi* are interchangeable terms. One can appeal to the development occurring during the New Testament period, as seen for example, in the letters of Ignatius with his 'high' doctrine of the bishop as a 'model of God' (*tupon tou theou*) without whom nothing might be done (*Epistle to the Trallians* 2 and 3); one can appeal to the great teaching fathers of the patristic period like Irenaeus and Ambrose and Augustine and the Cappadocians, though some of them turned out to be heretics, like Apollinarius; one can hardly fail to take note of the appalling record of medieval aberrations which helped to precipitate the Reformation (Luther's own bishop had also collected the archbishopric of Mainz by the age of fourteen); or one can examine the vast variety of bishops in the modern world, in Manchester and Hereford, in Chicago and San Paulo, in Cape Town and Jerusalem, in Dornakal, Tokyo and Nanjing, bishops Roman, Anglican, Lutheran and Methodist, and try to derive from them some common identifying factor (though some of them would not recognise others as being bishops); or one might be tempted to find secular analogues, and try to understand episcopal functions in terms, for example, of top management. No doubt the answer lies in trying to detect and identify the activity and purposes of God the Holy Spirit in and through this bewildering mass of evidence.

Deeply embedded in the tradition, from F. D. Maurice back to Ignatius is the conviction that bishops are signs and agents of unity and universality; of the universality of the saving work of Christ, which is itself based in the nature and operation of the Triune God. As Maurice put it in 1842:

> Bishops being as we believe the witness and representatives of Christ's universal kingdom, are the very instruments of our communion with other nations. If there be no such institution – no apostleship – in the Church now, then the Church has lost its universal character; then the idea of the Church as existing for all space, and all time, perishes; then the commission, 'Go ye into all nations,' has no persons to whom it is directed. We cannot then recognise a Church without Bishops.
>
> (*Three Letters to the Rev. W. Palmer*, p. 34)

Episcopacy is 'one of the appointed and indispensable signs of a spiritual and universal society' (*Kingdom of Christ* (Ev.) 2.91). The fact that bishops are called 'Fathers in God' is a reflection founded in the New Testament, of the universal Fatherhood of God:

> It is a sad day for churches, yes, and for nations, when men begin to regard themselves as officials sent forth by some central government to do its jobs, and not as men who are bound by sacred affinities and actual relations to those whom they preside over.
>
> (*Epistles of St John*, p. 54)

The episcopal succession Maurice regarded as an important witness to the permanence of the Church's constitution. He spoke of 'the necessity for Apostolic Succession and Episcopal Ordination' (*Kingdom of Christ*, (1838) 2.112); and the act of consecration through the agency of three existing bishops signifies 'that the person newly entering upon the function receives the same kind of authority and the same kind of gifts as those who were first endowed with it' (*Kingdom of Christ* (Ev.) 2.87).

In this matter Maurice is at one with Irenaeus for whom apostolic succession became a vital issue at the end of the second century when the church was threatened by heresy on a large scale. The purpose of succession (and for Irenaeus this is both presbyteral and episcopal) is to safeguard the truth of the tradition derived from the apostles. Irenaeus attaches particular importance to the tradition preserved in 'the greatest and most ancient church, the Church known to all men', and by way of emphasis he quotes the succession of bishops of Rome from the founders Peter and Paul down to Eleutherus in his own day. (*Adversus Haereses* 3.2.2 and 3.3.1–2) In order to safeguard the catholicity of ordination of bishops the Council of Arles in 314 decreed that an ordaining bishop must be accompanied by seven others, or if that is impossible, by at least three (Canon 20). In 325 the Council of Nicaea confirmed the necessity of a minimum of three bishops together with the written approval of all the bishops of the province, though ideally all should be present (Canon 4).

Sadly this provision did not act as the safeguard for which it was intended. In the fifth century the primacy of Rome turned into Roman imperialism with Leo (the Great, pope 440–461) declaring, 'through them (bishops in greater cities) the care of the universal church should converge towards Peter's one chair, and nothing anywhere should be separated from its head', thus claiming a universal extension for the pope's teaching office. (*Epistolae*. 14.11). (The same Leo also declared that to abandon one's concubine in order to take a wife in legitimate matrimony was 'not bigamy, but a sign of moral improvement' (*Epistolae*, 167).)

Equally sadly, the bishop today, so far from being a sign of unity, is often the exact opposite. In many of the big cities of England there are two bishops, and the fact that together an Anglican bishop and a Roman Catholic archbishop of Liverpool can write a book about their close co-operation (D. Sheppard and D. Worlock, *Better Together*, 1988) merely serves to underline the point. Nowhere else is the sin of Christian disunity so visible and so harmful. The ecumenical implications will be considered in Chapter 18.

A bishop is not an isolated unit. The episcopate is one, as Cyprian maintained, and today there is on many sides a rediscovery of the fact of collegiality. The Roman Church is finding its way there in the wake of Vatican II, and the Church of England has had bishops-in-synod since 1970, though England is one of the last parts of the Anglican Communion to attain synodical government: Australia has had it for over a hundred years. The General Synod is a legislative body with power to make canons and pass measures, but the House of Bishops retains a veto in matters of worship and doctrine. In 1985 the English House was asked by the Synod for an authoritative statement on the nature of Christian belief and of that assent which is to be required of ministers given a teaching authority. The matter was occasioned by a recurrence of questions about the virgin birth and the physical resurrection of Jesus, questions which have been raised with monotonous regularity each generation in this century. An answer was provided by the House in *The Nature of Christian Belief* published in 1986. Some surprise was expressed, and perhaps some disappointment, that the report was unanimous, with no signed minority appendix. This is a good example of the English bishops' exercising a wider 'catholicism' over against petty local 'catholicisms', a task with which diocesan bishops are confronted daily.

The teaching task is a complex one because it is never finished, and sometimes it has to be undone. (The process is easier for Anglicans than for Romans.) The Lambeth Conference Report of 1908 stated in Resolution 43:

> The Conference regards with alarm the growing practice of the artificial restriction of the family, and earnestly calls upon all Christian people to discountenance the use of all artificial means of restriction as demoralising to character and hostile to national welfare.

Whereas the Report of 1958 states in Resolution 115:

> The Conference believes that the responsibility for deciding upon the number and frequency of children has been laid by God upon the consciences of parents everywhere: that this planning, in such ways as are mutually acceptable to husband and wife in Christian conscience, is a

right and important factor in Christian family life and should be the result of positive choice before God.

Sometimes, however, the wider Anglican episcopate cannot agree. The ten-yearly Lambeth Conference is a consultative and not a legislative body, but has to make decisions about the common life and discipline of the whole Anglican communion. In 1978 it had to resolve differences about the ordination of women to the priesthood because women had been so ordained in Hong Kong, Canada, the USA, and New Zealand, and plans for their ordination were proceeding in eight other churches. The debate was long and hard but characterised by a serious doctrinal approach and a proper family charity. In the event a complex resolution (21) was passed by an overwhelming majority, to the effect that: to heal distress and strengthen fellowship is a primary pastoral responsibility of the bishops; each member Church has the right to make its own decision about the ordination of women although such provincial action has important consequences for the whole communion; the conference declares its acceptance alike of Churches which do and do not ordain women; and declares that the holding together of diversity within a unity of faith and worship is part of the Anglican heritage, and that 'we hope the dialogue [with other Churches] will continue because we believe that we still have the understanding of the truth of God and his will to learn from them as together we all move towards a fuller catholicity and a deeper fellowship in the Holy Spirit.'

A principal duty of bishops, then, is to conserve the apostolic and prophetic tradition of the whole church. This tradition, however, can never be fully and finally encapsulated in doctrinal formulae. People's understandings of God's actions and purposes are always conditioned by their own human nature and by the society of which they are a part. The titles of the last three major reports of Church of England Doctrine Commissions are significant: *Doctrine in the Church of England* (1938), *Christian Believing* (1976), and *Believing in the Church* (1981). They do not offer a definitive statement of doctrine as understood by that church. Rather, they state the foundations on which that doctrine is based, how it has come to be formed, and the limits of diversity which may and must be tolerated. This is not to the liking of some church members who would prefer it all cut and dried. But such is not the manner of Anglican believing, nor is it, the Church of England maintains, the manner of Christian believing.

Bishops have no monopoly as teachers of the faith. The majority of the commission-members responsible for these three books were not bishops (though it is said that had not the first been chaired by William Temple, it would never have reached final agreement – and that took sixteen years). Most academic theology is now done by men and women holding a variety of positions in a variety of churches. It is their responsibility to explore the boundaries of religious belief, and it is not surprising that their findings are often uncomfortable. It is noteworthy how in the last generation 'theology' at the university has now come to embrace also 'religious studies', that is to say, a serious theological concern with other major world faiths. Two eminent Roman university theologians, H. Küng and E. Schillebeeckx, have been called to account by the Curia, the former being deprived of his university chair and forfeiting the title of a catholic teacher.

The bishops, both Anglican and Roman, have largely delegated to others their responsibility for selecting and training women and men for the ministry, though they have a rather more direct say in the continuing education of ministers serving in their dioceses. The complexities involved in these areas will be examined in Chapters 25 and 26.

Closely allied to the task of teaching is that of administration, which St Paul is happy to class along with teaching as one of the gifts of the Spirit (I Cor. 12.28). Good administration facilitates the work of ministry. It sees that, as far as possible, the right persons are put in the right places, that they are adequately paid and housed during and after their active ministry, that they have opportunity to continue their training and education throughout their ministry, that they have proper periods of rest and holiday and retreat, and that they have a trusted person to whom they can resort to discuss the deep things of their ministry and of themselves as persons. The bishop also has to exercise discipline over his clergy, though this is best understood as the art of making and keeping disciples. The 1960s and the 1970s saw men leaving the ordained ministry in large numbers, not least in the Roman Church, but this was part of a much wider shaking of the foundations. There are cases where experience shows that a person does not have the qualities to sustain the exercise of ministry, and where a person altogether loses the sense of vocation which drew him or her to the ministry. It is a part of episcopal care that such people should be helped out of the ministry; the Anglican Church of Canada has a commendable scheme for re-training them for some other appropriate occupation.

There is also the question of the appointment of bishops. The Roman answer is straightforward – by the Pope. In most parts of the Anglican Communion it is by some sort of synodical election. In England it is by the sovereign on the advice of her (or his) Prime Minister, because, since the Reformation, the sovereign 'has supreme authority over all persons in all causes, as well ecclesiastical as civil' (Canon A7). Since 1976, however, when the General Synod established a Crown Appointments Commission, there is now a representative body to choose two names to be submitted to the Prime Minister on the understanding that she (or he) will submit the first to the Sovereign. A curiously Anglican device! In fact it seems to work better than most. Purely autocratic choice tends to breed discontent: synodical election tends to produce safe, unexciting candidates, and also the worst aspects of politicking.

A greater threat than political party influence is the ecclesiastical variety. There have been notorious instances in recent years in the Church of England where a diocesan bishop has spent a great amount of time and energy consulting with his diocese about the shape of its life and worship and mission and has then gathered his findings into a charge delivered to the diocese, and has set up structures and appointed persons to carry out this shared policy; and upon his departure, a

successor has been appointed of whom it was known that he
would have no sympathy with such a policy or even with the
way it was formed; and all this, it seems, to maintain some
sort of 'party balance' in the House of Bishops. Little wonder
that in some areas the church's mission makes little progress.

A diocesan bishop, in so far as he is a successor of the
apostles, is a missioner. He sets the tone and direction for
mission in the diocese. His place is on the ecclesiastical boundary as much as it is in the centre. It is his duty to get to
know, and to be seen among, all aspects and institutions of
secular life in his diocese so that he may interpret the critical
Christ in an informed way to the whole range of social situations and public bodies in a plural society. An important
part of his ministry will be to affirm what is good in society
and in the struggle by many people to make it better. As
Archbishop Helder Camara has said,

> The bishop belongs to all. Let no one be scandalised if I
> frequent those who are considered unworthy or sinful.
> Who is not a sinner? . . . Let no one be alarmed if I am
> seen with compromised and dangerous people, on the
> left or on the right . . . Let no one claim to bind me to a
> group . . . My door, my heart must be open to everyone,
> absolutely everyone.

The bishop is called to martyrdom. It may be the open
spectacle of a Romero in San Salvador or a Luwum in
Uganda, or it may be the unperceived agony of rejection,
misunderstanding and deferential defiance, particularly by
disgruntled clergy. His is 'the call to be a symbol of catholicity,
diversity, plurality in his fragile and broken particularity. His
authority is swathed in impressive impotence.' (A. Jones,
1978, p. 285.)

16
Models of Ministry

OVER the years the ministry has been modelled on prominent secular features of contemporary social life and has, often unconsciously, adopted many of their characteristics. We select here five such models, some with a long and honourable history, though the list does not claim to be exhaustive.

1. *Imperial*

The church of San Vitale in Ravenna, north-east Italy, was consecrated in 548. Dominating the beautiful mosaic wall decoration are two panels on either side of the apse: on the left the emperor Justinian and his leading courtiers and opposite, his wife Theodora and hers. He is portrayed in purple and gold with a halo surrounding his crown, giving much the same impression as the figure of Christ in the dome of the apse. With the reconquest of Persia, North Africa and Italy during his reign (527–565) east and west had been largely reunited under Byzantine rule, and the emperor devoted the early years of his reign to supervising the re-editing of the whole body of law, Roman, Teutonic and Christian, into a great Code, to be the universal and eternal law of the empire. His laws were divine, binding on all clergy, prohibiting, for example, any clergy of any rank from being present at the gaming-table or at any public spectacle. The bishop was an imperial officer for certain temporal affairs, such as sharing in the unusual inspection of accounts in each city, and for the discharge of these functions the bishops were answerable to the emperor. The law even limited the number of clergy to be attached to each church, with the great church at Constantinople having its quota reduced to 425, 60 presbyters, 100 male and 40 female deacons, 90 subdeacons, 110 readers and 75 singers. Justinian saw church and state as part of a single organism with himself as their earthly director. In his time eastern and western Christendom had become distinctive civilisations, and his death marked the failure of the last great effort to hold these together in unity.

At the end of that century, Pope Gregory I, the Great, the son of a wealthy, landed senator, left the cloister to discover a land devastated by flood, famine, pestilence, and invading Lombards, the whole made worse by the weakness and treachery of the Byzantine authorities. So he appointed governors to the Italian cities and provided them with war materials, and greatly strengthened the church in Spain, Gaul, and N. Italy. He also selected Augustine (of Canterbury) for missions in England. He was indeed the father of the medieval papacy, even though he took to himself the title of 'servant of the servants of God'.

Chapter 8 sketched the deformation of the ministry in the Middle Ages, when the Holy Roman Empire succeeded its 'secular' predecessor. For centuries the church in east and west had for its administration borrowed many features of the political and social scene until in 1077 at Canossa the emperor Henry IV stood (so it is said) for three days in the snow to await the pope's absolution. The church was the state: it was *the* society both here and hereafter; it was the society of rational and redeemed mankind. To provide an effective centralised government for ruling western Christendom was an enormous undertaking. Popes undertook wars, conducted campaigns and made treaties of peace, but they failed to gain widespread consent for this exercise of power. This church-state had neither army nor police of its own. Even the Inquisition was swallowed up by local interests. The worst terrors which people had to face were generally archdeacons or rural deans and most of those wanted a quiet life. The church, therefore, had to rely on secular states, and the ultimate sanction was excommunication. Actually King John lived for nearly four years as an excommunicate with all ordinary church services suspended; but life went on, and a contemporary chronicler says that the king thought of becoming a Moslem.

The Roman Church has never abandoned its imperial past. It is always happier dealing with an autocratic government, making concordats with a Mussolini or a Franco in a 'catholic' Italy or Spain, while the silence which the Pope maintained about Hitler's tyranny was deafening. Against communist tyrannies, however, it is sternly militant because they are 'atheist', and the Church was prepared to lend its full weight to Polish dissidents. Some of the ecumenical consequences of this attitude will be considered in Chapter 18.

2. *Military*

The military model, which is not unconnected with the imperial because every empire is kept in being by military power, has a long and fairly honourable history going back to the kings of the Old Testament and the Maccabean martyrs of the Apocrypha. Indeed St Paul gives us a detailed picture of the arms and armour of a Roman soldier in Eph. 6 as illustrating Christian equipment for the spiritual fight. Such is the theme of many popular hymns like *Fight the good fight* and *Onward, Christian soldiers*. There is even a mosaic picture at Ravenna in the Archbishop's Chapel of Christ in the uniform of a Roman soldier carrying a cross which looks remarkably like a sword.

Military organisation is based on a rigid chain of command with an appropriate officer or non-commissioned officer at each level. (It is interesting that for some years the Chinese army tried to do without ranks, but was compelled in 1988 to re-introduce them.) Uniform is worn to strengthen a corporate sense of belonging and diminish personal identity. Much basic military training is designed to instil immediate and unthinking obedience to orders. This may be necessary in the heat of battle, but it is a grave discouragement to creative thinking in larger matters of strategy and tactics. It was said of the British army in the Second World War that it was only when conscripted amateurs had gained sufficient experience and seniority to be able to take over from the professionals that the army became efficient.

Efficiency requires, amongst other things, an accurate knowledge of the enemy, his whereabouts, his strength and his nature. In the days of pitched battles, this was not too hard to discover, but has become increasingly difficult with highly mobile forces, and particularly so in operations against guerrillas and terrorists. In the days of Christendom the battle-lines were clearly demarcated, and people knew their places and the rules. It is not so to-day: the nature of the warfare has completely changed, and many Christians feel ill-equipped and ill-trained for it. The enemy remains the same, 'the deceits of the world, the flesh, and the devil', but to identify those forces and overcome them remains as hard as ever.

Indeed, talk of 'overcoming' may be positively misleading. To 'fight' a temptation may result in such concentration on it that it becomes stronger than ever. To overcome it may require a diversion of attention on to an alternative objective.

Military discipline is maintained by strong sanctions. To desert in the face of the enemy is punishable by death. Christians, however, are free to leave the field at any time, and if they do not take kindly to one form of ecclesiastical discipline they can, and do, go in search of a more agreeable one.

It has been wryly observed that all that happens after one war is finished is that allies are changed before the next one begins. The events following the Second World War are a case in point. Christians do not always find it easy to know who their allies are: in Poland Roman Catholics led the struggle against communism, whereas in South America in thousands of base-communities Roman Catholics serve side by side with communists in a struggle for a juster ordering of society. The military model for ministry needs careful handling.

3. *Industrial*

The difference between churches and factories
Everyone understands.

It's the difference between the laying on
And the laying off of hands.

(G. Ewart, *All My Little Ones*)

The church is frequently likened to a business, with bishops as top management, rural deans as middle managers, and vicars as local managers whose success in selling the product is to be judged by the number of customers sitting in their pews. Nothing could be farther from the concepts of the New Testament, and few models could be practically more injurious to clergy and laity alike. The purpose of business is to make and sell a product at a profit, and the shareholders who have provided the capital pay managers and workers to do the work for them. This executive hierarchy is the successor to the commodity hierarchy whose roots lay in the medieval guilds, and it was created as a means of organising and controlling increasingly impersonal systems of production. The complete work is broken down into a number of separate tasks of decreasing complexity, and the chief executive is responsible for delegating the work of the whole organisation to others. His authority reaches into every department, permitting him to monitor the limits of work and also to limit the judgment of his workers about how the work should be done. He must safeguard the values of the firm and communicate its general purpose to the workers. Employees are not members of the firm; they agree to work for x hours a week at £y an hour, and if their work is unsatisfactory they can, under certain conditions, be dismissed.

It is far otherwise with the church and its members. Here the laity are as much members as the clergy, and the New Testament is clear that every local church is, at least in embryo, *the* Church of Christ. The gospel is not a product, nor is it for sale. It is the free gift of God to be witnessed to by the lives and words of all church members, gathered and dispersed. Success is not to be measured by numbers, and J. B. Lightfoot when Bishop of Durham forbade his clergy ever to count heads in church lest they should be unduly elated or depressed. The vicar is not an employee either of the diocese or of the congregation (technically, in the Church of England, he is self-employed although his monthly cheque comes from the Church Commissioners), and his 'parson's freehold' gives him a great measure of real independence: he cannot be starved out by his church council, nor removed by his bishop except for a very grave offence. Sometimes the relationship between priest and people is poor, and sometimes a priest may relapse into idleness (it was H. H. Henson, also a bishop of Durham, who remarked that the Church of England contained the half-dozen idlest and the half-dozen hardest-working men in the country), but by and large the freehold has been a source of strength.

If it is supposed that the bishop is the chief executive of the diocese and that he will have *his* work done through *his* parish priests, then the pressure on himself will grow intolerably as he sees himself personally responsible for the work of two or three hundred branch offices in his diocese. Furthermore if the bishop sees himself as responsible for determining the particular theological or liturgical flavour of the diocese as being the company's policy, he will gravely inhibit the real catholicity of the church which is grounded, at least in the Church of England, in a fairly wide diversity.

It is generally supposed that a hierarchy is to be likened to a pyramid of command with the supreme authority at the top, and lower levels in subordination (does not the Book of Common Prayer speak of 'inferior clergy'?). In fact, the pyramid should be turned upside down, following Pope Gregory's title, with the bishop at the bottom, sustaining, with his fellow pastors, the laity who are in the front line of conflict.

4. *Professional*

Is a clergyman a professional? Ought he to be? Does he see himself as one? Do others see him as one? What, anyhow, is a professional? A. Russell has shown in *The Clerical Profession* (1980) how in the nineteenth century as British clergy were increasingly squeezed out of influential roles, as Poor Law administrator, political agent, teacher, registrar, policeman, and even sanitary engineer, by the growth of professions, so they responded by adopting many of the characteristics of a profession themselves, of which the establishment of theological colleges was a sign. The clergyman of 1860 was very different from that of the country gentleman of 1810. Russell offers the following as the ideal of a profession (p. 23, slightly adapted):

> an occupational group that has specialist functions, based on theoretic, esoteric knowledge;
> a prolonged training;
> a monopoly of legitimate performance;
> regulation of entry and expulsion;
> colleague-group solidarity;
> autonomy of role performance;
> a relationship of trust between practitioner and client;
> a distinctive professional ethic stressing altruistic service;
> a reward structure and career pattern;
> a research orientation and control of the institution within which the professional role is legitimated.

The institution itself is important because it is able to gain rewards and status in society which individuals could not hope to attain. Its natural history passes through four phases: the occupation is followed on a full-time basis; formal training is established; training is provided in a university; local and then national professional associations are established. The Church as an institution helped to perform this role for clergy from an early stage in the process.

This trend towards clerical professionalism has had its benefits, but at a cost. As early as 1906 G. B. Shaw observed through one of his characters in *The Doctor's Dilemma* that 'all professions are conspiracies against the laity', speaking with more theological profundity than perhaps he knew. The medical profession in the west has made enormous advances through scientific research and technological skill, but at the cost of dehumanising people and dividing itself into ever-narrower specialisms (in 1980 in the USA there was one general practitioner for every eight specialists). Wide public dissatisfaction with the state of medical care has resulted in a burgeoning 'alternative medicine' or 'complementary medicine' with all sorts of people with various or no qualifications setting up as therapists. The British Medical Association has reluctantly extended a measure of recognition to osteopaths, and many medical practitioners now give a qualified blessing to their patients seeking the help of chiropractors and suchlike. Even acupuncture is being seriously examined, and there is now a British Holistic Medical Association. A number of clergy have set themselves up as specialists in spiritual healing. It has been observed that the medical profession in the 1980s and '90s has been suffering the same sort of professional disillusionment that the clerical 'profession' suffered a generation before. Professions are also increasingly suspect because they have considerable access to power: in 1980 twenty-two per cent of Members of Parliament belonged to the legal profession.

Clergy once relied on their esoteric learning, and a 'learned clergy' has been an important tradition in the Church of England. To-day, however, it is not at all unusual to find a university department of theology where only one in ten of its undergraduate members is interested in the possibility of ordination; the rest find posts in education, industry, commerce or social work, much like other arts graduates. Many congregations contain lay members who are better educated theologically than their ministers. Is that an encouragement or a threat to the minister?

The sort of theology being taught at university may not be that most appropriate for the ministry, and a hundred years ago theological colleges were founded to rescue young men from the snares of such learning. Today some theological colleges award degrees validated by the Council for National Academic Awards, but it is very difficult to see such a college fulfilling the function of a 'universal' education to which a university by its very name is pledged.

One of the dangers of clerical 'professionalism' is the very narrowness of its concerns. The minutes of a clerical club in

Norfolk reveal that in the 1870s the two matters which were above all exercising the minds of its members were marriage to one's deceased wife's sister (for which legislation was being prepared in Parliament) and the burial in one's churchyard of those not baptised in the Church of England. More recently, a non-stipendiary minister has given up attending meetings of his deanery clergy because the ecclesiastical talk to which he was subjected bore no relation to the real world as he knew it. The arrival of non-stipendiary ministry on the clerical scene has been greeted with a good deal of suspicion because these persons do not fit the professional mould; in particular, they are considered 'part-time', a description which they would vigorously repudiate. (The implications of this will be considered in Chapter 23.)

All in all, then, the professional model has its hazards and limitations. In any case, professions are the product of, and are peculiar to, Western European and North American cultures.

5. *Family*

The family as a model for the people of God has a long and honourable history rooted in the concept of God as Father. One of the most distinctive Christian words is *Abba* (though scholars dispute whether it corresponds exactly with the colloquial word 'Daddy'), and Jesus taught his disciples to address their prayer to 'our Father' (Matt. 6.9) or 'Father' (Luke 11.12) which probably reflects *Abba*. The word occurs in the Old Testament of Israel's relationship with God, but not often.

Christians have been inclined to a romantic and a limited view of the family as a stable and mutually loving relationship of father, mother and two children, with grandparents, aunts, uncles and cousins in the background. This flies in the face of present-day evidence loudly proclaimed, if not relished, on all sides: a high rate of divorce, much marital instability especially in inner cities, an alarming rate of abuse of children by parents and near relatives, and widespread cohabitation outside marriage; so much so that secular prophets have been proclaiming the demise of marriage as an institution; though the latest signs do not bear out their gloomiest forebodings.

It is not clear, however, that overall the quality of partnerships and family relationships has declined. Although the family is a key element in fabric of social stability, it also reflects the kind of society we have built and are building. This is the common ground of innumerable novelists, and the subject seems to be one of eternal fascination. Some people chose not to marry as a conscientious protest against the long record of oppression, not least male oppression, of which many Christian societies have been guilty. The Biblical evidence is far from reassuring. Polygamy is a frequent feature of the Old Testament scene and is nowhere specifically repudiated. Levirate marriage was customary. Jesus himself was unmarried and childless, and warned that discipleship might very well precipitate family conflict (Lk 12.49–53). Certainly the demands of the kingdom took precedence over family loyalties (Lk 9.59–60).

The family has always had a tarnished record, not least in the Bible, but it remains the place above all places where people learn, or fail to learn, to become fulfilled human beings. It has one immensely strong claim to be the model for God's people in that (divorce apart) relationships are given, permanent and unalterable. A son or brother remains a son or brother whatever happens to him or whatever other members of the family make of him. There is no more telling parable than that of the prodigal son. Baptism is the witness and the pledge to every person, young or old, who receives it that he is a member of Christ, the child of God and an inheritor of the kingdom of heaven. It is, as F. D. Maurice put it, the sacrament of constant union not only with God but with the whole people of God. So long as we talk of God as Father, so long must we talk of the church as a family. In his diocese the bishop is father-in-God to his people, and every minister is ordained to the service of that divine society. Each circle is to be an image of the great family, each is to have its own father. Maurice comments that the Apostles loved and cherished that name:

They much preferred it to any title which merely indicated an office. It was more spiritual; it was more personal; it asserted better the divine order; it did more to preserve the dignity and sacredness of all domestic relations.

(*Epistles of St John*, p. 54)

All the models of ministry considered above are only models; each by itself is incomplete and if taken too far can become one-sided. None should be taken as *the* exemplar, but each has important truth to contribute. The ministry is witness to the church as the divine society, and so it is not surprising that it has no exact secular equivalent.

There is another factor, without which no model is valid:

6. *Doing and Being*

Some people attempt to define the ordained ministry in terms of function, to draw up for it a 'job specification'. It is clear that men and women are ordained to certain functions, to be 'messengers, watchmen, and stewards of the Lord', but it is equally clear that their office, be it bishop, priest, or deacon, is a peculiarly personal one. 'For you' said Augustine to his congregation at Hippo, 'I am a bishop, but with you I am a Christian. . . ', adding that he found the latter vocation altogether more agreeable and safer than the former. A priest may be ordained to preside over the sacraments; he is also called to be, in a manner of speaking, a walking sacrament, that is to say, someone through whom the reality of God discloses itself in unmistakeable terms. After all, most Christians are such because of someone, or some group, whom they have known well.

Austin Farrer, when preaching at the commemoration of a much-loved priest, Charles Linnell, described him as 'at once the most parsonical and the least parsonical of men'. Unlike those who try to make martyrs of themselves,

It was as native to Charles to be a parson as it is native to a foxhound to be a foxhound. He was enormously human, enormously alive to his whole human environment: but he saw it from the place where he actually was, his parson's place. For him to talk about his job was to talk about his world; they were the inside and the outside of the same thing. He was most happy in his calling, because it was a better excuse than any other for knowing everyone and everything. . . . He just found himself absorbed in people, and in all sorts of aspects of God's endlessly enthralling world.

Charles, he added had the secret of exercising influence. And what is that? Never to do it! The most he would do was to put himself unobtrusively in someone's way: he left himself about, so to speak. The rest lay with Providence. (A. Farrer, p. 214f.)

Or we may hear the witness of a Welsh priest-poet in more sombre terms from a harsher land:

> I take their hands,
> Hard hands. There is no love
> For such, only a willed
> Gentleness. Negligible men
> From the village, from the small
> Holdings, they bring their grief
> Sullenly to my back door,
> And are speechless. Seeing them
> In the wind with the light's
> Halo, watching their eyes
> Blur, I know the reason
> They cry, their worsting
> By one whom they will fight.
>
> Daily the sky mirrors
> The water, the water the
> Sky. Daily I take their side
> In their quarrel, calling their faults
> Mine. How do I serve so

This being they have shut out
Of their houses, their thoughts, their lives?

(R. S. Thomas, p. 39)

Every minister belongs to a community: it may be a local parish; for a prison chaplain it will be a prison; for a naval chaplain it will be a depot for Polaris submarines for an industrial chaplain a group of factories; for a non-stipendiary minister, an office block. In each his function is to be an *animateur*, a witness to the Lord the Spirit, who is also the life-giver. His mission is not only to people at their weak points, though he will find plenty of caring work to do among the world's casualties, but also at their strong points where he can rejoice with their successes and affirm their discoveries. Because he is at home there, because he knows his way around, he can demonstrate the church to be the family of God in that place; not a religious club for the like-minded, but a foretaste of the world redeemed.

Cardinal Suhard, discussing in his last pastoral letter the task of the priest in a proletarian world, talks of:

> . . . the double task which is given to the apostle in general and the priest in particular: renunciation and acquisition. It means *renunciation* of what is peculiar to himself: his education, tastes, culture, even perhaps his mother-tongue. But he also gains something from those whom he seeks to convert. He gives them the most essential things – the Gospel and the divine life. He absorbs from them what they have to give: thoughts and feelings hitherto unknown to him.
>
> (*The Priest in the Modern World*, pp. 143–4)

The function, then, of the ordained person is to be, as George Herbert put it, a window to God, and then, through Christ, so to open his congregation to the Spirit of the living God that they in their turn will become windows for others.

PART V – CURRENT ISSUES

17

Authority and Authorities

THERE is no doubt where ultimate authority lies. It lies in God's kingly rule, unhappily translated in most English Bibles as 'the kingdom of God'. It was the central feature of Jesus' teaching, at least according to the Synoptists, and it lies at the heart of the prayer which he taught his disciples. God's rule is not like that of ordinary rulers, as became abundantly clear from the culmination of Jesus' ministry where his throne proved to be a cross and his crown one of thorns. God rules among people by love and persuasion and will force his rule on no-one. God's rule is also to be seen in the whole created natural order to which, however, he has given a semi-autonomy: when St Paul speaks of the 'wrath of God' he seems to refer to a moral ordering of the universe which brings its own retribution. The authority which Jesus confers on his apostles is categorically different from the imperial rule which surrounded them: '. . . their great ones exercise authority over them. But it is not so among you . . .' (Mark. 10.42f.; Matt. 20.25f.; Luke. 22.25f.) It was, nevertheless, a remarkable authority, nothing less than the 'keys of the kingdom' (Matt. 16.19) with the power of binding and loosing (see also Matt. 18.18 and John. 20.23).

How was, and is, authority to be exercised? The whole story of the ministry is part of the answer, and a confusing one at that, but ministry is a second-order issue. The Church is primarily a missionary and witnessing body for which matters of structure and handing-on are secondary. The doctrines of ministry and sacraments took shape after those of God, Christ, redemption, and grace; they were means rather than ends; they were socially and culturally conditioned; and ever since apostolic times the Church has constantly struggled to adapt and update them. The exercise of ministry preceded any doctrine of ministry, just as the recognition of certain biblical documents preceded the canon of scripture. Apostolicity means the courage to take local initiatives which are then to be checked against the wider experience of the Church, a process classically portrayed at the Council of Jerusalem in Acts 15. For 250 years the Church coped on a local basis until the first 'ecumenical' council of Nicaea in 325 summoned by Constantine with at least one eye towards consolidating imperial unity.

The most important decisions must come locally first and local councils must act with high doctrinal responsibility. The local church may be wrong, but if it does nothing it will be wrong. The Church has power to construct and reconstruct its ministry, its sacramental forms and hierarchies, because it has always been doing so since apostolic times, and it is unlikely that the process will ever be complete. 'Ecclesiologically', says A. Hastings (Jeffery, 1987, p. 63),

> it is not wrong because it has not been done before. Ecclesiologically, it is not wrong because the *orbis terrarum* has not yet pronounced upon it. Ecclesiologically it would be wrong, after such a process, to be afraid to act for no other reason than that the universal Church remains partly uncertain, partly opposed. The rightness of the particular decision must be hammered out pastorally, christologically, soteriologically, anthropologically, but not ecclesiologically.

The Anglican communion has drawn up a statement about authority which has become something of a classic and is printed in full in Appendix 2. It is part of a report attached to the Lambeth Conference report of 1948, and, like most things to do with Lambeth Conferences, it carries moral, not legal, authority. Its manner of expression has to be read against the background of its time. The formulation of authority, it states, is an organic process, similar to the scientific method, contained in the process of life and thought in which religious experience has been, and is described, intellectually ordered, mediated, and verified. This experience is described in scripture, defined in the creeds and in theological study, mediated in the ministry of word and sacraments by commissioned representative persons, and verified in the witness of saints and in the *consensus fidelium*. The Christ-like life carries its own authority, and the authority of doctrinal formulations rests in part on their acceptance by the whole body of the faithful. Thus Anglicans see authority as dispersed, rather than centralised, having many elements which interact with and check each other.

It is wholly in line with this theory that the Lambeth Conference is seen as advisory and not legislative, that Canterbury carries a primacy of regard and not of law, that there is no appellate tribunal, and that the Anglican Communion is a family of local Churches and not a union. Cohesion was tested in 1978 in a long and searching debate about the ordination of women, but the outcome was clear and the resolution (21) was carried by a very large majority, to the effect that the Conference acknowledged the legal right of each Church to make its own decisions on the matter, encouraged all member Churches to continue in communion with one another notwithstanding, to promote dialogue between member Churches which differ, and extend the dialogue outside the Anglican Communion. A similar conclusion was reached in 1988 about women bishops.

The final Anglican appeal is sometimes described as a threefold cord of scripture, tradition and reason, with particular acknowledgement for the last to R. Hooker and the other seventeenth century divines. To appeal to reason and conscience, however, is not to set up a third source of Christian truth, but to emphasise the way in which all truth, under God, is to be recognised and obeyed. God's authority, as exercised in Jesus Christ, is the authority of love, and as such is always open to being challenged and misunderstood. It is a self-giving love, inviting discernment and a response which involves the whole person. It does not call for blind faith but a response which needs to be worked out in thought and action. On such a trust and on such an authority the Christian accepts the truth of a gospel, and not on any infallible knowledge either of scripture, or of Church, or of particular forms of religious experience. P. R. Baelz underlines the point:

> It may indeed be said that the response of love, if it is to be *truly* loving, requires the ascetical discipline of reason and conscience in order to purify and direct what may otherwise become inverted into sentimentality and illusion. Reason and conscience are rightfully the servants of love, not love's masters nor love's enemies.
>
> (R. Jeffery, 1987, p. 46)

God's authority, being mediated through human apprehension, can always be challenged. There is no place for infallibility this side of the Parousia. It is true that scripture has a unique authority as witness to God's self-giving in Christ, and the tradition of the Church has a unique authority as the continuing central reflection on God's self-giving both in Christ and in the life which is in Christ. But a simple appeal to that authority is not sufficient. Some attempt must be made to answer the questions, what exactly it is that they say, how it is to be understood, and why it is to be believed. The glorious liberty of the children of God is not, in M. Polanyi's phrase, 'the freedom of the subjective person to do as he pleases' but 'the freedom of the responsible person to act as he must'. (*Personal Knowledge*, 1957, p. 309)

It is sometimes assumed that the appeal to conscience is something private, set over against the claims of the community. Sometimes, it is true, a person cannot 'in conscience' go along with the majority, but to suppose that conscience is an infallible inner voice, or a private line to God, is highly misleading. Conscience is undoubtedly personal but it is certainly not private, cut off from the community. A prophet can only condemn aspects of his own community because he has roots in that community. The work of the Holy Spirit is no more private than the judgment of conscience. C. F. D. Moule has described the way in which the Holy Spirit may be expected to work as through the 'Christian worshipping congregation listening critically'.

In fact, however much Christians in a community may reason together, disagreement and conflict may occur and will then have to be resolved. A compromise may be possible, or a vote taken with the minority giving way; but on some matters which are deeply felt the community may have to be broken: truth may at times be reckoned more valuable than unity. But a community which is bound together by allegiance to a living Lord will do all it can to remain joined together, and any group within it will always remember that it may be wrong.

The bishop has always played a key part in the Church's quest both for truth and for unity. He stands in the centre of the debate about how the Church may recover its shattered unity, being himself a conspicuous sign of its disunity. Granted that there is a place for bishops, how are they best to exercise their spiritual authority? On that there is no general agreement, but there are signs of a convergence. It was the unanimous view of the Fathers, many of whom were bishops, that a bishop was not an isolated officer: *episcopatus unus est*, and even so autocratic a character as Cyprian said he would undertake nothing without the counsel of his clergy and the assent of the church (see page 44). No doubt 'consultation' was as unclear a process then as it is now. Vatican II re-emphasised the collegiality of bishops, but left it quite unclear how this should work out in practice, and the question of the primacy of the bishop of Rome will be considered later (pages 185–91).

Throughout the Anglican Communion the seat of authority is found in the bishop-in-synod. Synodical government, like other church institutions, grew out of the necessities of corporate life, and has assumed a variety of forms depending upon local contexts, the personal style of a bishop, constitutional procedures borrowed from the surrounding political society, and the local missionary task. When in the eighteenth and nineteenth centuries Anglican colonial churches gained their independence from the Crown they located their seat of authority in synodical government with houses of bishops, clergy and laity. Authority was shared between the episcopate and the synod, leaving a veto to the house of bishops, and reserving to bishops certain powers and responsibilities, like ordination, which they could not delegate. The reason for this was not simply a pragmatic one but it enshrined clear theological principles. (The Church of England is not typical of the Anglican Communion since it is the established Church of the land, and it only included lay people in its government as recently as 1965, whereas the Church of England in Australia convened its first General Synod in 1872. The tractarian George Selwyn, as first bishop of New Zealand, wrote synodical government into the original constitution of the Anglican Church in that country, building on the experience of the North Americans, and the first synod since the suppression of Convocation in England in 1717 met in his diocese in 1844.)

The principles and practices of the various Anglican Churches reveal a common pattern: that legislative authority lies neither in the 'house' of bishops nor in the various committees and councils of the Church, but in diocesan synods, and to a lesser degree in provincial and national synods. Other structures, like the Lambeth Conference, are advisory, relational and collegial, but not legislative. The constitution of the Anglican Church of Australia is quite clear: 'A diocese shall in accordance with the historic custom of the One Holy Catholic and Apostolic Church continue to be the unit of organisation of this Church and shall be the see of a bishop'. (*Section 7*)

The relationship between the bishop and his synod has no real parallel in parliamentary democracy, autocracy, oligarchy, or bureaucracy as found in the secular world, but is a complex one springing from a combination of theological principles held in balance. It is classically set out in the 1948 Lambeth statement (Appendix 2). The personal oversight of the bishop goes hand in hand with the corporate responsibility shared with other clergy and laity. The Holy Spirit is given to the whole Church as the guiding dynamic of its life, to be responded to in the *consensus fidelium*. Anglicans insist both on the exercise of real power by those entitled to claim it, and also on the necessity of open criticism of the quality of the exercise of that power.

This sort of consensus should not be understood as unanimity, nor is it shown by majority vote in synod: it emerges from time, patience and a costly love which is willing to defer to the common mind even when it has not yet emerged, and when it is genuinely free. Synods can be manipulated by bishops, theologians, lawyers, priests, lay people, and ecclesiastical parties, but this is a decline from true consensus. The safeguards against it are the example of Jesus Christ, the appeal of the gospel to the human will, openness to theological criticism, and time for people to reflect and reconsider. Tyrannous and psychologically manipulative uses of power are to be identified, criticised, and abandoned, though, of course, their recognition depends upon fallible judgement. 'Our Anglican experience is', writes K. S. Chittleborough from Adelaide, 'that the Christian Church requires *both* the discriminating exercise of authority *and* the discriminating exercise of criticism if Christ's work is to be done in the world.' (*Authority in the Anglican Communion*, 1987, p. 152.)

Discussion of authority is liable to end up in abstractions far removed from the realities of life, and so it may be helpful at this point to consider as an example one issue concerning the exercise of authority which is a current matter of debate, namely that of the ministry of homosexual clergypersons. It has long been recognised that the Church's ministry has contained many who are homosexual, but in recent years the homosexual community has come out much more obviously into the open, with claims that the homosexual relationship should be accepted as the equivalent of heterosexual marriage, and that therefore it might be proper for an ordained minister to live an open and sexually active life with a partner of the same sex. Some Christians agree with this position, while others find it personally repugnant and theologically untenable. Bishops have to make pastoral decisions about such matters. How is authority to be exercised? The matter first came to a head in the Church of England in 1974 when a letter was sent from the Conference of Principals of Theological Colleges to the Board for Social Responsibility asking for a study to be made for the Church's guidance. The Board set up a Working Party which four years later published its report *Homosexual Relationships: A Contribution to Discussion*. When the Board considered the report it was deeply divided, and went to the unusual lengths of appending a Part II of *Critical Observations*. When the General Synod came to debate the report, similar divisions were apparent, and the Church of England has not committed itself to the views expressed in the report.

The matter may be looked at sociologically, anthropologically, psychologically, theologically and pastorally. The sociologist observes the ways in which homosexual persons organise themselves as a minority group in society and how the society reacts to what it sees as a threat to its accepted arrangements concerning the family and marriage, concerning its understanding of gender, and concerning our own sexual experience. The resultant hostility tends to segregate homosexuals into a subculture where a person's sexual disposition becomes the central fact of his or her existence. Doctors no longer look on the homosexual condition as an illness to be cured. Its causes are uncertain and its very nature is hard to define. The word 'homosexuality' is commonly applied both to the practice of engaging in a sexual, perhaps genital, act in which both persons are of the same sex, and to the psychological state which moves them to desire it. There is, however, no objective test for sexual orientation and some people are neither exclusively homosexual nor exclusively heterosexual. The prevalence of homosexuality among different peoples is hard to establish, with reports of one African tribe where it is unknown, and one tribe in New Guinea where a marriage relationship is regularly accompanied by a homosexual one as well. It is generally accepted, however, that in Western European and North American societies 4 per cent of people are exclusively homosexual and another 29 per cent may have had homosexual experience but are capable to a greater or lesser extent of a heterosexual relationship. (These figures come from the Kinsey Report of 1948, and have been called in question.)

How does the witness of the Bible bear on this evidence? References are comparatively few, and they are condemnatory, in the Old Testament principally because homosexual practices are seen as peculiarly characteristic of heathen Canaanite society and religion. In the New Testament the key passage is Romans 1 where the context is the whole created order. Because humanity has departed from the knowledge of the one true God, so it fails to recognise the divine purpose in sex and hence misuses it, and of this misuse homosexual practices are the clearest example. Thus, for Paul, all such practices are 'unnatural', and again characteristic of the heathen world. It is not, however, clear that what is being condemned is the homosexual condition. In any case, we may not simply take over moral injunctions from the Bible without regard for their social and historical context, nor may we assume that the Bible has a static notion of nature. The question remains, if there are those who cannot find their sexual fulfilment with members of the opposite sex, is their condition an aspect of the fallenness of creation, or is there a place for their sort of sexuality in the divine order?

The Christian tradition is a complex one, but it has generally condemned homosexual acts as sinful. Nevertheless, tradition is not final and complete: for a long time it condemned contraceptive practices as sinful. The traditional arguments tend to fall into two groups, based on Bible and on nature, the former favoured by protestants and the latter by catholics. The Natural Law approach has been much debated in connexion with *Humanae Vitae*. This argues, in its simplest form, that as the sexual act is aimed at the transmission of life, to engage in sexual activity in which this aim is frustrated is against nature and completely wrong. The argument in this form is open to severe criticism in that such a requirement conflicts with the demands of the partners' own relationships and also with an adequate interpretation of the end of procreation itself since the rearing of responsible human beings requires a family of manageable size and a happy parental relationship. In short, the appeal to nature must be made in a broader context than the merely biological.

A personalist view argues that what matters in sexual behaviour is the quality of the personal relationship which it serves to express and confirm: a genuine love needs to be exclusive but it is debatable whether it has to be life-long. Many homosexuals argue that their relationship reflects this value to the same extent and in the same fashion as with heterosexuals, and claim that if the unitive end of marriage is seen to be independent of the procreative, then homosexual equality must be conceded, to the point of accepting 'homosexual marriage'.

Anglicans, however, continue to maintain that the norm for sexual relationships is one of mutual love, nurtured in life-long and exclusive marriage, based on the givenness of biological and psychological potential, with the couple taking responsibility for the use or non-use of contraception. Not everyone, however, is capable of entering into a heterosexual response, and many men and women feel that they are able to respond erotically only to members of their own sex. How can a homosexual witness to the sacramental mirroring of the divine love which the Christian Church sees in marriage? The Anglican Working Party concluded: 'In the light of some of the evidence we have received we do not think it possible to deny that there are circumstances in which individuals may justifiably choose to enter into a homosexual relationship with the hope of enjoying a companionship and physical expression of sexual love similar to that which is to be found in marriage'. (p. 52)

The Working Party did not, however, believe that such an arrangement was possible for its clergy because their domestic affairs inevitably affect their standing as leaders of the congregation and examples to the flock of Christ. 'A homosexual priest who has come out and openly acknowledges that he is living in a sexual union with another man should not expect the Church to accept him on the same conditions as if he were married' (p. 76.). The report recommends that a parish priest in this position should offer his resignation to his bishop. It is acknowledged that bishops vary in their views, but this only reflects the variety in the Church at large.

Many Anglicans were unhappy with the report's con-clusions, and in November 1987 a motion was introduced into the General Synod demanding a harder line, to reaffirm the Biblical standard that sexual intercourse should take place only between married couples; that fornication, adultery and homosexual acts were always sinful; and that Christian leaders were called to be exemplary in all spheres of morality, including sexual morality, as a condition of being appointed to or remaining in office. After a searching and sensitive debate an alternative motion was accepted by an overwhelm-ing majority which affirmed, amongst other things, that homo-sexual genital acts fall short of the ideal, and are to be met by a call to repentance and the exercise of compassion. The exer-cise of authority was left in the hands of the bishops.

In 1991 the House of Bishops published an authoritative statement, *Issues in Human Sexuality* in which they broadly sup-port the reasoning of the 1979 report and reach this conclusion (5.17):

> We have, therefore, to say that in our considered judge-ment the clergy cannot claim the liberty to enter into sexually active homophile relationships.
>
> Because of the distinctive nature of their calling, status and consecration, to allow such a claim on their part would be seen as placing that way of life in all respects on a par with heterosexual marriage as a reflection of God's purposes in creation. The Church cannot accept such a parity and remain faithful to the insights which God has given it through Scripture, tradition and reasoned reflection on experience.

In subsequent paragraphs the House rejects the proposal that bishops should be more rigorous in searching out and exposing clergy who may be in sexually active homophile relationships because it does not wish to subscribe to the suggestion that any two people of the same sex who choose to live together are therefore in an erotic relationship, and it eschews any general inquisition which would infringe their right to privacy and manifest a distrust which would undermine their ministry.

As for those clergy who wish to make known their orientation openly with a commitment to a life of abstinence, the bishops comment that any community which cannot accept such an honourable candour is not worthy of the name of Christian. As for those who are in an active homophile relationship and who proclaim the fact as a matter of personal integrity, the bishops call upon such clergy to live lives that respect the Church's teaching. Disagreement, however, over the proper expression of homosexual love will never become rejection of the homosexual person.

Many people, including Anglicans, find such a concept and exercise of authority too complex and too imprecise to be authoritative. They would opt for a more authoritarian one and would be prepared, they say, to pay the price. But they would be giving away a central feature of the Anglican tradition, perhaps one of its richest contributions to the ecumenical scene.

18

Ecumenical Aspects of Ministry

I T is a tragedy that the principal causes of division among Christians concern the ministry and the sacraments because these are the very gifts of Christ to his Church to ensure its unity. Great progress, however, has been made in recent years to face up to, and resolve, these difficulties with two notable documents both published in 1982, that of the World Council of Churches Faith and Order Paper *Baptism, Eucharist and Ministry*, and the Anglican-Roman Catholic International Commission's *The Final Report* which includes two statements on *Authority in the Church*. These are perhaps, the least satisfactory part of the Commission's work because they deal with authorities rather than authority, and then in such an abstract way that they never even mention the Roman Curia or Anglican synodical government, nor the process which led up to the publication of *Humanae Vitae*. The greater part of the second Statement concerns the papal primacy since, at the outset, the commission proclaims its agreement 'that a universal primacy will be needed in a reunited Church and should appropriately be the primacy of the bishop of Rome . . .' (para. 9).

This question of primacy must be examined, but what sort of question is it? Historical? Christological? pastoral? psychological? The papacy certainly has a history, and its origins and development have been sketched in the first part of this book. Whether from it one can deduce that papal primacy was a providential development depends upon one's reading of the history. At least it has to be borne in mind that in terms of maintaining the Church in the apostolic-prophetic tradition the reformation was as providential as the Roman Church; that in terms of maintaining the unity of the Church the

Roman Church was principally responsible for precipitating the first great breach between Catholic West and Orthodox East in 1054; and that the Eastern Churches have never (since the sixth century) accepted the need for a universal primacy, least of all that of the bishop of Rome, but have maintained a national or regional autocephalous system with a primacy of honour reserved for the Patriarch of Constantinople.

Is the question a Christological one? One of the official titles of the Bishop of Rome is 'Vicar of Christ' and this has traditionally been based on the Petrine texts of the New Testament and particularly on Mt. 16.18, '. . . thou art Peter, and upon this rock I will build my church . . .', with the corollary that this primacy was conveyed to all his episcopal successors. Today, however, the judgement of Roman New Testament scholars is far different: H. Fries and K. Rahner, for example, wrote in *The Tablet* of 6 November 1982,

> The unanimous view of to-day's Catholic exegetes is that on the basis of historical criteria, the so-called Petrine passages of the New Testament cannot be understood in the sense of the institution of a universal primacy for the post-apostolic Church and its equipment with universal jurisdictional plenitude of power.

The First Vatican Council was quite sure that this primacy derives from Christ, '*ex ipsius Christi Domini institutione seu iure divino*' – by divine right – and the ARCIC Final Report struggles hard to maintain that this categorical statement does not mean what it says:

> *Jus divinum* in this context need not be taken to imply that the universal primacy as a permanent institution was directly founded by Jesus during his life on earth . . . It is to a universal primate thus envisaged within the collegiality of the bishops and the koinonia of the whole Church that the qualification *jure divino* can be applied.
>
> (p. 86)

Similarly the Report struggles with the attribution of 'universal, ordinary and immediate jurisdiction' to the Bishop of

Rome defined by the First Vatican Council. It claims that 'Primacy is not an autocratic power over the Church but a service in and to the Church which is a communion in faith and charity of local Churches.' This is a fine sentiment, but hardly borne out by the facts. In particular, since the mid-fourteenth century in the Roman Church the pope has had power to appoint bishops to vacant sees, and in the seventeenth and eighteenth centuries this extended to the suppression of national episcopal hierarchies, such as that in Holland, and the conversion of their territories into missionary areas directly under the Curia. In more recent times the Holy Office in Rome issued in July 1949 a decree whereby Vatican envoys in China ordered Chinese Catholics not to collaborate with the People's government, nor to join any pro-government association or organisation on pain of suspension from the sacraments or even excommunication. (Chu and Lind 1983 p. 63.) On 6 June 1981 the Pope appointed Deng Yiming Archbishop of the Guangzhou (Canton) diocese (he had been a titular bishop there since 1951) apparently without consultation with the Chinese Catholic Patriotic Association, and on 11 June Bishop Yang Gaojian denounced the appointment as illegal, accusing the Vatican of interference in the 'sovereign affairs of the Chinese Church' (Whyte, 1988 p. 440). On 22 June the diocese removed Deng as bishop, thus ending all hopes of reconciliation between the Vatican and the Patriotic Catholics.

Closely allied to the concept of 'divine right' is the equally contentious one of papal infallibility, crystallised by the First Vatican Council in 1870, which affirmed that the definitions of the Roman Pontiff are 'irreformable of themselves, and not from the consent of the Church' but it restricted this infallibility to those occasions 'when he speaks *ex cathedra*. . . when . . . by virtue of his supreme Apostolic authority he defines a doctrine regarding faith or morals to be upheld by the Universal Church'. Such authority was invoked in 1950 by Pius XII when he defined as dogma the assumption of the Virgin Mary, body and soul, into heavenly glory. The papacy of John XXIII, however, culminating in Vatican II, marked a turning point: the old definitions were not withdrawn, but new (in fact very old) viewpoints were added. The Petrine ministry is seen as pastoral ministry, not dominion, arising from the whole Church and shared collegially with all bishops.

Vatican I breathed the atmosphere of its period, of romantic traditionalism and political absolutism. Today the whole approach to doctrinal definition is different. It has been well stated by H. Küng: 'It is a simplified view of the truth to suppose that every sentence in its verbal formulation must be either true or false. On the contrary, any sentence can be true *and* false, according to its purpose, its context, its underlying meaning'. (*The Church*, p. 343) Küng in that book (p. 342) wished to explain infallibility in terms of indefectibility: 'If it [the Church] is obedient, then all lies and deceitfulness are removed from it'. That was too much for ARCIC (Report p. 97 footnote), but they are also unhappy about the term 'infallibility' and wish to avoid it (p. 97). The fact is that the Roman Church is today moving out of one ecclesiology and has not yet found another.

The measure of the hiatus is vividly illustrated by the episode of the encyclical *Humanae Vitae*. The thorny subject of birth control had been removed from the agenda of Vatican II by John XXIII, and Paul VI set up a special commission of experts, including lay persons, to advise him, not on the subject of family planning which had been endorsed by the Council (*Gaudium et Spes* 50–52; 87), but on appropriate means. By 1967 it was known that a majority of the commission was in favour of change: the choice of means should be left to the individual, an opinion widely shared by clergy and laity alike. For long the Pope delayed. Finally he toed the line of Pius XI and XII and published *Humanae Vitae* in 1968. It was greeted with a chorus of opposition, including an outspoken interview given by Bishop Butler to the *Sunday Times* on 6 October, entitled 'The Dictates of Rome'. 'It seems to me', he said, 'that at the very point where authority fails to communicate its message to the conscience, it fails to *be* effective authority'. His conclusion was striking: 'The birth control encyclical may turn out to have been the occasion of a great ecumenical advance and not a regression. Because, it is already compelling the Catholic Church to face internal criticism of the encyclical thus making Vatican II a living reality.'

The reception accorded to a papal pronouncement is a crucial issue, and a difficult one, as ARCIC II acknowledges (pp. 96–7). The official Roman position is repudiated by the Anglican members: 'Anglicans do not accept the guaranteed possession of such a gift of divine assistance in judgement necessarily attached to the office of the bishop of Rome by virtue of which his formal decisions can be known to be wholly assured before their reception by the faithful'. The *Response* of the Church of England points out that 'If it took three centuries for the Canon of the New Testament to be finally received, and half a century for the Council of Nicaea, should we expect any papal utterances to be accepted overnight?' (p. 88) Yet Vatican II was quite clear:

> In matters of faith and morals, the bishops speak in the name of Christ, and the faithful are to accept their teaching and adhere to it with a religious assent of soul. This religious submission of will and of mind must be shown in a special way to the authentic teaching authority of the Roman pontiff, even when he is not speaking *ex cathedra*.
>
> (*Lumen Gentium*, 25)

But what if acceptance is not generally given, as has certainly happened in Britain and America in the case of contraception? (*Lumen Gentium*, in a footnote, dismisses this possibility as 'imaginary' since the same Holy Spirit guides the pope, bishops, and laity.) Perhaps the answer is suggested by the Vatican itself. The Roman Congregation for the Doctrine of the Faith has insisted (*Observations* B III 3) that infallibility 'refers immediately not to truth but to certitude'. The English Roman Catholic bishops in their *Response* also speak in this connexion of 'a certitude that enables the faithful to adhere more serenely to that faith'. It seems, then, that the doctrine of infallibility is more a psychological device to provide a sense of assurance for the laity than a principle for discovering and proclaiming the truth at any cost. If that is so, much argumentation has been in vain.

Late in 1991, ten years after the publication of the ARCIC *Final Report* the Vatican gave its considered reply which may be seen as hopeful or unhopeful according to the reader's ecclesiastical disposition. (It was published in *The Tablet* of 7 December.) It certainly valued the report as 'a significant milestone not only in relations between the Catholic Church and the Anglican Church but in the ecumenical movement as a whole.' But 'it is not yet possible to state that substantial agreement has been reached on all the questions . . .', and the reply goes on to list areas of disagreement. On eucharistic doctrine there is 'notable progress', and on the ordained ministry 'significant consensus'. Not surprisingly it is the area of authority which provides the stumbling-blocks with only 'certain signs of convergence'.

It acknowledges that ARCIC itself could not agree on papal infallibility nor find any real consensus on the Marian dogmas, and this, it says, illustrates the need for further work on the matter of the Petrine ministry in the Church. It asserts that certain knowledge of any defined truth does not depend on its reception by the faithful, but that the councils or the pope are able to teach definitively by themselves. It finds unsatisfactory ARCIC's understanding of Peter's 'special position', and relies on Vatican I's statement that the bishop of Rome inherits the primacy from Peter who received it immediately and directly from Christ. It also cannot subscribe to ARCIC's interpretation of *jus divinum*, nor ARCIC's judgement that its work is not affected by the ordination of women, and it states that the historical-critical method is not sufficient for the interpretation of Scripture.

Now the question which the Roman Catholic Church was asked (as was the Church of England) was: are the agreements contained in this report consonant with the faith of the Church? What they have answered is that some of the agreements are not in line with the formulated doctrine of that Church. That is a different matter, and it illustrates the quandary which the Church of Rome is in about who speaks for that Church on matters ecumenical: is it the Pontifical Council for Promoting Christian Unity or the Congregation for the Doctrine of the Faith? The response shows little evidence of the important distinction enunciated by Pope John XXIII at the opening of Vatican II, 'the substance of the ancient deposit of Faith is one thing; and the way it is presented is another.' The response looks very much as if the claims of ARCIC were checked with Roman Catholic definitions as found, for example, in Trent and Vatican I, and if not in line then dismissed. Thus the *modus operandi* endorsed by Pope John Paul in 1980 seems to have been forgotten: 'Your method has been to go behind the habit of thought and expression born and nourished in enmity and controversy, to scrutinise together the great common treasure . . .'.

Nevertheless if this response brings out into the open the need to discuss more frankly ecumenical method and an ecumenical doctrine of the Church, facing the question of where the living tradition of the Church is to be found, it may, for all its cautious hesitations, do much good.

Progress towards reunion with the Free Churches and others of the Reformed tradition has advanced somewhat but there are still major obstacles. The Church of South India was a notable achievement in 1947 bringing together Christians from Anglican, Methodist, Presbyterian, Congregationalist, Dutch Reformed, and Lutheran traditions, though the last four had already formed a United Church. Since then some negotiations have succeeded, like the Church of North India in 1970, and others have failed. In Britain particularly, the record is disappointing. True, in 1972 the Congregational Church in England and Wales joined with the Presbyterian Church of England to become the United Reformed Church, but even that left a remnant of some hundreds of congregations from the former to become the Congregational Federation.

In 1957 an agreement was actually reached between representatives of the Church of England, the Church of Scotland, the Episcopal Church of Scotland and the Presbyterian Church of England, called *The Bishops' Report*, but it was emphatically rejected by the Church of Scotland's General Assembly, and nothing came of it. How much of the opposition to the idea of bishops, consecrated by Anglicans, being appointed as permanent moderators of presbyteries in England and Scotland was theological, and how much sociological, it is hard to say.

In 1969 prospects for Anglican-Methodist reunion were wrecked by a vote in the General Synod. Negotiations had begun in the late 1940s, there had been an *Interim Statement* in 1958, a *Report* in 1963, and approval in principle in both Anglican Convocations and the Methodist Conference in 1965. The vote was lost by a strange alliance of some Evangelicals who claimed that the Service of Reconciliation was in fact an ordination and some Anglo-Catholics who claimed that it was not.

So hard is it to be clear about terms and meanings in matters of ministry! It is one thing for a committee of representatives to draw up a report; it is quite another to move a whole church with the weight of centuries of tradition often involving martyrdom, to a new form of ministerial order. There has been another report from an international commission of Anglicans and Reformed, *God's Reign and Our Unity*, published in 1984, which well illustrates the difficulties. The report tentatively suggests that the moderator of presbytery or synod might become a bishop-in-presbytery, along the lines of the ordination prayer for a bishop in the Alternative Service Book, and that Anglican Churches should reconsider its use of the diaconate, and take into account the Reformed experience of the eldership, while both commissions will have to take more seriously the role of the whole membership in the governance of the Church (pp. 72–77). The report comments:

'It is recognised, of course, that the words 'deacon' and 'elder' in the early Church stand for quite distinct offices. But it is also recognised (eg. in BEM, p. 24, para. 22) that 'The Spirit has many times led the Church to adapt its ministry to contextual needs'.

(p. 76)

An interesting observation comes from Australia where since the mid-1970s there have been Anglican-Uniting Church conversations (the Uniting Church comprising Presbyterians, Methodists and Congregationals). S. Murray, reflecting on Uniting Church experience since the union, has said in a paper to the Joint Committee,

> Neither the role of chairman nor the role of presbyter officer has more than very muted episcopal overtones. What is missing is an effective means for maintaining the purity of the faith . . . There is no person within the structure of the presbyter who is given authority to 'speak for the Church' . . . There is no authentically prophetic voice speaking out of the heart of the body. But the *episcope* of the presbytery has great strengths. Its greatest strength is its ability to discern the body.
>
> (*Episcope through Presbytery*, 8)
> (in S. W. Sykes (ed.) 1987, pp. 153–4.)

It is becoming increasingly hard to see separated churches being able to agree on tidy formulations of doctrine in matters ministerial partly because of the essentially imprecise nature of all theological doctrine and partly because of the suspicions engendered by centuries of separation and diverse usages. Two things seem necessary for reunion in any given place: first, sufficient agreement by the authorities of the Churches concerned about the vital content of the faith including sacraments and ministry (the paper *Baptism, Eucharist and Ministry* being an encouraging example); and second, wherever Christians are praying together, worshipping together, studying together, and doing mission together, there to have a commonly authorised ministry with shared sacraments. Such an arrangement would result in administrative untidiness, but would do justice both to the demands of serious theological appraisal and to the demands of an increasingly impatient laity.

A note needs to be added about the Eastern Orthodox Churches. Because of even longer historical separation they have only recently begun to enter the active ecumenical field, but they are now full members of the World Council of Churches (unlike the Roman Catholic Church) and were represented in the process which produced *Baptism, Eucharist and Ministry*. Not surprisingly they have great hesitations about any claims of Rome to primacy or infallibility, preferring to locate authority in the seven General Councils reckoned as Ecumenical, the criterion for such recognition being that the Council's decrees were accepted by the whole Church (though Chalcedon was rejected by Syria and Egypt). (See *Anglican-Orthodox Dialogue*, 1984, pp. 44–6.) The Orthodox would maintain that truth can have no external criterion; a Council is, or is not, ecumenical in so far as it bears witness to Him who is the way, the truth and the life. Bishops, as teachers, define and proclaim the faith, and the Orthodox attach great importance to the Fathers of the first five centuries of the Church's life. There are problems here, particularly concerning issues like the ordination of women which hardly entered the minds of the Fathers. The Orthodox are rightly suspicious of the ecclesial fundamentalism of Rome and the Biblical fundamentalism of Geneva, but they lay themselves open to a patristic fundamentalism with comparable limitations.

19

The Ordination of Women as Priests and Bishops

FEW issues have proved so contentious in recent years as the ordination of women, and it seems likely that the argument will continue. Many questions about ministry are focused in this one, and practical decisions have to be made. In England some Free Churches have had women ministers for over seventy years; in the Anglican communion Florence Lee Tim Oi was ordained priest by Bishop Hall of Hong Kong in 1944, though she resigned her priestly ministry two years later (but she remained a priest in her bishop's and her own eyes); Barbara Harris was consecrated the first Anglican bishop in the USA in 1989; and the second Anglican-Roman Catholic International Commission has the matter on its agenda. The Eastern Orthodox Churches are just beginning to grapple with it, reluctantly.

What sort of a question is it? How may it appropriately be handled? Which sides of it are theological, christological, pneumatological, sociological, psychological, or political? An attempt will here be made not just to go over familiar ground again, but to try to separate out the tangled strands in the debate and consider what are the appropriate criteria for handling them.

1. *Theological.*

First, then, theological – in the strict sense of the word: is there anything in the nature of God which makes the ordination of women *prima facie* impossible? It has been argued by eminent theologians (W. H. Frere for example) that God is male and it must follow that all priests (and bishops) must be male.

But Dame Julian saw it otherwise and more acutely in the fourteenth century: 'As truly as God is our father, so just as truly God is our mother'. Theologians like I. T. Ramsey in his *Religious Language* have demonstrated that all such terms are models and as such are inadequate and need qualification. Thus we are taught to address God as 'our Father', or rather 'our Father in heaven' to distinguish him from earthly fathers. If a child has only known a cruel father the model may be so inappropriate as to be unuseable; for that child 'mother' may be a better one. The Old Testament has over forty different models for God, and so there is a wide range of choice. It is true that most of the personal models for God in the Bible are in the masculine gender, but that is adequately accounted for by the fact that the society which produced the Bible was a sternly patriarchal one. Gender, however, is as irrelevant to the Trinity as is temporality. Relationship is not, and the threefold mutual love of the Persons is of the divine essence. God may be 'he' or 'she' but cannot be 'it'. Some play has been made with the gender of Greek and Hebrew nouns, but this is difficult since the Hebrew word for 'spirit', *ruach*, is feminine, whereas the Greek *pneuma* is neuter.

The first (later) creation story of the Bible tells how 'God created man in his own image, in the image of God he created him: male and female he created them' (Gen. 1.27). (In this respect there is a marked difference from the second, earlier, story (2.22) where woman is made from man's rib.) It is impossible for 'image' to be taken literally if man and woman both bear his image: the story of the Fall makes it much more likely that the image implies the possibility of a personal and moral relationship. In any case the Hebrew word *'adam* is a generic term for 'mankind'. In the previous verse God speaks in the plural, 'Let us make man in our image'. However this be explained (probably of a heavenly court of spiritual beings) it bears witness to a concept of plurality in the godhead. There can therefore be no simple deduction about a male ministry from the first person of the Trinity.

2. *Christological.*

God became man in Jesus Christ, but the classic statements of the incarnation avoid saying that he became a man. St John in his prologue uses the surprising, and rather shocking, word 'flesh' (Jn 1.14), used in the Old Testament of humanity over against God; the Nicene Creed keeps the same term and adds *enanthrōpēsanta* 'was made man', that is to say, shared our humanity; and the Athanasian Creed similarly, defines the divine-human Jesus as 'one; not by conversion of the Godhead into flesh: but by taking of the manhood into God'. It is true that the twelve whom Jesus chose to be with him were men, but it would have been unthinkable in the society of his day to have it otherwise. Women, however, were with them and ministered (*diēkonoun*) to them, Luke singling out for mention Mary Magdalene, Joanna, and Susanna (Lk. 8. 1–3). Women stood by the cross, helped to bury the Lord's body, were the first to discover that the tomb was empty, first encountered the risen Lord, and brought the news to the disciples.

Jesus' attitude to women was strikingly unconventional. He had a long conversation with a Samaritan woman, which surprised her and the disciples, as a result of which she became an active witness for him (Jn 4. 7–42). The Syro-Phoenician woman whose daughter he healed was a Gentile (Mk 7. 24–30). The woman with the haemorrhage was ritually unclean but he healed her when she touched him (Mk 5. 25–34). He graciously received an extravagant offering of devotion made by a disreputable woman, probably a prostitute, in the house of Simon the Pharisee, contrasting it with his host's frigid welcome (Lk. 7. 36–50). Among the pious, he commended Mary the theologian rather than Martha the traditional housewife, and overturned the norm of filial piety with his words 'whoever does the will of God is my brother and sister and mother.' (Mk 3.35).

There is here no hard evidence for or against the ordination of women, and it is a mistake to suppose that there could be, but the indications are firmly in favour of that which breaks convention, even the Law itself, in the service of God and of people who bear his image however faint or distorted.

An argument much used in the debate concerns the priest as the 'representative' or 'ikon' of Christ, but this needs careful handling. It is given great weight by the Eastern Orthodox for whom an ikon is not just a representation but a medium through which a devotee may come to see and experience some aspect of spiritual reality. The Vatican has spelled out this symbolic approach in its *Inter Insigniores* of 1976:

> The priest, in the exercise of his ministry . . . represents Christ, who acts through him . . . It is this ability to represent Christ that St Paul considered as characteristic of his apostolic function.

The supreme expression of this, it claims, is the eucharist where the priest takes the role of Christ to the point of being his very image when he pronounces the words of consecration: '. . . The Christian priesthood is therefore of a sacramental nature: the priest is a sign, the supernatural effectiveness of which comes from the ordination received, but a sign that must be perceptible and which the faithful must be able to recognise with ease'. If the role of Christ were not taken by a man, 'it would be difficult to see in the minister the image of Christ. For Christ himself was and remains a man'. The document goes on to suggest that Jesus did not choose female apostles because women could not be his image in the requisite way.

There are serious difficulties about this argument. An obvious rejoinder concerns the selection of the male characteristic alone. Why not also Jewish, celibate (no problem for Romans), young, and with a wood-working background? In fact this argument is not easily reconciled with traditional Roman Catholic teaching about the eucharist. In the mass the priest says to the congregation, 'Pray, brethren, that my sacrifice and yours may be acceptable to God the Almighty Father'. The sacrifice is offered by Christ himself, a re-presentation of the sacrifice of calvary, and the priest is the one who enables this to happen. But why does the priest have to be a man? Why not simply an authorised minister? In any case, Christ is present in the elements of bread and wine (or as most Anglicans would wish to say, in the whole eucharistic action including the bread and wine): how should he be particularly present in the figure of the priest? Curiously there is common ground here with some Protestants who see the eucharist as a re-enactment of the Last Supper with the minister playing the part of Christ. But this is to ignore the resurrection and ascension of Christ, not to mention Pentecost. The ordained minister is indeed the agent of the miracle; he is the representative of Christ but not his representation. To ordain women would in fact strengthen, not weaken, true Catholic tradition.

3. *Pneumatological.*

The *alter Christus* is the Holy Spirit, the Comforter or Paraclete or Advocate or Counsellor promised by Jesus to his disciples according to John 16: 'When the Spirit of truth comes, he will guide you into all the truth . . . he will take what is mine and declare it to you . . . A little while, and you will see me no more; again a little while, and you will see me.' Jesus did not leave his Church a constitution; he left it the assurance of his constant presence in the Spirit, and the Church has never found it easy to respond adequately. The doctrine of the Spirit has been, until recently, one of the most neglected areas of theological study. Much of the argumentation about the ordination of women has been in the area of 'tradition', strongest among the most traditional Churches. In fact, tradition for Christians is the record of the operation of the Spirit as perceived, responded to, and recorded by them: if it is less than this, if it is merely doing what has been always done, it falls under Jesus' condemnation of the Pharisees, 'You leave the commandment of God, and hold fast the tradition of men'. (Mark 7.8). For living tradition must be always changing because Christians are constantly opening up new aspects of the truth. Even J. H. Newman could write, 'In a higher world it is otherwise, but here below to live is to change, and to be perfect is to have changed often.' Earlier in his *Essay on the Development of Christian Doctrine* (1845) he said, 'From the nature of the human mind, time is necessary for the full comprehension and perfection of great ideas'. A. Bloom has well said that 'tradition is the living faith of the dead; traditionalism is the dead faith of the living.'

In the Acts and the Epistles of the New Testament there are graphic sketches of just such a development taking place, and its course as regards ministry has been traced in earlier chapters. The position of women is a prominent feature. In Romans 16. 1–3 Paul refers to Phoebe as sister and deaconess (*diakonos* is of common gender in Greek) of the church at Cenchreae, and he commends her to the church at Rome as a helper of himself and many others. A half a dozen other women receive honourable mention. Euodia and Syntyche have less honourable mention in Phil. 4.2 though they have laboured side by side with Paul in the gospel. From the reference in I Cor. 1.11 it seems that Chloe is an important figure in the church at Corinth. In the opening verses of Acts Luke portrays the eleven in Jerusalem devoting themselves to prayer 'with the women and Mary the mother of Jesus, and with his brothers'. In Acts 6 Stephen and six other men are appointed to help in the daily care of Greek-speaking widows. In Acts 9 Tabitha, or Dorcas, is commended for her charitable works. In 16, Timothy is introduced as 'the son of a Jewish woman who was a believer'. In Philippi Lydia is converted, offers Paul hospitality and it seems that her home became a Christian meeting place (16. 14–40). In Corinth (18. 1–3) Paul stays with a Jew, Aquila, and his wife Priscilla because they were fellow-tentmakers, and later takes them with him to Ephesus where they help to instruct Apollos in the faith (18. 18–26). When Paul came to Caesarea (21. 8–9) 'we entered the house of Philip the evangelist who was one of the seven (significantly not described as a deacon) and stayed with him. And he had four unmarried daughters, who prophesied.'

This evidence presents an impressive picture of the ministry of women as fellow-workers with the apostles in prayer, evangelism, teaching, prophecy and charitable works. They are ranked as *diakonoi*, but there is no mention of their ministering as *presbuteroi* or *episkopoi*. Since this development owed much to Jewish synagogue practice, women were *ipso facto* ruled out.

A deeper matter of principle is raised when Paul has to deal with the behaviour of women in worship at Corinth in I Cor. 11 and 14. Paul's rabbinic background appears at its prickliest in 11. 1–16 when he requires women to pray or prophesy with their head covered. He attempts to base his argument on 'natural theology', 'Does not nature itself teach you that for a man to wear long hair is degrading to him, but if a woman has long hair, it is her pride?' Paul seems, however, not to be convinced by his own argument, and lapses into a tame conclusion, 'if anyone is disposed to be contentious, we recognise no other practice, nor do the churches of God'.

His treatment of the question here does not easily harmonise with his injunctions in 14. 34–40: 'the women should keep silence in the churches. For they are not permitted to speak, but should be subordinate, as even the law says. If there is anything they desire to know, let them ask their husbands at home. For it is shameful for a woman to speak in church'. Paul speaks with all the authority he can, but again his conclusion is tame, 'but all things should be done decently and in order'.

The issue of subordination is an important one especially for some evangelicals who would accept the ordination of women as priests, so long as they hold no position which would require them to exercise authority over men. This would debar them from incumbencies and bishoprics. Codes of behaviour governing particular social relationships are to be found in several Epistles, and the form in which the different kinds of duties are expressed, the similarity of the teaching and the verbal parallelisms, especially the repeated use of some part of the verb *hupotassesthai* (to be subject to) point to a common source or sources. The evidence is conveniently summarised by E. G. Selwyn in his *Commentary on I Peter*, p. 423 where he sets out in parallel columns the obedience of everyone to civic authority, of slaves to masters, of wives to husbands (and reciprocal duties of husbands to wives), and of younger to elder, as presented in I Peter, Romans, Colossians, Ephesians, 1 Timothy, Titus and James. Similar kinds of presentations can be found both in Hebrew and in Greek writers, and indeed every one of the New Testament injunctions can be paralleled in Jewish or Greek teaching. It is disappointing that so little of the spirit of the Sermon on the Mount (for example) has found its way into these codes. But then the working out of the ethical implications of the gospel is an enormous task which will never be finished. There is no direct suggestion in the Epistles that slavery as an institution is contrary to the Gospel: slaves are bidden to obey and if they suffer unjustly they can bear this as Christ bore his cross (1 Pet. 2. 18–25). It took the Church nearly eighteen centuries to conclude that slavery must be abolished. A slave in New Testament times was in no position to do much about the institution which reduced him or her to a mere chattel, nor were women about the system which reduced them to being childbearers for their husbands. It is true that wifely obedience is sometimes tempered with reciprocal duties of husbands (as in 1 Pet. 3.7 and Eph. 5. 25–33) where a husband's love for his wife is compared with Christ's love for his Church, but the subjection remains. It is deeply embedded in the New Testament, and rooted in the Old. There is, however, no more reason to sustain it than there is to sustain slavery. In his best moments Paul recognised this: 'For as many of you as were baptized into Christ have put on Christ. There is neither Jew nor Greek, there is neither slave nor free, there is neither male nor female; for you are all one in Christ Jesus'. (Gal. 3.28.)

The 'tradition' was decisively broken by the young Christian church at the meeting of apostles and elders at Jerusalem described in Acts 15. They had to face the crucial question of whether a Gentile has to become a Jew in order to become a Christian. Does he have to be circumcised and keep the Law? The answer was clearly given that he does not, and if it had been otherwise the Church as we know it would not have survived.

The new growth away from Judaism and the Law of Moses towards the community of the resurrection and of the Spirit was (and still is) inevitably slow and painful. That is why ministers were and are needed. The early Fathers, many of whom were bishops, were not much concerned with answering the question of women priests because it was hardly raised. The evidence is set out in *The Ordination of Women to the Priesthood*, 1972 pp. 31–34 and may be summarised briefly. When the issue did arise it was generally in the context of heretical sects. Tertullian is clear that 'it is not permitted to women to speak in church, or teach, or to baptise or to offer, or to lay claim to a man's function or to the priestly office', and no doubt he had the Montanists in mind (before he became one). Irenaeus refers to the iniquities of the magus Marcus who led astray silly women, encouraging them 'to make their own thank-offering in his presence' and to prophesy, as well as behaving immorally with them. Chrysostom says 'let the whole female sex retreat from such an office . . . and similarly the majority of men'. Epiphanius says, 'Never anywhere has any woman, not even Eve, acted as priest from the beginning of the world. The *Apostolic Constitutions* debar women from teaching and priestly functions, though the deaconess had special tasks.

For the later scholastics women are incapable of receiving orders. Aquinas says, 'As it is not possible for the female sex to signify an eminent status, woman being under subjection, it follows that she cannot receive the sacrament of order.' Generally speaking, the early Fathers, as, for example, Augustine, believed that woman was made so that man should rule over her, though her servitude is the direct result of Eve's sin. In most basic endowments, however, they considered women to be equal to men, and tributes were paid to their spirituality, their courage (being certainly equal in martyrdom) and sometimes their intellect, as in Gregory of Nazianzus' reference to the debt his father owed to his mother.

4. *Sociological.*

But how much of this argumentation rests on theological foundation, and how much of it on the absorption of cultural patterns? And if the patterns are diverse, how is one to be valued above another? (There are diverse patterns within the

Bible.) The work of anthropologists has clearly demonstrated an infinite variety of patterning in the roles of the two sexes, with no one gift to be exclusively assigned to either sex. So it is probably necessary to see maleness and femaleness as a point on a sexual spectrum with wide normal variations tipping over in extreme cases to the trans-sexual. How far the variations are due to nature and how far to nurture has been widely debated without any clear conclusions. A psychologist writes, 'there is a traditional agreement on what are feminine personality attributes (i.e. affectionate, warm, dependent, sensitive, caring etc.) and what are masculine attributes (i.e. independent, assertive, dominant, competitive, forceful etc.), (H. Santer in *Feminine in the Church*, ed. Furlong, 1984, p. 146), but on such an analysis the personality traits of Jesus are more feminine than masculine, and would be at least as well represented by a female priest as by a male.

5. *Psychological.*

Whatever psychology has done to theology, it has opened up some areas which have been tabu for centuries, not least in the area of sexuality, and some of these have played an important part (consciously or unconsciously) in the debate about the ordination of women. How much influence still attaches to Levitical ideas of 'uncleanness' (Lev. 15)? In the Orthodox Church it is still the custom that women do not approach the sacrament during menstruation, and that only after the menopause may a woman enter the sanctuary; these customs claim some canonical authority.

Is it woman's sexuality which is the real bar to priesthood? One side of the stereotype concerns gentleness and humility, but another is demonic – the witch. Is there a deep unconscious fear of women and their sexuality, particularly in connection with the sacraments which involve physical touch? If so, it will need more than argument to exorcise it. Sometimes it takes a social upheaval on the scale of a world war to change people's perceptions, and it is interesting to note that in England the Congregationalists accepted the ordination of women in 1917, Baptists in 1918, and Presbyterians in 1921.

6. *Political.*

Many practical problems would attend such a decision for the Church of England, and these were faced at the Lambeth Conference of 1978 concerning ordination to the priesthood and at 1988 concerning ordination to the episcopate. Not all the Anglican Communion is similarly inclined but it was agreed that each province is and should be responsible for its own ordering. The bishops in 1968 observed in this connection that 'the New Testament does not encourage Christians to think that nothing should be done for the first time'. Some members are anxious about prejudicing reunion with Rome and the Orthodox east, to whom the reply may be made that any agreement on ministry without the inclusion of women is an act of disunity against mankind.

Conclusion

The key to the argument seems to be the inclusive humanity of Jesus Christ. The comprehension of this fact is so vast and difficult a task that truths which were there from the beginning have had to lie dormant until the social and psychological conditions have been right for them to be perceived. The time now seems to be ripe for the Church of England, at least, to ordain women as priests and bishops.

20

The Parish System

THE parish is an unmistakeable part of the English scene. Parish churches are a distinctive feature of the countryside, and to a lesser extent of the urban townscape. There is scarcely an inch of England which is not in 'somebody's parish'. The title 'vicar' is now the normal popular designation of a clergyman. The system is over a thousand years old originating in the desire to minister to small local communities (see p. 66). Boundaries soon became fixed and are difficult to unfix. (The present writer was vicar of a city parish whose medieval boundaries passed through the middle of a large chocolate factory.) In 1991 England was divided into 13,099 parishes with 16,425 churches, but with only 8,906 benefices, that is to say, bases for parochial clergy, and only 6,734 incumbents, that is to say, vicars or rectors.

The face of England was greatly changed by the so-called Agrarian Revolution of the seventeenth and eighteenth centuries and even more by the Industrial Revolution of the eighteenth and nineteenth, with the result that today at least 85 per cent of the population live in large cities. That is why the great majority of church-buildings in our industrial cities are Victorian, and why two-thirds of Anglican clergy minister to one third of the population. The parish system has been put under great strain by this development, and it is not unusual to find in such a city a large parish church (calling itself the Parish Church) drawing a congregation from a wide area, sometimes in competition with the cathedral, surrounded by a number of inner-city parishes with small and struggling congregations, generally in socially deprived areas often with large ethnic minorities; then a belt of suburban parishes sometimes clearly divided socially between privately owned homes and council estates, though some parishes have a mixture of both, where a vicar, with an assistant curate if he is fortunate, may find himself responsible for a population of fifteen or twenty thousand; then five miles further out, somewhat overgrown commuter villages, and five miles beyond that, small rural settlements, mainly agricultural, with populations of a few hundred. Few of these today remain independent parishes. Thus there is a vast variety of parishes, as great as the variety of men and women clergy who staff them. How can one generalise about such different units?

A useful distinction is that often made between two concepts of the local church, communal and associational (to avoid the more ambiguous terms parochial and congregational). The former starts from Richard Hooker's classic statement, 'With us one society is both Church and Commonwealth . . . which people are not part of them the Commonwealth, and part of them the Church of God, but the self same people whole and entire.' Thus the Church of England claims to be what its name implies; it is not a sect or a denomination; least of all is it a religious club. A vicar or rector is instituted to the cure (or care) of all souls in his parish, be they Anglican, Baptist, Roman Catholic, Hindu or atheist ones.

The associational mode is rather of a community of the like-minded who choose to associate out of preference. The preference may be for certain doctrinal formulations, or liturgical rites, or social milieux, and a high degree of commitment will be expected, which will set members over against outsiders. The two models are not entirely distinct, and both can be found among Anglican parishes.

The associational model lies behind the evangelical parish which advertises itself as disseminating the full gospel and behind the Catholic one which claims to offer full catholic privileges, while both ignore their social settings and draw their congregation from elsewhere. Both approaches were probably introduced by a strong incumbent, so much so that some congregations seem to incline to ancestor worship, forgetting that the only reason for having a church is to demonstrate that the Christian faith is true and that the Church manifests the nature of God by what it does and the way that it does it, as well as by what it does not do. To put all the emphasis on human commitment rather than on God's action in Christ runs the risk of turning justifying faith into a human work. Or as the teacher said to her children after studying the parable of the Pharisee and the publican, 'Now let us pray that we don't become like that nasty Pharisee.' By putting the emphasis on committed membership, the group runs the risk of ignoring the context in which it is set, tending to see it as all darkness in comparison with the light within. Here the doctrine of the Church has superseded that of the Kingdom. If the only reason for a Church is to make more converts so that they may make more converts, it needs to be remembered that the multiplication of cells unrelated to the purpose of the body is cancerous.

The communal model, on the other hand, takes seriously the complex interaction between the church and the community in which it is set. It is glad to welcome all comers who seek, in however muddled a way, some sort of consecration for the great moments of life, at birth and marriage and death. At baptism it will attach more weight to the promises of God in Christ than to those of the godparents, though it will do its best to ensure that the family concerned has some understanding of what God's promises are. It will be available for celebrations of joy like marriage without being too fussed about the sexual record of the parties involved, though helping them to face *frankly* what their vows to each other imply. It will welcome the mayor to a civic service where he kneels in worship to God so that he may have a truer idea of what his own title of 'Worship' means. It will be there for moments of tragedy: it is remarkable how at the great football-ground disasters at Bradford and Sheffield, thousands of those afflicted turned to the Church and its ministers, and the bishops automatically became those who spoke with authority and compassion.

The parish church has a complex interaction with the community in which it is set, and its members and minister must learn how to handle competently the dependent expectations of the parishioners (that is to say, all who live within its bounds) though often these are incoherent and sometimes unconscious. The term 'folk religion' is much used, often disparagingly, for this confused welter of religious or quasi-religious expectations, but this is the boundary on which the church stands and where the minister must operate. 'I will support the building fund but I don't come to church.' Or as Philip Larkin described himself, 'a member of the Church of England, albeit a non-believing one.' The communal model is truer to the gospel than the associational.

The parish church is an important sign, even if people do not intend to enter it, though its upkeep is often the despair of priest and people. It is important because it is there, a part of the parish consecrated for the sake of the whole, a focus of meaning confronting people with a distinctive presence, speaking of continuity and bidding people take a long view. It is only a building, if a sacred one, and it needs adapting to current needs of worship and perhaps for other aspects of the parish's mission. A medieval church, for all its beauty, can be a serious hindrance to worship with its long chancel and remote altar, but altars can be moved and furniture can be re-arranged. Large churches in down-town parishes can be re-ordered to provide several useful meeting-rooms while preserving an area for worship.

The key question which every parish must ask itself, not once but at regular intervals, is 'What is the church for, here?'. Indeed, the primary task of the incumbent is to see that the question is asked by the congregation, or its elected representatives, and to provide skilled help towards its being answered in the most adequate way. The answer must inevitably fall into two sections: the first 'churchly' and the second 'worldly'; the first to do with the inward journey of each soul as it seeks God, or is sought by God, and attempts to respond in the fellowship of the church; and the second to do with the outward journey of each soul as it works out its obedience to God's kingdom or rule in the secular world, a task which is impossibly hard for individuals to do on their own.

The first will have to consider matters of public worship. What services should we have and when? Should the principal service be the eucharist every Sunday if this means excluding the interested outsider? Should we encourage people to rely on a home-made 'family service' if they never move on to regular sacramental worship? If people are only ever going to hear small parts of the Bible selected for liturgical readings (perhaps no Old Testament at all) how are they going to be exposed to the whole range of Biblical insights? Should baptism normally be administered on Sundays at public worship when the most number of people come together (as required by Canon B. 21)? What sort of policy is the parish (not the vicar) to have about the preparation of parents who wish to bring their babies to baptism? What sort of hymns and other music are most suitable for public worship? How should the church be furnished and decorated so as to enrich worship? What sort of preaching do we want? What right do clergy have to introduce new pastoral techniques like counselling? Do we want shared leadership anyway? Why can't the vicar decide it all?: that is what he is paid for; and then we can blame him when it does not work.

It is clear that there are no easy answers to these questions. They raise fundamental issues of theology; they require a sensitive appreciation of local conditions; and they need a working knowledge of group psychology. No wonder that every incumbent supposes that he has the most difficult parish in the Church! Basic to this exercise is the concept of informed consent which more and more people are expecting and demanding in all sorts of areas, not least that of medical care. It is a practice in which the Church should be setting the lead. The consent needs to be informed otherwise it cannot be whole-hearted, and the ordained person is there to see that the necessary information is forthcoming. Many congregations have set up small working groups of lay members to look at issues like baptismal policy or the re-ordering of church buildings and to produce written recommendations, and this has been found to be a valuable educational process for them and for the wider congregation.

The love or *agapē* of Christian fellowship is based on will and not on emotion, but wills need to be nourished, and information is part of the diet.

This domestic life of the congregation is, however, only half of its total responsibility. The other half concerns the kingdom of God as it is experienced from Monday to Saturday. Here the Church's record is nowhere near so good. How much help does the average parish church give to its men as they face the responsibilities of secular life? How much do the clergy know about the pressures, sometimes very great, that their men work under? The questions are often so complex and so new that it is hard for clergy to keep up with them, and an important part of ministry is sitting down with groups of people in the same trade or profession to listen to their problems, (as well as to their satisfactions) and then bring to bear insights from the extensive Christian tradition. It may be that the parish is too small a unit for such groups, in which case the deanery might answer. The diocese is in a position to call together not only those of the same discipline but also those of different disciplines working in the same area of life to ask some fundamental questions, questions behind the questions, all of which finally come back to the basic one, 'What does it mean to be human?' Along the way many difficult ethical issues will have to be faced, and there will be genuine differences of judgment between Christians, but this is no reason for avoiding them because this kind of interchange can be one of the most valuable educative processes. It can also be a powerful evangelistic medium because it enables non-Christians to hear the gospel being worked out in terms which are familiar to them.

So every parish church will have to make some sort of organised survey of just what goes on inside its boundaries as a vital part of its understanding and responding to God's rule in that place. A specimen 'audit for the local Church' is printed as Appendix A in *Faith in the City*, though it contains surprisingly little reference to the paid work which takes place within the parish. The purpose of such a survey is to help the congregation form some objectives and priorities which can themselves be surveyed from year to year and strengthened or altered or abandoned as seen fit.

This kind of survey is valuable for two reasons: it earths any discussion of what the parish is about in undeniable realities. It also opens up the question of 'needs' which the Church may satisfy. There is likely to be a division at this point between those who think that the Church is only in the business of spiritual needs, since it is God that everyone really wants, and those who advocate 'social action', appealing to the parable of the Good Samaritan. The outcry which greeted the publication of *Faith in the City* that the Church should keep out of politics, is typical of the former viewpoint, but some of those who share the latter are less happy about some of the avowedly political recommendations made in the report, such as those concerning housing-finance, because they see those as representing a leftist view which would not be accepted by a good many rightist Christians.

The answer must be that there is no purely spiritual realm. At the very centre of Christian prayer and worship is bread, which is a manufactured substance. The whole process of its growth and manufacture and distribution is of concern to God and so must be of concern to us. Man does not live by bread alone, but he lives by bread, and will die without it, and we are our brother's keeper.

Some examples may help from parishes which feel the stress of changed circumstances most severely. In *Church and Politics Today* Ch. 7 (ed. G. Moyser, 1985) Gerald Wheale describes his ministry in Moss Side, Manchester, extending over 21 years. During that time the parish was cleared and re-developed because it suffered multiple deprivation. By 1975 the City Council declared that between 30% and 40% of all residents in the area were either first or second generation immigrants. Prostitution was the most visible social problem. The 1981 census revealed that 26% of the population were under 15; overcrowding was worse than in other areas of the city; 30% of the residents were born outside the UK; the overall unemployment rate was 24% and of youth 39%. Riots took place there in 1981. 'My commitment as a priest required me to preach the gospel and administer the sacraments but also carried a moral imperative to identify with and to struggle alongside my parishioners in their search for humanity'.

Impending redevelopment led the church council and the congregation to ask fundamental questions about the nature of the parochial system and the role of the church there. Neither the diocese nor the Town Hall was helpful in supplying information. At this point laity, feeling unsupported, usually either opt for the most conservative kind of non-involvement or move to more affluent churches. This parish's response was to create the Moss Side Pastoral Centre, on the site of an old church hall, which is home to a large number of groups sacred and secular. One of the groups is the Housing Association, sponsored by local churches in the 1960s, which has rescued and renovated nearly a thousand near-derelict homes, and rents them with a 'tenant-intensive' style of management. This, with the Moss Side Community Project, grew out of the conviction that the City Council's housing policy was leading to the destruction of the Moss Side community, and now the Parish Church, the Housing Association and the Community Project are all represented on the Moss Side Consultative Committee set up by the City Council. If asked about his involvement in politics, Mr Wheale replies that the exercise of ministry in itself generates a political stance on the part of the priest, and the activities of the parish are themselves a commentary on the outworkings of the political system as expressed in the life of the local community. He concludes, 'the great strength of the parish system is also the greatest potential weakness, for "parochialism" can sound the death knell of vision.'

At the other social extreme (though often sharing its multiple deprivation) is the remote country village, where once there were well-attended services every Sunday, a Sunday School and youth fellowship, uniformed organisations and a Mothers Union. The elderly can still remember when it had its own vicar (perhaps with a curate) and much of the village life circled around the church and its annual programme of activities. Traditionally the village church has been seen as coterminous with the community and deeply rooted in all aspects of local life. Every villager is thought of as belonging to the church, whether he or she attends or not, and this extends to members of other Christian bodies who still refer to the parish church as 'our church'. The church is dissolved in the veins of village society so that all village life may be baptised and hallowed by the church. The parish magazine reflects all the elements of the village. This, however, is not the view of many townspeople who have recently moved into the village. They think in terms of a gathered church as a separate organisation with its own life and membership. Recent liturgical developments like the Parish Communion have stressed 'the happy fellowship of the faithful few.' Any village church will have to work with both these models; on Christmas Day it will be the village church, and on Good Friday it will be the gathered church, and the clergyman has to understand and work with both.

The situation has been drastically altered with the decline in numbers of clergy. Hereford diocese had 320 clergy in 1932 but only 148 in 1985. The South Hereford deanery had a population of 10,700 in 1871 and was served by twenty-six clergy (a ratio of 412 to 1), whereas exactly a hundred years later the population had risen to 10,894 but the number of clergy had fallen to fifteen, (a ratio of 726 to 1). It is now impossible to envisage a stipendiary clergyman for every village parish, and in the 1970s solutions were canvassed with a new urgency, and three distinct pastoral strategies emerged. The first was to form groups or teams of parishes served by a number of clergy working closely together. This will be considered in more detail in the next chapter. The first such group was established by Lincoln diocese at South Ormsby in 1952 and the second by Norwich at Hilborough in 1961. By 1970 the latter diocese had a third of its clergy working in such collaborative ministries.

The second approach advocated the deanery rather than the parish as the basic pastoral unit for the countryside, and in the 1970s there was talk of rural deans being 'upgraded' to bishops. In fact deaneries proved to be too large areas to serve as a pastoral unit, and little was achieved in the Church of England. In Methodism, however, many small chapels were closed and the ministry was centralized in such country towns as Downham Market.

By the end of the 1980s the vast majority of small country parishes were served as part of a cluster under the care of a single stipendiary clergyman, a system widely known as multi-parish ministry. A cluster of four to six parishes has become the general rule, and those of eight to ten are not uncommon. There is an example of one of seventeen in Herefordshire. Village identity is a strong force, but with five or six or more parishes one clergyman cannot treat each parish individually. It is true that rural congregations are characteristically small, with about a third of all Anglican and non-conformist churches numbering under twenty-five people, but since the majority of rural settlements have a population of under 500, a congregation of twenty-five is a much better representation (upwards of 5%) than one of 250 in a suburban parish of 20,000 (1¼%). It is now established that the proportion of church-going increases as the size of the settlement decreases. In small rural settlements the proportion of regular worshippers is 10–15%; in larger ones with a population of about 1,000 it is 8–10%; whereas the national average is about 3%. Many small congregations do feel under threat and tend to dig in, but statistics are not the whole story. A small church is not a failed large church: it has the valuable virtues of intimacy, stability and simplicity.

The pattern of the church's life in the countryside, and its theological understanding, has been greatly affected by the Parish Communion movement which has tended to replace the community church with the eucharistic sect. The emergence of a pattern of worship more dependent on clergy has coincided with a sharp fall in their number, and the result today is an unholy rush for them from service to service, sometimes with the earlier part, the ministry of the word, having been started by a lay person. There is much to be said for the encouragement of local lay ministry (the question of local ordained ministry will be looked at in Chapter 24) so that each small church can have its service when it wants each Sunday, even if this means a less frequent celebration of Holy Communion. The pressing need is for the local church to take responsibility not only for its ministry but also for the quality of its local life.

When the Hilborough group was new in the 1970's the village pubs were being closed by the brewers because they were uneconomic and village schools by the local authorities for the same reason. The wife of the squire of one of the villages, Cockley Cley, with the active connivance of the clergy, bought the village school when it was put up for sale, and converted it into a pub, aptly named 'The Twenty Churchwardens', which very soon became a thriving social centre for an increasingly deprived area.

The English parish system is the product of a long history peculiar to England, and it cannot be exported just at it is (it died in the Episcopal Church of the USA in the 1930s). It needs supplementing, and the next four chapters deal with additional forms of ministry. It is under strain, particularly in the inner city and in the remote country, but that is no reason for abandoning it. It is unlikely to be abandoned. The English bishops are by no means convinced that its day is done, nor have they any agreed alternative. A great deal of money, tradition and sentiment is vested in parish churches and parsonage houses, and the present system is responsible for there still being a recognisable Christian presence in unpromising areas from which every other Christian denomination has withdrawn. The latest thinking about community development and community health stresses the importance of encouraging local responsibility, and in many deprived areas the Anglican vicar is the last 'professional' person to remain: the teachers, doctors, lawyers, police and social workers have all moved out to more salubrious areas. Life is hard for him, and for his wife and family if he is married, but the call to the parish ministry was never a soft option.

21

Teams and Groups

In 1961 Bishop Fleming of Norwich summoned the church councils of nine parishes (later ten) in the Breckland area of Norfolk to tell them of his proposal to amalgamate them into a group ministry. Later they were called again to meet their new leader, Canon Hugh Blackburne, and so was born the Hilborough Group, pioneer of groups in the diocese of Norwich which were to number seventeen during that decade. This group covered an area of 36 square miles with a total population of about two thousand souls. Most of the livings had been vacant for some time, and most of the ten churches were in bad repair and funds were minimal. Services had been kept going by faithful laity with some visits from neighbouring clergy. It was to be a training group of three clergy, the rector and two assistants, with services in all the churches. Every church had at least one service every Sunday except that on the first Sunday of the month a corporate communion was held in a different church each month, and a group evensong. A minibus was an early purchase. In 1962 a group council was formed though it did not supersede the ten church councils.

Nothing could be less natural than welding together ten fiercely independent rural communities, but two factors were vital: the fact that all ten villages were similar in character and size, and the personalities of the leader and assistants. The team spirit which obviously inspired the clergy was caught by the laity, and it soon became obvious that much could be achieved, both liturgically and socially, in community which could not be achieved individually. Narrow horizons were enlarged and closed minds were opened to a new consciousness of belonging to the universal Church. The ideal, however,

217

of training clergy for rural ministry under a group leader became impossible after ten years. The decreasing number of clergy (combined with the re-allocation of the 'Sheffield' quota), together with the great increase in the cost of transport, reduced the number of clergy to one by the mid-1980s, but much of the group spirit lives on among the laity.

The deep countryside was not the only setting for this new kind of collaborative ministry. In 1973 the Southampton Team Ministry was inaugurated to serve the major parish of the city centre, an area previously served by six parishes. The resident population was by then very small but the working population was very large. The new team ministry, in partnership with lay people, was designed to minister not only to the residents but also to the thousands involved in local government, commerce, education, health, and social services. Together the team has been held by a new vision, offering insights to those who are wrestling with the problems of today and shaping the society of tomorrow.

Groups and teams in the Church of England have multiplied steadily. Between 1975 and 1984 an average of 26 teams and 6 groups a year were established so that by the end of 1983 there were about 333 teams with 1,005 clergy of incumbent status and 81 groups covering 305 benefices. By the end of 1990 there were 430 teams with 910 clergy of incumbent status and 112 groups covering 371 benefices. Groups and teams are by no means the same; in fact in some ways they are opposite kinds of structure. Under the 1983 Pastoral Measure the two types are defined as follows:

> A *Team Ministry* comprises a Rector and one or two more Team Vicars, who share 'the cure of souls', and may have other lay or ordained ministers who share in the 'pastoral care'. There will be a single benefice comprising one or more parishes. The Rector may have a freehold or a term of years, while all other members of the team must be licensed or given permission by the Bishop. In the case of Vicars, their licence must be for a term of years.

A *Group Ministry* comprises a number of incumbents or priests-in-charge of independent benefices. They must meet as a chapter, the chairman of which may either be elected or appointed by the Bishop.

In either case there may be a Council – Team or Group – relating to the area as a whole exercising such powers as may be thought to be appropriate in each case.

The idea of a team of clergy is not new. The notion of team-working is fundamental to the New Testament conception of the Church as the body of Christ. Particular manifestations of it may be seen in the Saxon minster or the medieval collegiate church. A powerful modern example has been provided by the *équipe* of the Mission de France which in turn has influenced the base-communities of Latin America.

What is the case for group and team ministries? Undoubtedly in origin the case was a pragmatic one: how to staff a group of small and isolated rural parishes which had driven some incumbents to despair. A team of ministers, carefully chosen and working as a team, could provide not only support for each other, but also a critical appraisal of each other's methods and performance. They also had a wider field for deploying particular gifts. Many ventures became possible for a group which could never have happened alone. At Hilborough the group communion with a hundred taking part gave a vision of the Church which was not possible with a tiny handful of worshippers. A team ministry was likely to be more attractive to clergy, and it provided a good training base for younger assistants who wanted to devote themselves to rural ministry, an important factor in light of the fact that few ordinands today come from the deep country. It seems, however, that the enthusiasm for collaborative ministry, so marked in the 1970s waned somewhat in the 1980s. Perhaps the greatest contribution which this style of ministry has made is the encouragement of lay responsibility, where ministry is seen as not confined to the clergy, but where the laity are seriously considered to be a part of the team-working.

There have, of course, been drawbacks and criticisms. A

team or group may be constituted without a proper under-standing of the local social history, so that, for example, mutu-ally antipathetic villages are put together and expected to co-operate at once. This may put an impossible strain on the clergy. Teams and groups can encourage a new form of co-clericalism where the maintenance of the clerical team out-weighs care of the parish or parishes. This should not happen if the right priorities have been agreed and are kept to in close co-operation with the laity, and for this purpose the services of an outside consultant have been found useful, to help clarify priorities and ensure that they are observed. Criticisms have been made on the grounds of 'churchmanship', that extremes will be avoided, and a safe, colourless, middle path will become obligatory. Here again hard questions need to be asked and answered about the nature of the Church, its gospel, its worship, its common life, and its mission, not only by the clergy but by the laity as well. At the end of the day, however, many lay people will feel unhappy about not having 'their vicar'. This dependent relationship goes deep and a plurality of available ministers does not wholly meet it. The nature of the dependency is of great importance, and a wise priest will try to make it as adult as possible.

Teams and groups of clergy undoubtedly provide richer ministerial resources for a carefully selected area provided that at every point they work closely with the laity. They can set a good example of collaborative ministry, overcoming many of the problems of isolation; they can offer a wider range of personal gifts; they can offer the individual parishioner a wider choice of close relationship with a priest; and they can provide a useful base not only for the training of younger clergy but also for clergy working outside the parochial pat-tern. Two kinds of these, those engaged in specialised minis-tries and those in non-stipendiary ministry will be considered in the next two chapters.

22

Specialised or Sector Ministries

THE parish clergy are not the only clergy, even if they sometimes think they are. In 1991 in the Church of England there
were 1,669 non-parochial clergy of whom 1,400 were not part
of diocesan structures. Most of these clergy are employed and
paid by a secular agency to exercise their ministry there, as, for
example, chaplains to hospitals, prisons, or the armed forces;
but some are paid by the church, as for example, chaplains to
industry, the arts, the media, or holidaymakers. These are
specialised or sector ministries which attract clergy for various
reasons. Some feel a call because of particular skills or experience they possess; some feel a challenge to undertake what
seems important work; some prefer the firm framework of an
institution to the apparent lack of frame in a parish; others are
attracted by a much higher salary: motives are seldom
unmixed. In order to describe and assess this important exercise of ministry, it is convenient to consider two examples, the
hospital chaplain who is paid by the government, and the
industrial chaplain who is paid by the church. The issue of non-
stipendiary ministry (a kind of worker-priest ministry) is separate and will be the subject of the next chapter.

There were in 1991 nearly five thousand part-time hospital
chaplains in England and Wales of many Christian denominations and of some other faiths, but there were only 210
full-time Church of England chaplains together with 48 full-
time female Anglican Chaplains' Assistants. The chaplain has
the more limited task expected of any clergyman, that of
taking services in chapel and wards, and visiting patients. But
he also has a wider ministry to the institution as a whole as a
place of healing, even if he does not go as far as one American

chaplain who concluded that his ministry to the staff was what mattered because it was the staff who ministered to the patients. For this wider role he has no rights: they have to be earned by faithful service. He will find himself in conflict with many of the assumptions both of church and hospital, and his essential role is that of a walking question-mark. The staff will see him functionally, but the patients will see him personally. All too often the church's contribution is seen to be a tranquillising one, whereas in fact a person's stay in hospital, removed from the family, in a new corporate setting, confronted with some of the most intractable problems of life and death, and often with time to spare, can be an opportunity for profound learning. Not for nothing is M. Wilson's penetrating study of the role of the hospital chaplain entitled *The Hospital – A Place of Truth.*

The demands made on the chaplain as a person are testing. He has to move from life to death, from despair to hope, from sadness to joy, from tragedy to comedy and back again within minutes. He must know how to speak the appropriate word, and more importantly, how not to speak but only listen so that the patient may work out his or her own answer. The listening itself can often be an integral part of the healing process. In a place of high anxiety he must be at peace with himself in order that he may be a peace-maker. There is no alternative to personal integrity.

He will be concerned with persons who happen to be patients, whereas the hospital is concerned with patients who happen to be persons. Here many questions will have to be posed, and the chaplain will need a thorough knowledge of hospital procedures (short of a qualification in medicine and nursing) in order to pose them charitably but firmly. He must cultivate a working relationship with the ward sister, and he may, when he has proved his value, be accepted as a member of the 'healing team'. In M. Wilson's study, of 62 chaplains surveyed, one third felt a more or less continuous exclusion from a place in the hospital team; one third felt completely accepted; and one third experienced exclusion as incidental only.

Three assumptions underline the present work of hospitals, and all need to be challenged from a Christian point of view. First, hospital medicine focuses on the patient in isolation from family, friends and work, and then concentrates upon a particular lesion or system to isolate that for healing or removal. Such specialism has produced notable progress, but at a high cost, and against it a whole range of alternative therapies have sprung up in the name of a more holistic approach to the person. Second, the rapid growth of technology is widely supposed to lead to the good life, rather than decisions made in the light of human values. Doctors find it hard to accept that a particular patient will not recover, or that heroic care for a malformed baby may later lay intolerable burdens on the baby's family. Third, doctors are not clear about the difference between treating the disease and treating the patient. Success in disease-eradication is what is valued, and psychiatric, geriatric, and subnormality hospitals where care is more important than cure are poorer in esteem and in resources. Against all these assumptions the chaplain, as the authorised church figure, is, or ought to be, a walking question-mark.

Unlike the hospital chaplain who is paid by the health authority, the industrial chaplain is paid by the church or churches and is invited into industrial plants and complexes by the management in consultation with the unions. This goes back to Bishop Hunter of Sheffield who in 1944 responded to an industrialist's request to 'send us one of your men in here if he can talk a language we can understand' by sending E. R. Wickham as his Industrial chaplain, the first step towards the Sheffield Industrial Mission. In 1985 Industrial Mission in England felt that it was still pioneering and experimental, but felt also tired and beleaguered, neither valued nor supported properly by its sponsoring churches. It published *Industrial Mission – An Appraisal* in 1988 to help itself rediscover its aims and objectives.

It sees itself as 'Industrial' because it sets high store in analysing that part of local industrial society with which it is dealing in order to provide primary data. This has been particularly difficult in the last twenty years because the scene has been one of rapid and relentless change – not least in the steel industry in Sheffield. Unemployment rose to unprecedented heights up to 1987 and then declined steadily to 1989; there has been a large-scale privatisation of nationalised industries; there has been a marked change from heavy manufacturing to light engineering, high-technology and service industries; and there has been a decline in the power of the unions. In its first two decades Industrial Mission operated mainly in the large, unionised, heavy industries, working closely with union leaders; now their work is more with industrialists, managers and local government officers, much concerned with training and community development schemes.

They see mission not as taking Christ into industry but rather as uncovering his presence there so that others can see it and respond, and to help to bring the industrial world nearer to the standards of the kingdom of God. In the 1960s and 1970s this was worked out largely in terms of reconciliation in industrial relations and in organisational development, but by the mid-70s it was losing its sense of direction and purpose, though it felt, that it had 'earned the right to be creatively critical.' The more conservative sought to influence those who held the power; the more radical put question-marks against the whole capitalist system. In the 1980s they were facing a 'new harsh realism' and the popular theological terms were crucifixion, judgement and even apocalypse.

The most radical critique of Industrial Mission has come from Roman Catholics, much influenced by their experience in France with *Action Catholique Générale* and *Jeunesse Ouvrière Chrétienne*. They claim that the appointment of industrial chaplains is a retrograde step because the field of industrial affairs belongs to the lay apostolate; the task of the clergy is to enable, form, and animate the laity for this work, but the priest 'leaves his people at the factory gates'. This criticism deserves to be taken most seriously, and points up the enormous need for world-of-work groups where lay workers from a particular sphere can meet with a priest as theological consultant for joint study on a 'story-reflection-action' model. Industrial

Mission depends upon the church, and its anxiety mirrors the church's own lack of theological understanding and agreement.

The hospital chaplain and the industrial chaplain alike with other 'specialists' exercise a ministry of authorised presence to people who happen to be patients, factory workers, sailors, prisoners, or undergraduates. For this they need to be closely acquainted with the ways of that sector of society just as a foreign missionary has to learn the language of his people. They also have a ministry to their institutions to help to make them more humane. (There is no contradiction here between Christianity and humanism). They also have the important task of interpreting to the church the problems and the opportunities encountered in their sector of society, just as they have the right to expect from the church proper support and the provision of theological insight. It is unfortunately clear that much remains to be done in these spheres.

23

Non-Stipendiary Ministry

THE idea that clergy could be financially self-supporting, earning their livelihood in a secular occupation, still strikes most people as strange and improper: if it has to be, then such a form of ministry is reckoned to be a sort of second-best, so strong has the professional image of the clergy become, at least in the western world. The Churches which have such ministers are not at all sure what they should be called, as witness the terms, non-stipendiary ministers, self-supporting ministers, supplementary ministers, auxiliary pastoral ministers, honorary ministers, ministers in secular employment, part-time priests, worker-priests; and others could be added. In fact this kind of ministry is nothing new, though it has only been fully authorised in the Church of England since 1970, and the recent debate about it serves to focus sharply various social and theological issues which are central to the understanding of priesthood.

The debate is already under way in the ministry and writings of the apostle Paul. He is clear that stipendiary ministry has dominical authorisation: 'the Lord commanded that those who proclaim the gospel should get their living by the gospel.' (1 Cor. 9.14), but in the next verse he renounces the exercise of this right, downgrading a command to mere permission. It was his deliberate strategy, as he points out to the Corinthians from Ephesus, 'To the present hour . . . we labour, working with our own hands' (1 Cor. 4. 11–12), and to the Christians in Thessalonica, 'You remember our toil and labour, brethren; we worked night and day, that we might not be a burden to any of you, while we preached to you the gospel of God' (1 Thess. 2.9). In both cases he includes his fellow-workers.

226

Luke tells us that Paul stayed at Corinth for eighteen months teaching the word of God, and achieved his economic independence by joining up with the refugees Aquila and Priscilla, 'and because he was of the same trade, he stayed with them, and they worked, for by trade they were tentmakers' (Acts 18.3). Only from the church at Philippi does he consent to receive his full pay as a token of special favour! (Phil. 4. 14–20). Paul's decision was no doubt in part a pragmatic one, but there may well have been deeper motives to do with the value of labour which he would have shared both with rabbis and with wandering Cynic philosophers. There is evidence that the latter used the workshop as a setting for intellectual discourse. Such an attitude was unthinkable to an educated Roman. 'All artisans are by their profession vile', remarked Cicero, 'for a workshop can have nothing worthy of a freeman' (*de Officiis*, 1.42). At that time virtually all manual work was done by slaves. Class distinction ran deep in the empire and at the end of the fourth century Chrysostom was at pains to extol the life and dignity of the working members of his congregation:

> When you see a man driving nails, smiting with the hammer, covered with soot, do not consider him cheap, but rather for that reason admire him. For even Peter girded himself, and handled the dragnet, and went fishing after the Lord's resurrection. And why do I say Peter? For Paul himself . . . standing in a tentmaker's shop, sewed hides together . . . He gloried in this very fact.
>
> (*Sermons on 1 Corinthians*, 20. 5–6)

The situation changed dramatically in AD 313 when Constantine legalised the Church as an institution and it began to receive all kinds of monies, lands and privileges which had previously belonged to pagan institutions. New endowments made it possible for some clergy to be paid, but others preferred to work for their livelihood. Bishop Epiphanius of Salamis in Cyprus writes, about 375:

> Those of God's priests who according to the word of
> the gospel imitate their father-in-God in the following of
> Christ (I mean St Paul) – not all of them, but most of
> them as they are able – work with their hands at what-
> ever sort of work is befitting their worth and they find
> consistent with the mind of the Church, so that their
> understanding of the word and gospel may grow and
> bear fruit through the work of their hands, and that,
> replenished in this way, they may help the brethren and
> those that lack.
>
> (*Patrologia Graeca*, 42. 764–5)

Of Spyridon the Cypriot bishop of Trimithus who attended
the Council of Nicaea in 325 it was written:

> So great was his sanctity while a shepherd that he was
> thought worthy of being a pastor of men; . . . on account
> of his extreme humility he continued to feed his sheep
> during his incumbency of the bishopric.
>
> (Socrates, *Historia Ecclesiastica*, 1–12)

Another fourth-century bishop, Zeno of Majuma (Gaza), by
'pursuing his trade of weaving linen continued to earn the
means of supplying his own wants and of providing for others'.
(Sozomen, *Historia Ecclesiastica*, 7–28). Non-stipendiary
bishops, however, were not always a success: Gregory the
Great wrote a strong letter (13.26) about a bishop of Naples
who spent his time in shipbuilding and forfeited the respect
of his people.

The canons of the early Councils (for example that of Elvira
in 304) allowed the possibility of clergy engaging in trade but
limited the amount of their travel. They firmly forbade their
holding state offices, though as the western empire's administration collapsed from 410 onwards clergy frequently found
themselves in positions of civil administration by virtue of
their ability to read and write Latin. In the east the tradition
of clergy supporting themselves never died out and most of
them were ordinary citizens engaged in humdrum tasks of
agriculture and craftsmanship. In the west in the sixteenth

and seventeenth centuries many country clergy farming their glebe had a style of life not unlike their peasant parishioners. An English Act of 1529 limited the number of benefices that could be held in plurality and forbade trading in detailed terms. Its object was to create a clerical caste and to foster 'the good opinion of the Lay-fee towards spiritual persons'. It was modified by the Pluralities Act of 1838 which allowed a clergyman to run a school, farm up to eight hundred acres, sell books, be a director of an insurance company, and sell minerals mined under Church land, though he could not on his own account 'engage in or carry on any trade or dealing for gain or profit or deal in any goods, wares, or merchandise'. This remained the law until 1964. The teaching profession has always been a major exception to the parochial principle in England and indeed the very existence of the universities of Oxford and Cambridge depended upon it because ancient statutes required most college fellows to be in holy orders – until, at Oxford, 1877.

From the middle of the nineteenth century, however, new voices were heard, for the clerical profession was seen by some to be inadequate for, if not counter-productive to, the Church's mission. Three names stand out. Thomas Arnold, who was headmaster of Rugby School from 1828 to 1841, in his book *Principles of Church Reform* of 1833 likened the Church to 'an army destitute of non-commissioned officers' and advocated as remedy the revitalising of the order of deacons. In a letter to A. P. Stanley in February 1839 he envisaged many lay men in large towns being able and willing to undertake the office out of pure love, with an immense gain to the Church 'by softening down that pestilent distinction between clergy and laity, which is so closely linked to the priestcraft system.' His advocacy attracted wide interest, even being discussed by Convocations of clergy, but to no effect.

The second episode surrounds the strange figure of Roland Allen, an Anglican priest who served in North China as a missionary with the Society for the Propagation of the Gospel from 1895 to 1903 when he was invalided home. He then served as vicar of Chalfont St Peter but resigned in 1907 because he could not convince his parishioners of the wisdom of a rigorous baptism policy. He subsequently held no official post but devoted himself to the cause of non-professional clergy, publishing in 1912 a searching book *Missionary Methods: St Paul's or Our?*, and in 1930 *The Case for Voluntary Clergy*. Thanks largely to his advocacy the matter was placed on the agenda of the 1930 Lambeth Conference which gave 'auxiliary priests' a lukewarm sanction. On that basis the Chinese Church altered its canons in 1934 and the first non-stipendiary clergy were ordained in Hong Kong.

The third influential, figure is F. R. Barry who was vicar of the University Church in Oxford and later Bishop of Southwell. His book *The Relevance of the Church* (1935) contains the earliest systematic attempt to offer a rationale of work-focused non-stipendiary ministry 'not on grounds of expediency but of ultimate Christian and sacramental principle.' He stressed the great danger of ministry becoming the preserve of a clerical caste concerned narrowly with ecclesiastical affairs, with a consequent disastrous rift between religion and the life of the world.

> The real strength of the case is the principle. It is the desire to exhibit the Ministry as the consecration and focus of the ministry of the whole Christian body in the normal activities of life . . . The suggestion violates no catholic principle: it involves merely a change in accepted custom and a partial reversion to apostolic practice.
>
> (Chapter 6)

Actions, however, speak louder than words, and the 1940s witnessed a remarkable phenomenon in the Roman Catholic Church in France, the rise of the worker-priest movement. It was occasioned by the misfortunes of war, with the Germans conscripting large French labour forces to work in munitions factories in Germany but refusing provision for spiritual care by French chaplains. During 1943–44 twenty-five priests were chosen by French bishops to serve there disguised as workers. In these factories and labour camps the priests' rediscovery of the worker by complete participation in his life was most complete. H. Perrin wrote in his diary, 'These people are dechristianised, yes, but they are not against Christ. Often it does not take so very much to uncover the true, face of Christ to them and awaken their love for him.'

The experience was so valuable that after the war some of the priests concerned felt called to continue as 'worker-priests', and received strong support from Cardinal Suhard, Archbishop of Paris, who wrote in his Lenten pastoral of 1949:

> In too many so-called Christian countries, particularly in France, the Church, in spite of the existence of many ecclesiastical buildings and many priests, has ceased to exist for the majority of people. They no longer have the chance of deciding for or against Christ. A vast accumulation of prejudice has completely distorted the face of the Church in their eyes. The priesthood is still less accessible to them. Therefore it is a good thing that priests should become witnesses again, less to conquer than to be a 'sign'. They have been told that to be a witness does not mean to spread propaganda, nor even to stir up emotions, but to keep the mystery of God present'. This means so to live that one's life would be inexplicable if God did not exist.

The worker-priests had a rough ride ahead of them. They found themselves in conflict with the hierarchy and with parish priests (Suhard died in 1949), with factory management and with the police. In 1952 worker-priests took part in a demonstration against the setting up of NATO headquarters in Paris and two were arrested. On 23 September 1953 the verdict from Rome was announced that worker-priests should be stopped as the dangers to the Church outweighed the gain, and on 15 August 1954 the bishops wrote a letter to each ordering him to give up work – though not all did. Everything was not lost. In 1965 the French episcopate decided that a few small teams of worker-priests might be formed and their members were authorised to join, but not hold office in, trades unions. About fifty new worker-priests now joined the forty or so already active. By 1988 there were about six hundred in all, including one worker-bishop, operating under an episcopal commission.

Another important contribution came from the Lutheran pastor, theologian and martyr, D. Bonhoeffer in prison in Berlin. In the summer of 1944 he sketched the outline of a book he wanted to write and its conclusions were these:

> The church is the church only when it exists for others. To make a start, it should give away all its property to those in need. The clergy must live solely on the free-will offerings of their congregations, or possibly engage in some secular calling. The church must share in the secular problems of ordinary human life, not dominating, but helping and serving. It must tell men of every calling what it means to live in Christ, to exist for others. In particular, our own church will have to take the field against the vices of *hubris*, power-worship, envy and humbug, as the roots of all evil . . . It must not under-estimate the importance of human example.
>
> (*Letters and Papers from Prison*, pp. 382–3)

In England after the war successive Lambeth Conferences gave increasing support to 'supplementary ministries'. Resolution 89 of 1958 referred to the permissive resolution of 1930 and stated that it 'now wishes to go further and to encourage provinces to make provision on these lines.' The 1968 Conference recommended 'a wider and more confident use of the ministry', while its committee asserted that 'the part-time non-stipendiary priest is in no way inferior to his full-time stipendiary brother . . . In some areas the part-time non-stipendiary minister could become the norm'. (*Report*, pp. 39 and 102)

In 1960 the diocese of Southwark under its bishop M. Stockwood and its suffragen, J. A. T. Robinson, set up the Southwark Ordination Course to train men and women part-time, while they remained in their secular occupations, as ministers both stipendiary and non-stipendiary, and by 1983 a network of fifteen such courses had grown to cover every region of England. The bishops issued regulations in 1970 for what was then called Auxiliary Pastoral Ministries, but the revised regulations of 1987 refer to Non-Stipendiary Ministry.

How then does it actually work in the Church of England? The answer is not simple and some non-stipendiary ministers find it hard to produce a clear explanation, which is not surprising in view of the lack of firm theological foundation, and sometimes of sympathetic episcopal support. Some facts, at least, are clear. The original intention of the bishops was for a ministry which would supplement parish clergy: its earliest appellation was Auxiliary Parochial Ministry, and the Advisory Council's report *A Supporting Ministry* (1968) had no brief for ministry outside the parish boundaries, though it regretted this limitation. The Council produced a review of progress in 1977, *An Honorary Ministry*, based on enquiries addressed to 164 such ministers of whom 131 sent back full details. Their average age was 48; 42 were engaged in some form of teaching; the hours spent in secular employment averaged 47 and in parish work 12.8; when asked whether they saw the main emphasis of their ministry in place of work or in parish, the answer was 50:50 (though there was some unclarity about interpretation here). It was clear, however, that a considerable number of these ministers did not see themselves as merely auxiliary to the parish system; and it should be noted that 1970 was not a time of shortage of ordinands: the 1960s had been a peak period of ordinations averaging around 600 a year from 1960 to 1966, with a decrease to the 400s from 1967 to 1969. By 1988 about 150 ministers preferred the title of Ministers in Secular Employment to stress the fact that they saw the main thrust of their ministry to be in the work place. The Bishops' *Regulations* of 1987 recognise this title, and place this category before those whose chief area of ministry is in the context of a parish.

In fact this distinction is arbitrary and many would not want to press it. All are based in a parish, and have some share in its worship and communal life, even if their work is some way away. Most do not have the opportunity of regularly presiding at the eucharist at work, and value the opportunity of doing so in the parish church where they can share intercessions for the working world, and in their preaching can present the gospel in terms of that world. There can be no question of being a part-time priest: one can no more be a part-time priest than one can be a part-time parent.

A non-stipendiary minister is an authorised representative of the church and of Christ in the church, and his task at work, as anywhere else, is to promote the gospel. He will seldom do this in formal preaching but he has innumerable opportunities in private conversation or group discussion. A university teacher comments, 'It is not necessary to be confrontational: the subtle footnote or appropriate analogy may be all that is required to encourage thought or to stimulate questioning.' An ordained person, if he or she has responsibility for policy-making, may well not be satisfied with the questions put but will pose questions behind the questions, and will be expected to do so. Most of these questions concern basic issues about being human and shaping a humanly responsible society. Answers are not easy. An ordained town-planner may have to advocate a new motorway which will demolish some people's homes in the interests of the travel of the majority. A minister may have to dismiss an employee knowing that this will further strain an already precarious marriage, and the same evening go round to his home to give pastoral help. The minister's own example will be under constant observation, and above all it is important that he be good at his own job, and be willing to praise all good work well done. J. Rodwell, who is an ordained university research biologist, has said:

> It is blessing in this sense [giving thanks for God's great generosity] which I take to be one of the distinctive marks and purposes – perhaps the most distinctive – of the priesthood. The priest is called to make explicit what many others do implicitly, to bring, from a creative perception of the world, a renewed awareness of God's active presence and his invitation to participate in it. That is, to proclaim its inherent redeemability and so convene a relationship within which the old innocence may be revealed.

The minister will not bless indiscriminately: the created order is fallen as well as redeemable. Another has said, 'The prophetic role is central – a stance of critical reflexion arising from a particular vision of the nature of things, from a detailed knowledge of the present context.' His concern is to interpret people as people to one another and he hopes that this concern will be infectious. Most ministers steer clear of pious groups of Christians in the work-place because they tend to be divisive and concerned with issues unconnected with work; rather, they will try to conscientise, encourage, and strengthen those whom he knows to be Christian.

The task of a non-stipendiary minister is an onerous one, particularly if he is married with a family. He constantly has to re-assess his priorities, and time-off for leisure is an important one. He may well meet with incomprehension and suspicion from his stipendiary brethren, hearing such comments as 'a back door into the ministry'. On one occasion when a deanery chapter meeting was moved to the evening to accommodate a non-stipendiary, only one stipendiary turned up. Some non-stipendiaries (as in Southwark diocese) have a chapter of their own, and some diocesan bishops meet regularly with theirs, but too often they are left without effective pastoral support.

Their own spiritual life is all-important, and the normal pattern of daily mattins and evensong is for many either impossible or inappropriate. M. Hatt has written that his spiritual life is under constant threat, but he regards the opposite danger of having too much time as the greater. Spirituality is exercised in responding to events as they arise. Prayer happens in snatched minutes of unexpected quiet. No formula guarantees success. He manages some theological reading but also finds much important input from the reading which his work requires. He feels the lack of refresher courses, but he goes into retreat with his team who take days off together, and those days come out of his holiday allocation.

Upon what theological foundation does such a concept of ministry rest? An important clue is contained in J. A. T. Robinson's dictum, 'Just as the New Testament bids us have as high a doctrine of the ministry as we like, as long as our doctrine of the Church is higher, so it commands us have as high a doctrine of the Church as we may, provided our doctrine of the Kingdom is higher.' (*The Historic Episcopate*, ed. Carey, p. 17). By the same token, we may have as high a doctrine of redemption as we like, as long as our doctrine of creation is higher. (This emphasis on a cosmic perspective to both redemption and creation is fundamental to eastern orthodox theology and urgently needs to be recovered in the west.) The meaning of 'the world' in the New Testament is ambiguous: it often carries a sinister connotation from which is derived 'the world, the flesh and the devil', but it was the world which God loved so much that he gave his son for its salvation (John 3. 16–17). God's presence and power are not limited to either the religious or the ecclesiastical departments of life: the holy and the secular are not mutually exclusive because God is both transcendent and immanent. The notion of being 'set apart' can be dangerous if it implies a lack of concern for a world in which God was pleased to become incarnate. Material things can only become sacramental because this is a sacramental universe.

Within such a context one may properly speak of ministers in secular employment celebrating secular sacraments when they help those around them to see an ordinary event take on an extra depth and significance on occasions of celebration, forgiveness or renewal. Such a minister, employed in the Department of Health and Social Security, was responsible for the ambulance service in England. It was awarded a royal warrant, and it wished to celebrate this special recognition. Representatives discussed with him what form the celebration should take and they decided to have a great service in York Minster and asked him to preach at it.

Such a ministry, often humdrum and seeming to be a matter of bits and pieces, is not different from any other form of sacred ministry. It is a preparation for the coming of the Kingdom. Non-stipendiary and stipendiary ministry alike are for the communication of the gospel in word and deed. Each needs the other.

24

Local Ministry

IF the Church of England is unclear about non-stipendiary ministry, it is even less clear about 'local ministry', which also appears as 'local ordained ministry' or 'local non-stipendiary ministry'. The bishops published their *Guidelines for Local Non-Stipendiary Ministry* in 1987 (with the admission that there were divided views on the matter) to help dioceses devise the pattern appropriate to their circumstances. The distinctive marks of this form of ministry are fivefold:

(a) The call of God to this ministry comes to the candidate, in the first place, through the local congregation of which the individual is a member . . . Ordination is the Church's validation of this call, to which the individual has responded.

(b) A Local Non-Stipendiary Minister exercises this ministry as part of a team of people, ordained and lay, working together in the same parish or locality.

(c) This team may include lay people, with whom the Local Non-Stipendiary Minister has trained . . .

(d) The training of a Local Non-Stipendiary Minister does pay particular attention to . . . the local situation . . .

(e) The ministry is local, in that it is confined by Licence.

The earliest such scheme in England to attract attention was at Bethnal Green in the Stepney Area of London diocese where in 1971 four men were called by one parish (in two congregations) and were ordained five years later. They were aged between 30 and 60 and were settled in the locality with no desire to move. They were working-class, though not manual workers, and their ministry was to be unpaid. The aim was to produce an indigenous church with an indigenous ministry since the working-class was largely estranged from the church. The image of the church was one of wishing to help people better themselves, whereas this group wished to retain their class and culture as something to be proud of. The training was designed to be local, practical and realistic with every situation an opportunity to learn, so that their education would not alienate them from their fellows. They were encouraged to think biblically rather than concern themselves with the 'niceties of critical scholarship'. In fact, as their training developed and opened their eyes to wider horizons they realised that the local context was not enough, and they made some use of the Southwark Ordination Course.

There were difficulties, not least in their relationship with stipendiary clergy many of whom had not encountered a working-class priest. There was talk of ordination on the cheap, or the place being flooded with clergy. Would all readers become clergy? There were great demands on time because neighbours assumed that a clerical collar signified the availability of an unlimited amount of pastoral time. Pressure on family life was considerable, and the wives had to be prepared to give full support. By 1989, after a good deal of personal turmoil, two had settled back in their old church and were performing a valuable ministry there, one had left to become a hospital chaplain, and the fourth had died.

The experiment carries more questions than answers. It was on too small a scale; the congregations were too little involved in the training; there was not enough support before and after ordination; and there needed to be more partnership between 'locals' and 'outsiders'. It stands, however, as a milestone towards a clearer understanding of shared ministry.

During the same period another experiment was under way in a context which was the antithesis of Stepney, the diocese of Lincoln, which in 1988 listed 664 churches, 550 parishes and 260 stipendiary clergy. During the 1970s growing concern was expressed at the diminishing number of clergy many of whom found themselves responsible for four or five or more small village churches. (Half of Lincoln's parishes have fewer than a hundred civil voters.) The ideal was held up of a sacramental priestly presence in every community. This was impossible to achieve with stipendiary clergy, and so the only possible answer was the provision of non-stipendiary clergy with a limited local responsibility. A scheme for their selection and training was set up in 1980, though only in 1987 was a full-time director appointed with four assistants, all of whom held small parishes, and a diocesan budget. By 1989 fourteen men and two women had been ordained.

The shortage of clergy was not the only motivation for this scheme; there was also a growing demand from lay people for training and education for deeper involvement in ministry. So parishes are invited to explore and with the incumbent's support, choose a team of up to twelve, some of whom, it is hoped, will be candidates for ordination: the church council recommends these after a year's training. Training is done in groups of six to twelve. For two years the course is general, with specialisms provided for in the third year. Lay ministers are commissioned, and ordinands deaconed, after two years, and after three the deacons are ordained priest and given a three-year licence, though they continue training for a fourth year.

The training pattern has come under a good deal of criticism. Up to 1987 it relied largely on an existing educational course which was not related to the particular pastoral and administrative gifts of the students. It was both too wide and too academic for a working-class parish, yet it was not of high calibre, and certainly not comparable with training courses for non-stipendiary ministers. It had no examinations or formal essays, and assessment was made by a continuing profile of a student's progress. Its aim was to relate learning to ministry, to help reflect upon life's experience, to build up confidence in faith, and to prepare people to exercise a parochial ministry under a parish priest.

The theory was that a parish team should number not less than four, and the supervision of such teams is important if the team is not to institutionalise the views and prejudices of the incumbent. There is a corresponding need for training for incumbents and tutors, particularly to avoid the possibility of creating a lay élite which would depress rather than vitalize the ministry of the rest.

Many rural villages still possess a rigid class structure inherited from medieval times. An incumbent who comes in from outside does not have the advantage of being indigenous but he does have the advantage of standing outside that local structure, even if his background and education are likely to be nearer that of the squire than that of a pigman. If the pigman were to be ordained as a local minister he would, no doubt, find readier opportunities for ministry among farm-workers than with the squirearchy. An answer might be a team ministry with both pigman and squire – or perhaps the squire's wife.

During the 1980s a small scheme known as the Brandon scheme was set up in an inner-city area covering four parishes just south of the Elephant and Castle in Southwark diocese. Its population in 1981 was 23,000, 84% of whom lived in council housing. It was predominantly working-class yet the 1981 census revealed that 21% had lived elsewhere the previous year. The idea was conceived by the four incumbents, who had constituted an informal group for some years, principally in order 'to bring the working-class into the ordained ministry': they were to be 'indigenous' in contrast to the stipendiaries who were 'apostolic'. In 1980 each congregation elected its own candidates, two from two, and one each from the other two, with one not accepted by the bishop, thus by-passing the national selection process. The men were aged between 28 and 76; one was a churchwarden, two were servers, and two were active members of their church council. Three had considered ordination earlier.

Their training was local, mainly through the Readers' Course, and did not approach the standard of the General Ministerial Examination. There was no systematic programme of reading or essay-writing and no external assessment. The five were ordained deacon after one year in 1981 and priest in 1983. Soon after, when three out of the four incumbents moved and group relationships became severely strained, the local ministers provided a focus for unity and continuity. Their ministry has not extended beyond their parish churches (no emphasis was placed on work-based ministry) though it has released the stipendiaries for more work outside. There are few indications that the scheme has furthered the concept of every-member ministry. In 1988 the three younger men were contemplating other forms of ministry, two of them stipendiary.

A very different approach has been tried in Liverpool. A working party was set up in 1980 by the bishops of Liverpool and Manchester, 'to consider the case for and against ordaining men to the priesthood who would have particular gifts for their own urban area'. A report was submitted in 1982 which led to the creation in Liverpool in 1984 of the Group for Urban Ministry and Leadership. (Manchester began on different lines in 1988 and ordained its first four local ministers in 1991.) Its purpose was to stimulate the development of local Christian leadership in the inner-city areas and outer-city estates characterised by multiple deprivation which have come to be called 'urban priority areas'. Behind it lay the conviction expressed in the report that in these areas 'there are networks, assumptions, attitudes which the full-time, fully stretched, predominantly middle-class professional ministry only touches peripherally and rarely penetrates in effective depth'. Again, 'At present far too many of our inner-city churches are financially and physically dependent on former residents now living in suburbia. Nostalgic loyalty, status seeking, religious conservatism, possibly a fear of the "posh" suburban congregations, bring back these former members Sunday by Sunday. They inhibit the emergence of a truly local congregation.'

The purpose, therefore, of the Group is the selection and training of local ministry teams with the expectation that out of them will emerge some candidates for ordination as local non-stipendiary ministers. Church councils have to make an act of commitment to the scheme when they nominate members. Training is done in teams of between five and twelve, culturally representative of the parish and not of the congregation. Tutors and trainees travel to the parish, and the manner of training is oral rather than written. Each tells his or her own story, and this is put up against other stories from the tradition, which of course includes the Bible, and discussed. (Biblically speaking, the method has much to support it.) The training lasts eighteen months at the end of which the team is commissioned for a five-year period. In 1988 there were thirteen teams in training with an average size of eight, an average age of forty-three, equal numbers of women and men, and a good spread of types of employment and unemployment. The aim is to recruit ten teams a year with a target of reaching 90 out of the 240 parishes in the diocese. Significantly, up to 1988 the organisers had not proceeded to the second stage of ordination-training.

There have, needless to say, been difficulties. There has been a temptation to accept more candidates from less deprived parishes; clergy-tutors tend to slip into traditional pedagogical methods; problems arise when parish clergy leave; the focus tends to be too much on the congregation and not enough on the world around; and programmes of empowerment can seem subversive. Results, however, are encouraging, with hopes of an 'authentic urban theology' emerging.

These experiments, more and less successful, focus to burning point the main theological issues of ministry and the practical ones of selection and training. What is a priest for? Is he just another pair of sacramental hands? Can a priest ever be merely local? (In fact, in the Church of England if a priest moves to another diocese and is approached by a patron of a living to be its incumbent, it is hard for the bishop to refuse.) What sort of priest does a parish want or need? Will local ministry prove to be a charter for a congregationalism of self-opinionated congregations? What expectations does the public have of a priest? Is it proper for a priest always to be only an assistant? Does this make him second-class? What if a 'local' priest wants to become stipendiary? Granted the advantages of being indigenous, how is he to represent in himself and in his teaching the full range of the Christian tradition? The arguments advanced in previous chapters offer some answers to these urgent questions. Issues to do with selection and training remain to be dealt with in the next two chapters.

25

Vocation and Selection

THE rise of local ministry brings into sharp focus the connected issues of vocation and selection. Its claim that the local church should call out men and women for the ministry, and that these should be locally selected and locally trained is in sharp contrast with the traditional Anglican idea of vocation as an inner call experienced by the individual and then tested by the Church.

The idea of calling is a central one in the Bible in the two senses of 'giving a name to' and 'summoning'. The senses are linked because name-giving implies a claim of possession: 'I have called thee by thy name, thou art mine' says the Lord to Israel through the unknown prophet called Second-Isaiah (43.1). Even more striking is God's call of Cyrus, the Medo-Persian king, as agent of the liberation of exiled Israel: 'For Jacob my servant's sake, and Israel my chosen, I have called thee by thy name: I have surnamed thee though thou hast not known me.' (Is. 45.4). Israel is called to be a people of divine destiny though all too often they fall short both corporately and individually. Some of the most striking individual calls are those of the prophets: Amos as he was tending his sheep in the barren Judean hills (7.14f.); Hosea through the circumstances of his unhappy marriage (1–3); Isaiah amid the Temple ceremonial (6); and Jeremiah with his conviction that his call antedated his birth (1. 4–10). The priesthood, however, seems to have been purely hereditary, being reserved to the tribe of Levi, or later to Aaron's sons. (Deut. 18. 1–8, Lev. 1.5.)

In the New Testament Jesus proclaims the good news of the near-arrival of the kingdom of God, (Mark 1. 14–15) calls his first disciples (Mark 1. 16–20), and horrifies the scribes and Pharisees by the company he keeps, underlining his action with the words 'I came not to call the righteous, but sinners.' (Mark 2.17). 1 John 3.1 sums up the work of Jesus: 'Behold what manner of love the Father hath bestowed upon us, that we should be called children of God: and such we are.' God calls everyone into his kingdom, or to salvation, or to eternal life (depending on the author) based on his free grace in Christ. In addition, he calls some to particular work, notably Paul to be an apostle, by virtue of his encounter with the risen Lord. In his epistle to the Galatians Paul is adamant that his apostleship came 'not from men, neither through man, but through Jesus Christ, and God the Father, who raised him from the dead' (1.1) After the lapse of more than three years during which he had been preaching, he went up to Jerusalem to visit Peter, and saw also James the Lord's brother, and spent a fortnight with him, but we know nothing of what transpired. Some fourteen years later he again went up to Jerusalem, met James and Peter and John and received from them the 'right hand of fellowship' that Paul should undertake his mission to the gentiles while they went to the Jews (Gal. 2. 1–10). The selection of Matthias however, as an apostle to replace Judas Iscariot is strikingly different. Soon after the ascension, according to Acts 1, Peter recommended to the brethren (about a hundred and twenty) that one should be chosen from those who had kept company with them throughout Jesus' ministry, and two were put forward, Joseph Barsabbas and Matthias. After prayer, lots were cast, and the lot fell upon Matthias. The Lord had shown whom he had chosen (Acts 2. 15–26). In each case much lay behind the choice, of which we have only a few indications.

Earlier chapters of this book have traced the way in which the medieval 'double standard' developed whereby first ordained ministers and later members of the religious orders came to be regarded as first-class Christians with a guarantee of salvation while the laity ranked as second-class, wholly dependent on the clergy for theirs. It was against this concept that Luther made his vehement protest, asserting that all ethically acceptable work, and the married state, could properly be seen as a vocation from God: so much so that today in German *beruf* (calling) is the normal word for 'occupation'. In this sense the Book of Common Prayer has the collect on Good Friday 'for all estates of men in thy holy Church, that every member of the same, in his vocation and ministry, may truly and godly serve thee'. Similarly the Catechism in defining duty towards neighbour includes 'to do my duty in that state of life, unto which it shall please God to call me' (though it is often misrepresented as if it were 'unto which it *has pleased* God to call me').

At the Reformation the Anabaptists took the principle of an inner call to the extreme, and allowed as minister anyone who claimed such a call along with some spiritual gift like that of preaching. This was opposed by Luther, and the Augsburg Confession lays it down in paragraph 14 'no one ought to teach publicly in Churches, or to administer the sacraments unless duly called'; and Calvin also stipulated that 'No one must be elected who is not of sound doctrine and of saintly life'. (*Institutes*, 4.3.12.) To this end both reformers put great emphasis on a thorough theological education for aspiring ministers, a tradition maintained to the present time.

When Cranmer wrote the Ordinal for the 1549 Book of Common Prayer, he included a question for deacons (probably under the influence of Martin Bucer, the German divine), 'Do you trust that you are inwardly moved by the Holy Ghost to take upon you this office and ministration . . . ?' in addition to 'Do you think that you are truly called according to the will of our Lord Jesus Christ, and the due order of this Realm, to the Ministry of the Church?' (The first question is not repeated at the Ordering of Priests.) There is no doubt here about the double aspect of 'calling': it is both inward, from God, and outward from the Church, and *Article 23* emphasises the latter: 'It is not lawful for any man to take upon him the office of publick preaching, or ministering the Sacraments in the Congregation, before he be lawfully called, and sent to execute the same'. The emphasis on the inner call in the rite of ordination is unique to the Church of England among all the Anglican, Reformed and Lutheran Churches. The Roman Church still states that the call comes from the bishop.

All the main-line Churches agree that some form of selection is necessary because individuals may be mistaken. Those who are most certain about their sense of vocation are sometimes found to be the least satisfactory, and in extreme cases the sense may be pathological. The Church has always retained the right to test vocations. How may this be done? The main Churches in England have reached a common pattern of a residential conference of two or three days where a group of candidates live together with three or four selectors, ordained and lay, and information is gathered by personal interviews, group activities, written submissions, the common life, external references, and sometimes psychological tests, at the end of which the selectors confer together and try to come to a common mind about each candidate. The remarkable experience of the Church of England is that the selectors who represent a wide range of tradition fail to reach unanimity only about once in five hundred cases. Then the decision is referred back to the sponsoring bishop who in any case has the final responsibility.

Two areas call for examination. First, the candidate must be sure that it is God who is calling. The call may have been articulated by another person ('Can you think of any good reason why you should not be ordained?') but if ministers are to help others discover their vocation they must be sure of their own. The church context is important, but not all-important. On occasion ministers may have to stand against their own congregation or against church authorities for which they will need the assurance of a call from a source higher than either, as they will also if they are to endure in a downtown parish where the congregation is small and dispirited and where vandalism to the church and break-ins to the parsonage are regular occurrences. Problems arise with candidates who have been converted, say, at college and have only ever known a university Christian fellowship: the realities of parish life can come as a shock. Those who recommend candidates for a ministry which is to be prophetic as well as apostolic must welcome symptoms of a divine discontent with established forms of church life. The local church has a limited view and a restricted image. The ministry is necessarily about something larger.

Second, any candidate must display some personal qualities, both natural and supernatural, which will equip him or her for ministry. One senior Anglican incumbent has been fairly described in these terms: 'He seems unable to listen properly to anyone and probably as a result of that he never reaches the same conclusions. He seems to look on the black side of everything and he seems absolutely unaware of anyone's feelings while being almost totally absorbed in his own. He recovers from one disaster only to walk straight into another.' The selectors need to make sure that a candidate's relationship with God is matched by a relationship with other people which is sensitive, loving and humble, and that he or she has an ability to enter strong emotional fields with sufficient detachment to be able to help.

Candidates single or married must have come to terms with their own sexuality, and if married must present a reasonably stable married life. Such at least is expected in 1 Timothy 3. Intellectually what matters is not so much a candidate's educational qualifications (if any) as his or her educability. A man with a first-class honours degree in theology may manifest a closed mind outside his subject, and a working man who left school at fifteen may after a year or so prove capable of writing a first-class essay. A minister does not have to be a teacher in the professional sense (though many are); he or she does have to be able to release the manifold opportunities for education which lie, often undiscovered, in every Christian congregation.

In a word, selectors will look for integrity in their candidates, manifested in a deep honesty and a thorough consistency. There is no final guarantee of success and mistakes are made. The Church of England allows candidates who are not recommended to return to one or two further conferences if sponsored by their bishop. Not even Jesus succeeded with all of his twelve.

26
Training for Ministry

MOST of the problems about the ordained ministry are high-lighted when the question is posed, How should ministers be trained? Indeed, the very title is problematic because the term 'training' normally presupposes a clear-cut end product, and ordained ministers are hardly that. A broader term is 'education', a process concerned with the discovery of truth and with the development of a truthful enquirer, but this lacks the vocational element. Roman Catholics prefer the term 'formation' for the development of both clergy and laity since this term puts emphasis on the involvement of the whole person, but others shy away from it as too suggestive of brain-washing. The case will here be presented that the key process for ministers is induction into a tradition, and in so far as this has a testable result, the term 'training' is still useful.

The tradition is a living and therefore a constantly changing one since it is prophetic as well as apostolic, and over the centuries it has developed a pluriform shape. A non-conformist minister will have been trained to give primary importance to the Bible and to preaching, with a particular relationship to a given congregation; a Roman Catholic will have been trained to give primary importance to the sacraments, and to a relationship with a world-wide church under a universal pope, with celibacy as a voluntary but necessary aspect of his vocation. An Anglican will try to keep a balance between word and sacraments, and will see his parochial cure as extending beyond the confines of his congregational life.

The purpose of the ministry is to bring others into this living and life-giving tradition, to nurture them and equip them to bring others in. The method of ministerial training is important because ministers tend to use on others the methods used on them. One perplexed young curate was heard to exclaim, 'All that my training did for me was to teach me how to lecture, and no one here wants to be lectured.' The laity are not to be clericalised, and too much emphasis on lay education may produce a deprived underclass who do not attend classes or courses. They also have their place in the church.

If the argument of this book is anything like correct, it follows that three things are basic for the training of ministers: spirituality, or the awareness of God in himself; the awareness of God's activity in his world; and a striving for wholeness, in the individual and in groups small and large.

The word 'spirituality' gained currency in the late 1970s in reaction, no doubt, to the shallow secularism of the previous twenty years and to the quest for deeper inner satisfaction in eastern religions. In 1980 the Advisory Council held a seminar and published a small book *Spirituality in Ordination Training* (ACCM Occasional Paper No. 9) which repays attention, particularly the introductory essay *What is spirituality?* by P. R. Baelz. He defines it as the relationship with God which is the fundamental context for all other human relationships. It is right for the church as trainer to pry into this private area because it is the guardian of a rich, though diverse, communal tradition. Life in the spirit involves a proper love of self, of God, and of neighbour which together produce growth towards wholeness. God is at the centre of the Christian's spiritual life, and we search for him only because he first has searched for us. He has put an ultimate restlessness into our hearts, and he keeps us in being even when he seems absent. Life in the spirit involves a redirecting of the will and all other human elements in a total response where good desires may have to be sacrificed for better. Sin is important, but grace precedes sin and is not its consequence. The Christian gospel is not simply a remedy for sin; it is good news of God's continuing creative and redemptive work in the world.

The second basic concern, then, must be a study of that world, which for Europeans means the western culture, in which the faith has to be earthed and contextualised. This culture has three salient features. First it is pluralistic; that is to say, there are a number of optional ideologies of belief and action, and there is, it is claimed (though Christians would not agree), no rational way of choosing between them. So, for Christians, simple proclamation is not enough; any attempt to make more sense of things cannot proceed by way of knock-down argument. Second, contemporary culture has a growing ecological sense. Any theology must do justice to the findings of natural science and to the traditional doctrine of God as creator. It must see nature as the matrix and instrument of the spirit rather than its enemy. Third, in the ecclesiastical context, greater importance is being given to the role of the laity, and all ministry is now being seen as shared ministry. So ministerial theology needs to be earthed and contextualised in the world as it is and cannot be learned by rote at some abstract level. If it is a function of theology to articulate the vision of God's presence in the world, the minister needs to be familiar with the Christian tradition in its wholeness.

The third basic concern in training must be in the area of personal growth, individual and corporate. Here the impor-tance of a training community becomes over-riding, because self-knowledge is best acquired in the mirror of charitable but critical friends and colleagues. The soul-friend who stands apart from the community, is of no less value. Psychologists have produced tests for self-awareness, but so subtle and com-plex is the notion of personality that one sometimes feels that these tell more about the originator than the user. Much work has been done in the area of group dynamics, and useful insights may be gained experientially about the forces at play in any group behaviour. Ministers need to know how to handle conflict because they will certainly encounter it, and should expect and even welcome it as a sign of a lively community. Amid much talk of the Church's ministry of healing it is essen-tial for ordinands to know what goes to make a healthy com-munity, and to be at least as much concerned with that as with the eradication of disease. The insights of psycholo-gists and sociologists are valuable but stand in need of

Christian critique. Amid all talk of growth, maturity and student-centred learning, the gospel insistence remains that life has to be lost in order that it may be found, that growth is to be measured by the stature of the fulness of Christ, and that the ministry we share is the ministry of Christ crucified, risen and ascended.

How has the Church of England attempted to implement the training of its ministers? It must be said, until very recently in a remarkably haphazard way. Readers of Jane Austen's *Sense and Sensibility* will remember how the hero, Edward Ferrars, on being cut off from the family fortune through his attachment to the wrong lady, was offered by a friend a nearby living with a rectory and two hundred pounds a year, to prepare for which meant two or three months' return to Oxford. That was in 1811, and attendance at half a dozen theological lectures would have sufficed. What mattered was the classical education which the university was supposed to purvey, and more particularly the status and accepted value which went with it. Charles Kingsley wrote in the 1840s to his friend F. D. Maurice asking his help in finding him a curate: 'I only ask three things: 1. No extreme opinions. 2. To be a gentleman. 3. To have on the whole the habit of speaking the truth. Ignorance and inexperience will be rather liked than not.' As late as 1868 Mark Pattison wrote, 'Theology has not begun to exist as a science among us', and he feared that it would continue to occupy 'its present degraded position of an extraneous appendage tacked on to the fag-end of every examination in every other subject.' An Honours School was founded at Oxford in 1870 and a Tripos at Cambridge in 1871 (though Durham had pioneered the way in 1842), but since the Universities Tests Act of 1871 opened all degrees and offices to men of any religion or of none, teaching moved from the passing on of established doctrine to the more investigative approach of the historical method.

It was during this period, from 1830 to 1880, that the Church of England took to founding theological colleges. Motives were mixed: the growing trend towards the supposed secularisation of the ancient universities (until 1871 in order to be a college

Fellow a man had to be in holy orders); the desire to keep up with 'other professions'; party enthusiasm, and at least in the case of one college anti-party enthusiasm; and fear of the incursions of the Ecclesiastical Commissioners who were set up in 1835 to examine, in particular, the scandalous state of cathedral finances with power to prepare schemes for their redistribution, which led to the sudden appearance of colleges in closes – at Chichester in 1839 (Durham had preceded it in 1831), at Wells in 1840, at Lichfield in 1856, at Canterbury in 1860, at Salisbury and Exeter in 1861, at Gloucester in 1868, at Lincoln in 1874, and at Ely in 1876. Cuddeson in 1854 was different, being ten miles out of Oxford and opposite the bishop's palace, and it bore the marks of European Roman Catholic seminaries.

These colleges are private bodies (like the missionary societies) and have never taken kindly to central control. They are self-governing and rely for capital expenditure on a constituency of supporters. Their students receive only grants for fees from central church funds. Only in 1921 did the bishops corporately require ordinands to complete a period of residential training and pass an examination, and only in 1946 did they require all candidates to attend a national selection conference if they wished to receive help from central church funds. In each case a world war seems to have been a necessary preliminary.

The situation was fundamentally altered in 1960 with the establishment of the Southwark Ordination Course by the then bishop M. Stockwood and his suffragen J. Robinson. The main practical reason for this was acknowledgment of the harm done to married men's families by their uprooting to go to a residential setting. But there was a deep dissatisfaction with many aspects of residential training, and it was hoped that a new pattern based on weeknight classes, residential weekends and a residential summer-school each year for three years would not only keep families more united but would earth theology in the realities of the working world. This experiment for older candidates (over thirty) was successful and was followed by the establishment of the North West

Ordination Course (later the Northern Ordination Course) in 1970, both of which trained candidates for stipendiary and non-stipendiary ministry side by side. By 1989 there were as many courses as colleges, fourteen of each, covering most parts of England.

Up to 1960 the typical pattern of the residential college had altered little since the nineteenth century. Most were small, forty to fifty students, with three full-time staff all male graduates and all priests of the Church of England, resembling a cross between a monastery and an Oxbridge college. (It was assumed that all students were graduates, though not all were.) The principal was the eldest, a venerable father-figure; the vice-principal was younger; and the youngest, perhaps the chaplain, was only recently a curate. The staff were devoted and the mood was for the most part courteous and friendly. The syllabus consisted of a reduced version of a university theological education together with some historical study of liturgy, ethics (if it had not disappeared through lack of examiners), preaching practice, some lectures on the minister's task, some visiting lecturers on social work and church music, two or three chapel services a day, three meals eaten in common, and a parish visit in the vacation. The university nearby was regularly visited for its lectures. It was assumed by the staff that the students would enter a ministry very like their own of three or ten or twenty years earlier. It was widely claimed that the worship in the college chapel was the clue to its life but more critical observers maintain that it provided spiritual legitimation for an unquestioned curriculum and ethos. (See A. O. Dyson 1982).

More serious criticisms may also be brought against it. Whereas, on the surface the college had the appearance of providing a liberal education with its relatively loose and broad approach, in fact by eschewing hard doctrine and concentrating on an apprentice-style of learning it powerfully reinforced traditional attitudes and played down innovation. In addition, the main theological study taken in university lectures was not directed towards ministry: the teacher was seen as scholar, not pastor, and the different subjects were not only distinct but also on occasion in competition. Both sets of factors, for quite dissimilar reasons, were powerfully dissuasive of any systematic thinking about the practice of ministry and training appropriate to it.

This state of affairs was bad enough in England, but over half a century it had been widely exported to most parts of the Anglican communion and also copied in other parts of the world. Soon radical criticism was being heard in third world countries that this pattern of training was producing an alien type of leadership; that ordained ministers were being turned into a professional élite; that the church was showing itself to be allied with privilege; and that it must be realised that our own practice of theology was encapsulated in our own culture, and was therefore not for export in its present form.

Between 1969 and 1971 the same protest was making itself felt at home. It was a period of student rebellion and riots; of student demand for relevance and authenticity; of the challenge to traditional academic theology posed by the rise of Religious Studies in British universities; of growing dominance of counselling techniques over against dogmatic proclamation; of puzzled debate about the nature of ordained ministry and experimentation with local ministry; of the popularity of secular theology; of frustration, anxiety and iconoclasm. The shock waves were by no means confined to Britain or Europe: the Anglican Central Theological College in Tokyo had to close for a period while its governors and staff rethought and rewrote its aims and methods.

Many ordinands found theological college life too oppressive and leapt over the wall in search of freedom; wives and small children played an increasing part in college life; premarital sexual and homosexual activity became more obvious; practical field-placements were allotted more time; students demanded sensitivity training; the skills of the liberated adult educator came to be valued more highly than academic scholarship. The minister was now seen to be a comprehensively trained practitioner and communicator, aware of relevant theory, ready to work with other professionals and showing prophetic impatience with the ills of society and of the church.

To this end new syllabi were created which endeavoured to integrate practical and theoretical. These depended upon a clear ruling idea, without which confusion and disorder result: in this case it was the norm of practical ministry. The changes were profound. The old 'academic' approach implied specialisation in isolated subjects, suspicion of new forms of knowledge, a long growth before the fruits could be plucked, and strong control over the process. It was reflected in its production of the minister as *persona*, inheriting traditional patterns of ministry which gave more importance to intellect and words than to emotions. It was necessarily cautious about social change because it provided no means of diagnosing what was happening in society.

The new 'integrated' approach shaped its syllabus around a ruling idea of the task of the minister. But where did this idea come from? It was plucked from a fairly superficial reading of the state of society and church at the time. Appeal was made to the liberation theologians of Latin America who started from an analysis of deep injustices in their society and used theology to support it. Thus in the Bible the determinative story became the exodus of Israel from Egypt rather than the exodus of Jesus from Jerusalem. It was removed from its context so that no notice was taken of Israel's subsequent conquest of Palestine and subjugation of its tribes. It is significant that Chinese theologians who had experienced liberation in 1949 were not impressed by liberation theology. They were aware that much more liberation needed to be done – years before the popular demonstrations of 1989. Deep investigation into individual subjects, Bible or doctrine or even church history soon showed up the inadequacies of this short-cut theology, and attempts to combine elements of the academic and the integrated approach produced frustration and perplexity.

Some Anglican scholars (like S. W. Sykes in *The Integrity of Anglicanism*) have argued that the solution to the problem lies in the recovery of a 'systematic theology' by and for the Church, but there are difficulties about that. Most 'systems' are the result of a founding father like Luther or Calvin or of a dominant thinker like Thomas Aquinas, but the Church of England has none such, and many of its distinguished sons, such as F. D. Maurice, have rejoiced in its calling to be unsystematic. In recent years German theological teachers have become increasingly unhappy about the restrictions of the Augsburg Confession, and the Roman Catholic Church has largely abandoned the philosophy of Aquinas as the basis for its ministerial training. The last forty years have witnessed a revolution in the understanding of the nature of theology and, as if that were not bad enough for theological educators, there has been a similar one in the field of education.

The former has been succinctly stated by F. W. Dillistone: before the Second World War theology was deductive, descriptive, and definitive, but since the 1960's it has become inductive, empirical and involved. In education, the old model of the learner has given way to the sleeper to be awakened, or the child to be helped to grow, or the right environment to be created which will encourage the right conditions of growth, or the learning community to be formed. There are also close connections between the way in which the nature of God is understood and the way in which people understand his communication. If, for example, the emphasis is on a God of order, clarity and unambiguity, then God's clear purposes are clearly communicated. If, however, God is seen as revealed in an unfolding or apparently ambiguous way, then communication and learning may be exploratory and open-ended, and ambiguity will itself be material for study.

Whether we believe that God communicates himself through a flash of insight to an individual or in the meeting of a group, there will be educational repercussions affecting the style of teaching and the assembling of experiences which may lead to moments of disclosure. If the view is held that God communicates after long and disciplined study of scripture, then planned accumulation of learning is appropriate. If God is understood to communicate himself through the experience of continuing corporate worship, emphasis will be put on patterns of liturgy and the permeation of study by the community's worshipping life. Others may see God communicating with his people in a challenging and risky way as they engage with difficult secular issues. That type of learning will tend to encourage engagement in contentious social and political questions.

The Biblical witness is that God communicates himself in all these ways 'at sundry times and in divers manners', and that therefore a great variety of methods needs to be employed, none of which can be guaranteed foolproof. The Bible must be known in all its breadth, from Leviticus to Job and from St John to the Pastoral Epistles, if only to underline the pluriformity of the Judaeo-Christian tradition. Church history and doctrine show how for better and for worse how the tradition has been continued, and they erect important signposts through ecclesiastical minefields. The study of liturgy is important for the effective arranging of worship services formal and informal. The study of ethics is vital for the equipping of lay people to face up to their secular responsibilities. These areas of study have their own intellectual disciplines (which are not unchanging), and it is important that each stands on its own feet so that together they can act as a series of checks and balances to each other. In addition, there are insights from the fields of psychology and sociology, though the theories and practices here are at least as diverse as those of theology.

The difficult task for the training of ministers is to bring these studies together in a context of worship, personal growth, and corporate awareness. Some integration may be achieved thematically, but to build a syllabus on themes alone puts undue responsibility on those who choose them and select the material for comparision. Much of importance is likely to be excluded. Team-teaching can be helpful, as is the teaching by staff in areas of others' specialisms so that the division between subjects is seen not to be watertight. Continuous discussion by staff among themselves and with students about the syllabus, its presuppositions, and about teaching methods is essential.

Tension is often felt between the kind of teaching offered in university lectures and that in theological colleges. It might be claimed that the former is concerned with truth, the latter with orthodoxy; the former objective, the latter subjective. In fact there can be no hard and fast disjunction between pure objectivity and pure subjectivity. The difference is, rather, that a university student has to be critical and detached whereas the college student should be critical but engaged: the latter has to inhabit his theology whereas the former can remain outside it.

The fact remains that many of those who read theology as a university degree exhibit great resistance to the programmes of theological colleges. (This is true of many graduates also in Germany and Japan.) During the 1980s many complained that the theology offered by colleges was of a lower standard, and that there was little for them to do of a challenging or useful nature. In response, the authorities relaxed the formal requirements offering instead a programme of projects each centred on a major area of 'theology-as-experienced', one per term for five out of the six terms. Only one college accepted it and the results have not been encouraging. It seems that degrees cause a kind of fatigue or loss of appetite for theology, which leads students to demand practical or doctrinal training with more informality and less rigour. It seems very difficult for them to move from the study of separate subjects to the theological study of experience. Perhaps it cannot be done at this stage of a person's career but can only be creatively accomplished much later.

Here the part-residential courses have much to offer. All their students are (or are meant to be) over the age of thirty and most are under forty-five. Nearly all of them are in secular employment, many in positions of responsibility – which certainly is the case for mothers of families. Many have experienced higher education though some have left school without any formal qualifications. The author's experience over eleven years with the Northern Ordination Course led him to conclude that a rigorous study of formal theology, even to the point of writing a long essay in each subject, is possible and useful for a wide variety of students, and the teaching of it amid the hurly-burly of family life, secular job and church engagement added a dimension of reality to the undertaking. The whole training programme was set in a context of worship and prayer and one of the unique features of the Course, and one most remembered by former students, was the Quiet Morning which occupied the Sunday morning of every residential week-end. It was something of a misnomer, because for an hour and a half a devotional topic was presented by speech or acting or music or exhibition, led by staff or students or visitor, drawing from a wide range of history, drama, poetry, art, biography, novels, music and the sciences, with silence, followed by a silent break, and then a celebration of the eucharist at which the sermon gathered up the presentation and placed it in the context of worship. Here was an important opportunity for integration to take place at the deepest level.

The merits and demerits of residential and part-residential training have been widely debated, and the Advisory Council published a report in 1986, '*Patterns of Ministerial Training in the Theological Colleges and Courses*'. The main argument adduced in favour of residential training concerns the nature of its community life. There is time and space for study; there is easy access to the minds of staff and fellow-students; the lesson of tolerance has to be learned; and the training is firmly based in a discipline of regular prayer and worship. The argument is impressive, but is not altogether borne out by the facts. That half of all residential students are married, and three quarters of those live with their family away from the college, poses a major question about the notion of a residential community. Many students found their community to be isolated from ordinary life, tense and oppressive. Some described it as sub-Christian, given to party wrangling, and rife with homosexual practice. Particular difficulties were experienced by older women.

The main argument advanced for the part-residential course is that it provided rich opportunity for the weaving together of theological study and secular life and work, often bringing with it new insights into the work situation. There was the stimulus of a wide variety of student backgrounds including differing church traditions. The residential week-ends and summer-schools provided an intensive and formative experience. The spirituality acquired was more appropriate. On the other hand, some students complained that little use was made of the experience which they brought with them, and others that the course was theologically lightweight, did not stir their imagination, and did not provide enough opportunity for reflection. There is no doubt that this manner of training is very demanding, not least on the family-life of married men, and sometimes on their employers also. That is why it is a condition of entry that candidates shall be well established in their family life and in their secular work. The strains cannot be too disastrous because one Course, at least, is receiving as students spouses of former students.

It is true that in terms of staff-student contact-hours a three-year part-residential course is equivalent to about half of a two-year residential course, but against that must be set the fact that the motivation of the part-timer is often much higher than the full-timer, and the learning process more intense. There is some evidence that those who have done it the hard way are more efficient at continuing their study after ordination than those trained residentially.

No scheme of education is ideal, and much can be said for both of these types. The fact that nearly one third of all in training are in Courses (373 in 1992 as against 761 in colleges) must make a considerable difference to the clergy of the Church of England in coming years.

The aim of theological training then, is to produce men and women of integrity as ministers. The process is helped (it cannot be guaranteed) by a syllabus which seeks to hold together theory and practice, heart and mind, academic rigour and personal development, theological insights ancient and modern, eastern and western, to be held only after critical examination. The training process thus begun in course or college must go on throughout a person's ministry, and dioceses are beginning to make better formal provision for this. The success of the initial phase can well be measured by the degree to which it produces men and women of deep confidence founded on faith in God and issuing in love of the world. Having faced the worst and found God in it (training may well prove to be a wilderness experience) they will continue in growth, adaptation and flexibility, knowing where to find resources and glad to welcome challenges. Such confident clergy can produce confident laity.

Conclusion

1. *Apostolic and Prophetic*

A survey of the development of the ordained ministry, even a cursory one like that attempted in this book, shows that almost every conceivable form has been tried somewhere at some time by some company of Christians. All have had to wrestle with the question of authority and how the divine dimension may be preserved and authenticated.

The one feature which is common to all the major traditions, Eastern Orthodox, Roman Catholic and Anglican (and to some extent Lutheran and Methodist) is episcopacy, although they are not agreed among themselves about the authenticity of those in that order. All would maintain that the responsibility for conserving and handing on the apostolic tradition lies primarily with the bishops, though some would be less sure about combining the apostolic tradition with the prophetic. Is not the apostolic for conserving, and the prophetic for upsetting? But that reflects the nature of the tradition.

The good news is that God is, that God acts, and that God has acted decisively in Jesus Christ. The foundation document for this claim is the Bible, and a working summary of the doctrine deduced from it is found in the Apostles' and Nicene Creeds. But the interpretation of this evidence, and the working out of its implications for Christian living, is a complex task which will never be complete partly because concepts of language and meaning are not fixed, and partly because the societies in which Christians are set are perpetually changing, never more so than at the end of the twentieth century. The apostolic element is there to ensure that the tradition is Christian; the prophetic element is there to see that it is appropriately related to the society in which it is set. The apostolic element tends to be tied to ecclesiastical systems; the prophetic element reminds the church that primary objectives are more important than systems. It is not surprising that great prophetic figures have often not been bishops, or even priests, as for example Francis of Assisi.

As far as Anglicans are concerned, they are resolved to stand firm on episcopacy, but not equally so on the three-fold mninistry. The classic statement is the Chicago-Lambeth Quadrilateral of 1886–1888 (see Appendix 1, p. 300), the four points constituting the minimum basis for reunion. The document itself has an interesting history. The Quadrilateral first appeared in a committee report at the General Convention of the American Episcopal Church at Chicago in 1886 when the first clause read, 'The Holy Scriptures of the Old and New Testaments as the revealed Word of God'. A committee of the Lambeth Conference of 1888 adopted this document but amended the first clause to avoid the implication of a literalist approach to Scripture. Here is an important example of apostolic authority in interpretation. Its understanding of what it calls the Historic Episcopate is an empirical rather than a theoretical one, acknowledging that the system necessarily undergoes adaptation in different social settings. The mission is constant; the form of its out-working is variable.

Bishops clearly need to be competent theologians, and if they are to understand the society in which they are set they will also need some working knowledge of sociology and economics. Since modern thought is heavily dominated by the language of the physical sciences, they need some familiarity with that as well. The task is immense, too great for any one man: but the episcopate is one, as Cyprian maintained, and it is important for bishops to confer so that their common mind may be as well informed as possible.

They also need to be in touch with universities and their

teachers, particularly at a time when theological faculties are
concerned less with handing on traditional doctrine and more
with exploring frontiers with other subjects and other
religions. The burden of fostering doctrinal studies lies
increasingly with theological colleges and courses where the
clergy are trained.

As the conclusion of his *A History of English Christianity 1920–
1985* Adrian Hastings compares two well-known clergymen
from fiction, Anthony Trollope's Archdeacon Grantly, confi-
dently astride his highly secularised ecclesiastical world of
Barsetshire in the 1850s, and Graham Greene's Monsignor
Quixote a century later; forbidden by his bishop to celebrate
mass, he sets off on a strange journey with his friend the
communist mayor who is finally converted at a kind of imaginary eucharist. The former knew more of the ways of the world:
the latter's religion proved more powerful. Hastings sees the
Church's visible history as a perpetual oscillation between
these two principles.

2. *Variable Shape.*

If some measure of variation is built into the episcopacy, it is
even more so with the other two orders of ministry as we now
have them. In England the parish system is the product of a
long history, and the variety of parishes is as great as the
variety of the men and women who staff them. The case for
the continuance of the system has been argued in chapter 20,
and parishes are unlikely to disappear in the near future
because the bishops corporately are not agreed on any better
system. It certainly needs supplementing, and is being sup-
plemented by sector ministries and non-stipendiary ministry,
and more recently by local ministry, all of which have an
important part to play in their own right and not merely as
'supplementary' or 'supporting' ministries.

The importance of the parish and the parish clergy is that
they are there, a visible presence in every acre of English soil
or asphalt. The maintenance of the ministry is the responsibility of the whole church and not just of the local church. The

diocese is an important unit not least because within it more prosperous parishes can support the ministry and mission of less favoured ones. That is why Anglican clergy, and often they alone, are still found living in socially deprived inner city areas as well as in remote rural areas which suffer their own form of deprivation.

The education and training of the clergy both before and after ordination is of vital importance. On the one hand they must know the tradition and be able to operate freely within it; and on the other they must know the locality and be at home within it so that they can interpret the signs of the times to the people who live and work there. They need also to be able to trace the structures which hinder justice and responsible freedom and to act as catalysts for their improvement or replacement.

Their task has no secular equivalent, and it is an advantage that it appears unclear, even marginal, because then it will pose no obstacle to membership either of the working men's club or of the local branch of Rotary, or preferably of both. One recalls the figure of the jester at the medieval court who was able to speak the painful truth to the highest authority just because he was marginal. The role or roles assigned to clergy by popular opinion are often not far removed from the caricatures of stage and screen, and clergy will always have to bear the tension between these fantasies and the tasks for which they were ordained, to be messengers, watchmen, and stewards of the Lord.

From time to time the Church of England, along no doubt with other ecclesial bodies, asks itself how many clergy it needs (see the report *The Ordained Ministry: Numbers, Cost and Deployment* of 1988). The question is unanswerable. In some ways the need is limitless, though no one would want to return to the thirteenth century scale of four paid clergy to each parish. Vocations will happen through the agency of lively and visionary congregations, and any policy of 'recruitment' is likely to be disastrous. As things are, half the population is debarred from the possibility of having a vocation, and if women are made eligible for ordination to the priesthood the situation might well arise where there are too many candidates for the number of stipendiary posts available. That in turn raises the question of money available for stipends, and here the Church of England is in the uniquely favoured position of having nearly half that money found by its dead and not by its living members: that percentage, however, will steadily decline as more has to be found for clergy pensions.

Most of these considerations are peculiar to the Church of England in England, and would be unfamiliar to Anglican Churches elsewhere. This is but one example, on a large scale, of the variable shape which the ordained ministry has taken, and must always take. Flexibility is a condition of survival.

3. *A Trinitarian Foundation.*

Such flexibility was built into his Church by Jesus' promise to the Twelve at the Last Supper (as recorded in John 15–16), fulfilled at Pentecost, of his abiding presence with them as the Advocate, the Spirit of truth, who would guide the Church into all the truth. The Spirit is both transcendent and immanent, coming from God and bestowed on Christians at their baptism. In the same way ministerial authority is both from above and from within; not from God without the Church, nor from the Church without God, but from God within the Church.

A proper doctrine of the Holy Spirit allows for new developments in the forms of the Church's life and for revivifying old ones: the (supposed) work of the Spirit must always be tested against the biblical record and the incarnation in particular. The clergy as *animateurs* are releasers of the Spirit, not so much calling him down but rather calling him out of the congregation where often for too long he has lain dormant, his many gifts unused.

The spirituality of the clergy, therefore, is central to their ministry. It is both personal and corporate; it must be real to each person but also nourished and developed by a long and rich tradition which needs to be familiar both to the clergy and to those to whom they minister because no two persons will follow exactly the same pattern. It will not be isolated but involved, serving people who are involved and ought to be involved in the world which God has visited and redeemed.

At the end of his chapter on 'Religion and Science' in *Science and the Modern World* A. N. Whitehead observes, 'That religion is strong which in its ritual and its modes of thought evokes an apprehension of the commanding vision'. Clergy are there because they have, in the context of the Christian community, been given such an apprehension, together with the conviction that in some way they are custodians of it and responsible for its furtherance. They are ordained to preside over each local manifestation of the Church of God to ensure, so far as they may, that by its worship, its thinking, and its common life that commanding vision may continue to be evoked, the vision of nothing less than, and nothing other than, the kingdom of God and of his Christ.

Appendix 1
The Lambeth Quadrilateral, 1888

(Part of a Committee Report approved by the Lambeth Conference of 1888.)

That, in the opinion of the Conference, the following Articles supply a basis on which approach may be, by God's blessing, made towards Home Reunion:

(*a*) The Holy Scriptures of the Old and New Testaments, as 'containing all things necessary to salvation', and as being the rule and ultimate standard of faith.

(*b*) The Apostles' Creed as the Baptismal Symbol; and the Nicene Creed, as the sufficient statement of the Christian Faith.

(*c*) The two sacraments ordained by Christ himself – Baptism and the Supper of the Lord – ministered with unfailing use of Christ's words of Institution, and of the elements ordained by Him.

(*d*) The Historic Episcopate, locally adapted in the methods of its administration to the varying needs of the nations and peoples called of God into the Unity of His Church.

Appendix 2
Lambeth On Authority, 1948

(A Committee Report approved by the Lambeth Conference of 1948.)

THE MEANING AND UNITY OF THE ANGLICAN COMMUNION
The world is in grievous disorder and needs to be restored to the order which God wills. A perplexed generation is in search of an authority to which to give its allegiance, and easily submits to the appeal of authoritarian systems whether religious or secular in character.

The question is asked, 'Is Anglicanism based on a sufficiently coherent form of authority to form the nucleus of a world-wide fellowship of Churches, or does its comprehensiveness conceal internal divisions which may cause its disruption?'

Former Lambeth Conferences have wisely rejected proposals for a formal primacy of Canterbury, for an Appellate Tribunal, and for giving the Conference the status of a legislative synod. The Lambeth Conference remains advisory, and its continuation committee consultative.

These decisions have led to a repudiation of centralized government, and a refusal of a legal basis of union.

The positive nature of the authority which binds the Anglican Communion together is therefore seen to be moral and spiritual, resting on the truth of the Gospel, and on a charity which is patient and willing to defer to the common mind.

Authority, as inherited by the Anglican Communion from the undivided Church of the early centuries of the Christian era, is single in that it is derived from a single Divine source, and reflects within itself the richness and historicity of the divine Revelation, the authority of the eternal Father, the incarnate Son, and the life-giving Spirit. It is distributed among Scripture, Tradition, Creeds, the Ministry of the Word and Sacraments, the witness of saints, and the *consensus fidelium*, which is the continuing experience of the Holy Spirit through His faithful people in the Church. It is thus a dispersed rather than a centralized authority having many elements which combine, interact with, and check each other; these elements together contributing by a process of mutual support, mutual checking, and redressing of errors or exaggerations to the many-sided fullness of the authority which Christ has committed to His Church. Where this authority of Christ is to be found mediated not in one mode but in several we recognize in this multiplicity God's loving provision against the temptations to tyranny and the dangers of unchecked power.

This authority possesses a suppleness and elasticity in that the emphasis of one element over the others may and does change with the changing conditions of the Church. The variety of the contributing factors gives to it a quality of richness which encourages and releases initiative, trains in fellowship, and evokes a free and willing obedience.

It may be said that authority of this kind is much harder to understand and obey than authority of a more imperious character. This is true and we glory in the appeal which it makes to faith. Translated into personal terms it is simple and intelligible. God who is our ultimate personal authority demands of all His creatures entire and unconditional obedience. As in human families the father is the mediator of this divine authority, so in the family of the Church is the bishop, the Father-in-God, wielding his authority by virtue of his divine commission and in synodical association with his clergy and laity, and exercising it in humble submission, as himself under authority.

The elements in authority are, moreover, in organic relation to each other. Just as the discipline of the scientific method proceeds from the collection of data to the ordering of these data in formulae, the publishing of results obtained, and their verification by experience, so Catholic Christianity presents us with an organic process of life and thought in which religious experience has been, and is, described, intellectually ordered, mediated, and verified.

This experience is *described* in Scripture, which is authoritative because it is the unique and classical record of the revelation of God in His relation to and dealings with man. While Scripture therefore remains the ultimate standard of faith, it should be continually interpreted in the context of the Church's life.

It is *defined* in Creeds and in continuous theological study.

It is *mediated* in the Ministry of the Word and Sacraments, by persons who are called and commissioned by God through the Church to represent both the transcendent and immanent elements in Christ's authority.

It is *verified* in the witness of saints and in the *consensus fidelium*. The Christ-like life carries its own authority, and the authority of doctrinal formulations, by General Councils or otherwise, rests at least in part on their acceptance by the whole body of the faithful, though the weight of this *consensus* 'does not depend on mere numbers or on the extension of a belief at any one time, but on continuance through the ages, and the extent to which the *consensus* is genuinely free.'

This essentially Anglican authority is reflected in our adherence to episcopacy as the source and centre of our order, and the Book of Common Prayer as the standard of our worship. Liturgy, in the sense of the offering and ordering of the public worship of God, is the crucible in which these elements of authority are fused and unified in the fellowship and power of the Holy Spirit. It is the Living and Ascended Christ present in the worshipping congregation who is the meaning and unity of the whole Church. He presents it to the Father, and sends it out on its mission.

We therefore urge the whole Conference to call upon every member of the Anglican Communion to examine himself in respect of his obligation to public worship.

We recognize that our fellow-Churchmen in some parts of the world do not always express themselves in worship according to Western patterns, and that they must have generous liberty of experiment in liturgy; and we therefore reaffirm Resolutions 36 and 37 of the Conference of 1920.

But we appeal to those who are responsible for the ordering and conduct of public worship to remember how bewildered the laity are by differences of use, and with what earnest care and charity they should be helped to take their full share in liturgical worship.

We consider that the time has come to examine those 'features in the Book of Common Prayer which are essential to the safeguarding of the unity of the Anglican Communion' (Resolution 37, 1920) and the Recommendations of Committee IV of 1920.

Appendix 3
Chinese Church Order, 1991

(H) CHURCH ORDER FOR TRIAL USE IN CHINESE CHURCHES
Passed by the Standing Committee of the Chinese Christian Three-Self Patriotic Movement (TSPM) and the China Christian Council (CCC), December 30, 1991.

PREFACE

Under the loving guidance of our heavenly Father, the vast majority of local churches in China have already embarked upon the path of church unity. In order to strengthen self-government so that 'all things be done decently and in order' in Christ's Church, Christian Councils and Three-Self organisations in more than twenty provinces, autonomous regions and municipalities have, since 1984, drafted church orders of their own for trial use. In 1987, the Standing Committees of the CCC and the TSPM passed the 'Resolution on the Advancement of Self Government through the drafting of a Church Order' and established a 'Committee on Church Order' to promote and assist local Christian church affairs organisations in the drafting and perfecting of church orders, and to draft a model church order for use all over China as a standard for the reference of local churches. The basic content of this church order is drafted in accordance with the teachings of the Bible, the inheritance of church tradition and the life of the Church ecumenical, and integrated with the actual context of the Church in China today; it has its own Chinese characteristics. According to present needs, there are special sections on the Church, believers, the sacraments, ministry, churches and meeting points and administration. Because there are differences in the history, denominational background and pattern of development of churches in different parts of China, church affairs organisations in different provinces, autonomous regions and municipalities may draft or revise their own church orders according to this one, or implement thier own rules and regulations. Because some churches and meeting-points have significant differences in viewpoint and tradition with the Church as a whole, they can develop according to their own traditions, providing they do not violate the Three-Self principle. Where there is the need, the local church affairs organisation should serve and resolve differences with these churches and meeting-points.

MINISTRY

1. Ministerial Designations:

The ministry refers to ordained church workers who can administer the sacraments. Churches in China at present use the following ministerial designations which follow the Bible and church tradition:

Bishop (two different Chinese terms are used, reflecting different church traditions) – where conditions permit and there is a need, provinces, municipalities and autonomous regions may consecrate bishops. A bishop has a wider area of pastoral responsibility, but does not have special administrative authority.

Pastor (including specially ordained elders whose function is similar to that of pastors, here and in what follows) – responsible for church work of all kinds, the management of churches and meeting points, the administration of sacraments, the nurture and teaching of believers.

Teacher (or Assistant Pastor) – assists the pastor in the nurture and teaching of believers, the management of churches and meeting points, and may also administer the sacraments.

Elder – assists pastors and teachers in the management of churches and meeting points, where his or her responsibility is limited to a specific church and related meeting points. If needed, elders may also take part in the nurture and teaching of believers, and the administration of sacraments.

In addition, there may be church workers who have not yet been ordained, and who do not administer the sacraments, but who have been appointed or elected by the church and approved by the church affairs organisation, and are designated as follows:

Preacher (Missionary) – Preachers who have received theological education or special training may preach and nurture believers.

Deacon – a believer responsible for church affairs. Clergy and preachers (missionaries) are commonly called pastoral workers.

The foregoing designations may be adopted by churches according to their original traditions and actual conditions.

2. Qualifications for Ministry:

2.1 The Bible requires that all male and female ministers should have (i) a pure Christian faith and a rich spiritual life; (ii) an excellent character, behaviour and witness; (iii) a will to serve Christ and experience in church service; (iv) the love and esteem of the majority of believers.

2.2 Clergy should be patriotic and law-abiding, with a good reputation in church and society.

2.3 Clergy should uphold the Three-Self principle in running the church well, uniting believers on the road of love-country and love-church, glorifying God and serving humanity, and should practice mutual respect regarding the special characteristics of different Christian beliefs. These three qualifications also apply to preachers.

2.4 A bishop should have a solid theological background, should have been a pastor for at least ten years, and should have rich pastoral experience in church work and be held in high esteem by believers.

2.5 Pastors should have had formal theological education, and about three years of experience in church work. Teachers should also have some formal theological education, and about two years of experience in church work. Those who have studied the Bible and theology on their own should pass an examiniation to make sure they are up to standard.

2.6 Elders are not required to have theological education, but they should uphold orthodox teaching and have many years' experience of service to the church. Elders should have some training before they are eligible to preach.

3. Procedures for the Ordination of Ministry:

3.1 The consecration of bishops should be proposed by the provincial church affairs organisation, after due consultation and discussion with the national church bodies.

3.2 Candidates qualified to be pastors or teachers should first apply in writing for ordination, and, following approval by their local church, should be recommended by their local church affairs organisation or two pastors to the provincial church affairs organisation. The provincial church affairs organisation shall select three or more pastors to form an ordination committee and examine the candidate(s). If the candidate is qualified, the ordination will be held within a fixed period of time.

3.3 Candidates qualified to be elders should apply with the recommendation of their local church organisation. The local or city church affairs organisation shall select three or more pastors and elders to form an ordination committee and examine the candidate(s). If the candidate is qualified, the ordination will take place within a fixed period of time, and it will be reported to the provincial church affairs organisation for the record.

4. The Liturgy for the Ordination of Ministry:

4.1 At least three bishops and other respected pastors of high standing, all of whom take part in the laying on of hands, are required for the consecration of a bishop.

4.2 At least three pastors are required for the laying on of hands in the ordination of a pastor.

4.3 At least three pastors and elders, one of whom must be a pastor, are required for the ordination of an elder.

4.4 The liturgy of ordination should be solemn and conducted openly within the church. Clergy should not receive or give private favours for ordination.

Select Bibliography

BOOKS
(Published in London unless otherwise stated.)

Ainslie, J. L., *The Doctrines of Ministerial Order in the Reformed Churches of the 16th and 17th Centuries*. T. and T. Clark, Edinburgh, 1940.

Allen, R., *Missionary Methods: St Paul's or Ours?* R. Scott, 1912.

Allen, R., *The Case for Voluntary Clergy*, Eyre and Spottiswoode, 1930.

Althaus, P., *The Theology of Martin Luther*, (Eng. Trans.) Fortress Press, Philadelphia, 1970.

Anderson, R. S. (ed.), *Theological Foundations for Ministry*, T. and T. Clark, Edinburgh, 1979.

Arnold, T., *Principles of Church Reform*. SPCK, 1833/1962.

Aune, D. E., *Prophecy in Early Christianity and the Ancient Mediterranean World*. Eerdmans, Grand Rapids, 1983.

Baelz, P. R. and Jacob, W., *Ministers of the Kingdom: Exploration in Non-Stipendiary Ministry*. CIO, 1985.

Baillie, D. M., *The Theology of the Sacraments*. Faber, 1957.

Bainton, R. H., *Studies on the Reformation*. Hodder, 1964.

Barry, F. R., *The Relevance of the Church*, Nisbet, 1935.

Barry, F. R. *Vocation and Ministry*. Nisbet, 1958.

Bernstein, B. B., *Class, Codes and Control, Vol. III*, Routledge, 1975.

Bonhoeffer, D., *Letters and Papers from Prison*. (Enlarged ed.) Ed. E. Bethge, SCM, 1971.

Browne, R. E. C. *The Ministry of the Word*. SCM, 1958/1976.

Campenhausen, H. von, *Ecclesiastical Authority and Spiritual Power in the Church of the First Three Centuries*. (Eng. Trans.) Black, 1969.

Card, T. *Priesthood and Ministry in Crisis*. SCM, 1988.

Carey, K. M., *The Historic Episcopate*, Dacre, 1954.

Carr, W., *The Priestlike Task*. SPCK, 1985.

Chadwick, O., *The Victorian Church*, Parts I and II. Black, 1966 and 1970.

Chu, T. and Lind, C., *A New Beginning*. Canada Church Programme of the Canadian Council of Churches, Canada, 1983.

Collins, J. N., *Diakonia*, OUP, Oxford, 1990.

Cooke, B., *Ministry to the Word and Sacraments*. Fortress, Philadelphia, 1976.

Cross, F. L. (ed.), *The Oxford Dictionary of the Christian Church*, OUP, 1957.

Delorme, J. et al., *Le Ministère et les Ministères selon le Nouveau Testament*. Seuil, Paris, 1974.

Dickens, A. G., *The Counter Reformation*. Thames and Hudson, 1968.

Donovan, V. J., *Christianity Rediscovered: An Epistle from the Masai*. SCM, 1978.

Dulles, A., *The Catholicity of the Church*. OUP, Oxford, 1987.

Dunstan, G. R. (ed.), *The Sacred Ministry*, SPCK, 1971.

Ecclestone, G. (ed.), *The Parish Church?* Mowbray, Oxford, 1988.

Farrer, A., *A Celebration of Faith*. Hodder, 1970.

Francis, L. J., *Rural Anglicanism: A Future for Young Christians?* Collins, 1985.

Frend, W. H. C., *The Rise of Christianity*. Darton, 1984.

Fuller, J. and Vaughan, P. (edd.), *Working for the Kingdom: The Story of Ministers in Secular Employment*. SPCK, 1986.

Fung, R. (ed.), *Households of God on China's Soil*, WCC, Geneva, 1982.

Furlong, M. (ed.) *Feminine in the Church*. SPCK, 1984.

Gerbé, P. and Daniel, Y. (edd.), *Aujourd'hui la Mission de France*. Le Centurion, Paris, 1981.

Gray, D. *Earth and Altar: The Evolution of the Parish Communion in the Church of England to 1945*. Canterbury Press, Norwich, 1986.

Grollenberg, L. et al., *Minister, Pastor, Prophet?* (Eng. Trans.) SCM 1980.

Gunton C. E. and Hardy, D. W. (edd.), *On Being the Church: Essays on the Christian Community*. T. and T. Clark, Edinburgh, 1989.

Habgood, J., *Church and Nation in a Secular Age*. Darton, 1983.

Haendler G., *Luther on Ministerial Office and Function*. (Eng. Trans.) Fortress, Philadelphia, 1981.

Haig, A., *The Victorian Clergy*, Croom Helm, 1984.

Hardy D. W. and Sedgwick, P. H. (edd.), *The Weight of Glory: A Vision and Practice for Christian Faith: The Future of Liberal Theology*. T. and T. Clark, 1991.

Hastings, A. *A History of English Christianity 1920–1985*. Collins, 1986.

Hastings, A. (ed.), *Modern Catholicism: Vatican II and After*. SPCK, 1991.

Heaton, E. W. *The Hebrew Kingdoms*. OUP, 1968.

Herbert, G., *A Choice of George Herbert's Verse*, ed. R. S. Thomas, Faber, 1967/1988.

Hill, D., *New Testament Prophecy*. Marshall, Morgan & Scott, 1979.

Hopko, T., *Women and the Priesthood*. St Vladimir's Seminary Press, New York, 1983.

Hurst, A., *Rendering unto Caesar: Towards a Framework for Integrating Paid Employment with Christian Belief*. Churchman, Worthing, 1986.

Hylson-Smith, K., *Evangelicals in the Church of England 1734–1984*. T. and T. Clark, Edinburgh, 1988.

Kinsler, F. R. (ed.), *Ministry by the People*. WCC, Geneva, 1983.

Kirk, K. E., *The Apostolic Ministry (2nd edn)*. Hodder, 1962.

Kruse, C. G., *New Testament Foundations for Ministry*. Marshall, 1983.

Küng, H., *The Church*. Burns & Oates, 1969.

Küng, H., *Why Priests?* Collins, 1972.

Lambourne, R. A., *Explorations in Health and Salvation: A Selection of Papers, edited by M. Wilson*. University of Birmingham, 1983.

Lightfoot, J. B., *The Apostolic Fathers*. Macmillan, 1891/1926.

Lightfoot, J. B., *The Christian Ministry: A Dissertation, in St Paul's Epistle to the Philippians*. Macmillan, 1868/1890.

Luther, M., *Werke, Kritische Gesamtausgabe*. Bohlau, Weimar, 1883-.

Luther, M., *Werke: Briefwechsel*. Bohlau, Weimar, 1930–1948.

Luther, M., *Works, (American edition)*. Fortress, Philadelphia, 1955-.

Maurice, F. D., *The Kingdom of Christ: or Hints on the Principles, Ordinances and Constitution of the Catholic Church in Letters to a Member of the Society of Friends*. Darton & Clark, 1838, 2nd edn, revised, Rivington, 1842.

Moberly, R. C., *Ministerial Priesthood*. 2nd edn, SPCK 1910/1969.

Moore, P. (ed.), *Bishops: But What Kind?* SPCK, 1982.

Moore, P. (ed.), *The Synod of Westminster: Do We Need It?* SPCK 1986.

Moule, C. F. D., *The Sacrifice of Christ*. Hodder, 1956.

Moyser, G. (ed.), *Church and Politics Today*. T. and T. Clark, Edinburgh, 1985.

Niebuhr, H. R., *The Purpose of the Church and its Ministry*. Harper, New York, 1956.

Norman, E. R., *The Victorian Christian Socialists*, CUP, Cambridge, 1987.

Paton, D. M. (ed.), *The Ministry of the Spirit: Selected Writings of Roland Allen*. World Dominion Press, 1960.

Pattison, S., *A Critique of Pastoral Care*. SCM, 1988.

Peberdy, A., *Women Priests?* Marshall Pickering, Basingstoke, 1988.

Penhale, F. *Catholics in Crisis*. Mowbray, Oxford, 1986.

Perrin, H., *Priest Workmen in Germany*. Sheed & Ward, 1947.

Pickering, W. S. F., *Anglo-Catholicism: A Study in Religious Ambiguity*. Routledge, 1989.

Polanyi, M., *Personal Knowledge*. Routledge, 1957.

Preston, R. H., *Church and Society in the Late Twentieth Century: the Economic and Political Task*. SCM, 1983.

Quick, O. C., *Doctrines of the Creed: Their Basis in Scripture and Their Meaning Today*. Nisbet, 1938.

Rack, H. D., *Reasonable Enthusiast: John Wesley and the Rise of Methodism*. Epworth, 1989.

Ramsey, A. M., *From Gore to Temple*. Longmans, 1960.

Ramsey, A. M., *The Christian Priest Today*. (2nd edn) SPCK 1985.

Ramsey, A. M., *The Gospel and the Catholic Church*. Longmans, 1936/ 1964

Ramsey, I. T., *Religious Language*. SCM 1957.

Roberts, T., *Partners and Ministers*. CPAS, 1972.

Rowell, G. (ed.), *Tradition Renewed: The Oxford Movement Conference Papers*. Darton, 1986.

Rudge, P. F., *Ministry and Management*. Tavistock, 1968.

Russell, A., (ed.), *Groups and Teams in the Countryside*. SPCK, 1975.

Russell, A., *The Clerical Profession*, SPCK, 1980.

Russell, A., *The Country Parish*. SPCK, 1986.

Santer, M. (ed.), *Their Lord and Ours: Approaches to Authority, Community and the Unity of the Church*. SPCK, 1982.

Schillebeeckx, E., *Ministry: A Case for Change*. SCM, 1980.

Schroeder, H. J., *Canons and Decrees of the Council of Trent*. Herder, St Louis, 1941.

Selwyn, E. G., *The First Epistle of St Peter*. Macmillan, 1947.

Shaw, G., *The Cost of Authority*. SCM, 1983.

Sheppard, D. and Worlock, D., *Better Together*. Hodder, 1988.

Siefer, G., *The Church and Industrial Society* (originally *Die Mission der Arbeiterpriester)*. Darton, 1964.

Smyth, C., *Simeon and Church Order*. CUP, Cambridge, 1940.

Steele, D. A., *Images of Leadership and Authority for the Church: Biblical Principles and Secular Models*. University Press of America, Lanham, 1986.

Stevenson, J., *A New Eusebius: Documents Illustrative of the Church to AD337*. SPCK, 1957.

Suhard, E., *The Pastoral Letters of Cardinal Suhard*. Chapman, 1955.

Swete, H. B., *Essays on the Early History of the Church and the Ministry*. Macmillan, 1917.

Sykes, N., *Church and State in England in the Eighteenth Century*. CUP, 1934.

Sykes, N., *Old Priest and New Presbyter*. CUP, Cambridge, 1956.

Sykes, S. W. (ed.), *Authority in the Anglican Communion*. Anglican Book Centre, Toronto, 1987.

Sykes, S. W., *The Integrity of Anglicanism*, Mowbray, Oxford, 1978.

Teilhard de Chardin, P. *Hymn of the Universe*, Collins, 1965.

Terwilliger, R. E. and Holmes U. T. (edd.), *To Be a Priest: Perspectives on Vocation and Ordination*. Seabury, New York, 1975.

Thomas, R. S. (ed.), *A Choice of George Herbert's Verse*. Faber, 1967/1988.

Thomas, R. S., *Not That He Brought Flowers*. Hart-Davis, 1969.

Thurian, M., *Priesthood and Ministry*. Mowbray, 1983.

Ting, K. H. (Ding Guangxun), *No Longer Strangers: Selected Writings of K. H. Ting, ed. R. L. Whitehead*. Orbis, Maryknoll, 1989.

Vidler, A. R., *Essays in Liberality*. SCM 1957.

Vidler, A. R. *The Theology of F. D. Maurice*. SCM, 1948.

Warkentin, M. *Ordination: A Biblical-Historical View*. Eerdmans, Grand Rapids, 1982.

Welsby, P. A., *A History of the Church of England 1945-1980*. OUP, Oxford, 1984.

Wendel, F., *Calvin: The Origins and Development of His Religious Thought*. Collins, 1963/1972.

Whitehead, A. N., *Science and the Modern World*. CUP, Cambridge, 1926.

Whyte, B., *Unfinished Encounter: China and Christianity*. Collins. 1988.

Williams, G. H., *The Radical Reformation*. Weidenfeld, 1962.

Wilson, K. (ed.), *The Experience of Ordination*, Epworth, 1979.

Wilson, M., *The Hospital – A Place of Truth: A Study in the Role of the Hospital Chaplain*. University of Birmingham, 1971.

Young, F. M., *Sacrifice and the Death of Christ*. SPCK, 1975.

REPORTS

Anglican-Lutheran Dialogue. The Report of the Anglican-Lutheran European Regional Commission, Helsinki, August-September 1982. SPCK, 1983.

Anglican-Orthodox Dialogue: The Dublin Agreed Statement, 1984. SPCK, 1984.

Baptism, Eucharist and Ministry. Faith and Order Paper No. 111, World Council of Churches. Geneva, 1982.

Believing in the Church: the Corporate Nature of Faith. A report by the Doctrine Commission of the Church of England, SPCK, 1981.

By What Authority? The Open Synod Report on Authority in the Church of England (ed. R. Jeffery). Mowbray, Oxford, 1987.

Call to Order: Vocation and Ministry in the Church of England. Advisory Council for the Church's Ministry, 1989.

Children in the Way: New Directions for the Church's Children. National Society, 1988.

[The] Church in the Mining Communities: The Report of a Working Party appointed by the Diocesan Social Responsibility Committee, Sheffield, 1988.

Deacons in the Church: The Report of a Working Party set up by the Advisory Council for the Church's Ministry, CIO, 1974.

Deacons in the Ministry of the Church: A Report to the House of Bishops of the General Synod of the Church of England, 1988.

Doctrine in the Church of England: The Report of the Commission on Christian Doctrine Appointed by the Archbishops of Canterbury and York in 1922. SPCK, 1938.

[The] Documents of Vatican II ed. W. M. Abbott. Chapman, 1967.

Education for the Church's Ministry: The Report of the Working Party on Assessment. Advisory Council for the Church's Ministry, 1987.

Episcopal Ministry: A Report by the Archbishops' Group on the Episcopate. Church House Publishing, 1990.

Experience and Authority: Issues Underlying Doing Theology. Advisory Council for the Church's Ministry, 1984.

Faith in the City: A Call for Action by Church and Nation. The Report of the Archbishop's Commission on Urban Priority Areas. Church House Publishing, 1985.

[The] Final Report. Anglican-Roman Catholic International Commission, SPCK and CTS, 1982.

For the Sake of the Kingdom: God's Church and the New Creation. Inter-Anglican Theological and Doctrinal Commission, Church House Publishing, 1986.

God's Reign and Our Unity: The Report of The Anglican-Reformed International Commission. SPCK, 1984.

Guidelines for Local Non-Stipendiary Ministry. Advisory Council for the Church's Ministry, 1987.

Homosexual Relationships: A Contribution to Discussion. General Synod Board for Social Responsibility, CIO, 1979.

[An] Honorary Ministry. W. H. Saumarez Smith, for the Advisory Council for the Church's Ministry, 1977.

Industrial Mission – An Appraisal. Board for Social Responsibility, Church House, 1988.

[An] Integrating Theology. Advisory Council for the Church's Ministry, 1983.

Inter Insigniores. In 'Vatican II: More Post-Conciliar Documents', ed. A. Flannery. Fowler Wright, Leominster, 1982.

Issues in Human Sexuality: A Statement by the House of Bishops of the General Synod of the Church of England, December 1991. Church House Publishing, 1991.

Lambeth Conference 1948; Encyclical Letter from the Bishops together with the Resolutions and Reports. SPCK 1948.

Lambeth Conference 1958; The Encyclical letter from the Bishops together with the Resolutions and Reports, SPCK, 1958.

Lambeth Conference 1968; Resolutions and Reports. SPCK, 1968.

Lambeth Conference 1978; Report. CIO Publishing, 1978.

Learning and Teaching in Theological Education. Advisory Council for the Church's Ministry, 1982.

[The] Ministry in the Church. Roman Catholic/Lutheran Joint Commission. Lutheran World Federation, Geneva, 1982.

[The] Nature of Christian Belief: A Statement and Exposition by the House of Bishops of the General Synod of the Church of England, Church House Publishing, 1986.

Non-Stipendiary Ministry in the Church of England. M. Hodge for the Advisory Council for the Church's Ministry. CIO, 1983.

Ordained Ministry in Secular Employment. Advisory Council for the Church's Ministry, 1989.

[The] Ordained Ministry: Numbers, Cost and Deployment: A Discussion Paper from the Ministry Co-ordinating Group, General Synod of the Church of England, 1988.

Ordained Ministry Today. Advisory Council for the Church's Ministry. CIO, 1969.

Ordination of Women in Ecumenical Perspective. ed. C. F. Parvey. Faith and Order Paper 105. WCC, Geneva, 1980.

[The] Ordination of Women to the Priesthood. Advisory Council for the Church's Ministry, CIO, 1972.

[The] Ordination of Women to the Priesthood. A Second Report by the House of Bishops. General Synod, 1988.

Patterns of Ministerial Training in the Theological Colleges and Courses. M. Hodge. Advisory Council for the Church's Ministry, 1986.

Patterns of Ministry. M. A. H. Melinsky, for the Advisory Council for the Church's Ministry. CIO, 1974.

[The] Place of Auxiliary Ministry, Ordained and Lay. Advisory Council for the Church's Ministry, 1973.

Regulations for Non-Stipendiary Ministry. Advisory Council for the Church's Ministry, on behalf of the House of Bishops, 1987.

Report to the Bench of Bishops of the Working Group on the Self-Supporting Ministry. The Governing Body of the Church in Wales Publications, Penarth, 1981.

Response of the Holy See to the Final Report of ARCIC. Catholic Truth Society, 1991.

Selection for Ministry: A Report on Criteria. Advisory Council for the Church's Ministry, 1983.

Specialised Ministries. Advisory Council for the Church's Ministry, CIO, 1971.

Spirituality in Ordination Training. Advisory Council for the Church's Ministry, 1981.

[A] Strategy for the Church's Ministry. J. Tiller, for the Advisory Council for the Church's Ministry. CIO, 1983.

[A] Supporting Ministry, being the Report of a Working Party of the Ministry Committee of the Advisory Council for the Church's Ministry on Priests in Auxiliary Parochial Ministries in the Church of England. CIO, 1968.

Team and Group Ministries. General Synod, 1985.

[The] Theology of Ordination: A report by the Faith and Order Advisory Group. General Synod, 1975.

[The] Time is Now. Anglican Consultative Council First Meeting, Limuru, Kenya. SPCK, 1971.

Today's Church and Today's World, with a Special Focus on the Ministry of Bishops. Preparatory articles for the Lambeth Conference 1978. CIO, 1977.

Towards a Church of England Response to BEM and ARCIC. Faith and Order Advisory Group. CIO, 1985.

ARTICLES

Dyson, A. O., 'Theology and the Educational Principles in Ministerial Training: Problems of Collection Codes and Integrated Codes.' *Kairos* No. 6, 1982.

Hollenweger, W. J., 'After Twenty Years Research on Pentecostalism.' *Theology*, November 1984, SPCK.

Hollenweger, W. J., 'Creator Spiritus: The Challenge of Pentecostal

Experience to Pentecostal Theology.' *Theology*, January 1978, SPCK.

Jones, A., 'New Vision for the Episcopate?' *Theology*, July 1978. SPCK.

Lambourne, R. A., 'With Love to the USA' in *Religion and Medicine. Vol. I*, ed. M. A. H. Melinsky, SCM, 1970.

Mathers, J. R., 'The Pastoral Role: A Psychiatrist's View.' in *Religion and Medicine, Vol. II*, ed. M. A. H. Melinsky, SCM, 1973.

Melinsky, M. A. H., 'One Anglican's Experience of Non-Stipendiary Ministry.' *Epworth Review*, January 1981. Methodist Publishing House.

Ramsey, I. T., 'Durham', in *All One Body*, ed. T. Wilson, Darton, 1969.

Ranken, M., 'A Theology for the Priest at Work.' *Theology*, March 1982, SPCK.

Schillebeeckx, E. and Metz, J. B. edd, 'The Right of the Community to a Priest.' *Concilium*, March 1980, T. and T. Clark, Edinburgh.

Thrall, M., 'Christian Vocation Today.' *Theology*, March 1976, SPCK.

(Note: In 1991 the Church of England's Advisory Council for the Church's Ministry was re-named Advisory Board for Ministry.)

Index

Aachen 61
Abba 'Father' 166
Act of Uniformity (1662) 97
Action Catholique Générale 224
Actius, archdeacon 132
Adam 'mankind' 196
adult education
    affected by theology 257
    beginnings of 48
    bishops' teaching ministry
        151–155
    continuing ministerial education
        261
    danger of too much 250
    in parish 210
    methods of 143
    minister as enabler 248
    purpose of 143
    role of universities 165
    theology in universities 155
    world-of-work groups 224
Agrarian Revolution 206
Alexander, bishop 132
Allen, Roland 229–230
Alternative Service Book (1980) 104,
    106
Ambrose, bishop
    achievements re church and state
        58
Anabaptists
    and vocation 246
    flight to Bohemia and Moravia 84
    in England 84
    origin of name 81
    persecution of 83
Andrewes, Lancelot, bishop 96
Anglican-Reformed reunion 191–3

Anglo-Catholicism (see also Oxford
    Movement) 104–7
    A–C Congresses 106
    A–C priests in slum parishes 109
Anselm, archbishop
    doctrine of atonement 65
apostle (Greek, *apostolos*)
    authority of 17–25
    meaning of word 6
    Paul and James 245
    Paul and the Twelve 19, 245
    Paul's call 245
    the Twelve 17
Apostolic Constitutions 203
apostolic succession
    at Trent 90
    in 2nd century 36
    for Irenaeus 152
    for Keble and Newman 104
    for Maurice 151
Aquila and Priscilla 200, 227
A.R.C.I.C.
    Reports xii, 185–6, 189–90
Arles, Council of (314) 152
The Army and Religion 105
Arnold, Thomas
    and the diaconate 229
Athanasian Creed 197
Athanasius, bishop 132
audit, parish 211–13
Augsburg Confession
    and vocation 246
    Lutheran dissatisfaction with 257
Augustine, bishop of Hippo
    and ordination of women 203
    on the eucharist 52–3
Austen, Jane 252

Australia
Anglican-Uniting Church
conversations 193
C. of E. in 178–9
Authorised Version (of Bible) (1611) 98
authority 173–184
a. of apostles 17–25
a. of Jesus 11–16, 173
Anglican doctrine of 174f., 270–2
Authority in the Anglican Communion
179
Authority in the Church
ARCIC Report 185
Auxiliary Pastoral Ministry 233
(see Non-Stipendiary Ministry)

Baelz, P. R. 176
on spirituality 250
baptism
administration by laity 140
by immersion 86
preparation for 140, 208, 210
the primary sacrament 140
Baptism, Eucharist and Ministry
(W. C. C. Report, 1982) 185,
192–3
Baptists
founding of first B. church 86
indirect heirs of radical reformers
82
Use of deacons 133
Barry, F. R., bishop
advocate of N. S. M. 230
base communities
of Latin America 219
basilica (see Church Buildings)
Believing in the Church
(C. of E. Report, 1981) 154
Benedict XII, pope 64
Benedictine Order
symbol of stability 60–1
Bethnal Green
local ministry at 237
Bible Churchmen's Missionary
Society
split from C.M.S. 103
bishop (Greek *episkopos*) 150–7
meaning of word 8

and early reformers 94
appointment of 156
as administrator 155–6
as conserver of tradition 154–5
as disciplinarian 156
as father-in-God 167
as imperial officer 158
as judge 31
as martyr 157
as missioner 157
as sign of unity 150–1
as sign of disunity 152
as 'superintendent' 94
as teacher 154–5
in *1 Clement* 27–8
in *Didachē* 24–5
in Ignatius 28–30, 150
in China 118, 120–1, 274
in N. Africa in 5th cent. 56
in synod 153f.
intellectual demands on 264
Luther's bishop 150
monarchical system of 31
qualities of, in 1 Tim. 31
b's seat in basilica 56
succession of, in C. of E. 93
The Bishops' Report (Scotland, 1957)
191
Blackburne, Hugh, Canon 217
Blaurock, George 83
Bloom, Anthony, archbishop 200
Bogo de Aare 67
Bonhoeffer, Dietrich 232
Book of Common Prayer
on vocation 246
Bramhall, John, bishop 96
British Holistic Medical
Association 165
British Medical Association 165
Bronte sisters 103
Bucer, Martin
Anabaptist leader 83
at Ratisbon 88
influence of on Cranmer 246
Butler, Christopher, bishop 188

Caecilian, bishop 132
Callistus, deacon 132

Calvin, John 77–81
  and Geneva magistracy 78–9
  and formation of colleges 81
  and ministry 77–8
  and parity of ministers 80
  and spiritual authority 80
  and total depravity 81
  and vocation 246
  Institutes 77–8
Calvinism
  dress of ministers 79
  emphasis on preaching 80
  in England 80
  in Scotland 80
  in South Africa 81
  ministerial authority in 80
  pastoral care by ministers 80
Camara, Helder, archbishop 157
Cambridge
  theology at 252
Cambridge Inter-Collegiate
    Christian Union
  split from S. C. M. 103
Camden Society
  formed, Cambridge, 1839 105
Canton, R. C. archbishop of 187
Cartwright, Thomas
  Puritan divine 95
The Case for Voluntary Clergy 230
Castellum Tingitanum
    (Mauretania)
  basilica at, AD 324 57
celibacy of clergy
  debate at Nicaea, 325 54
  emphasised by Clichtove 91
  example of apostles 54
  of English clergy in 13th cent. 68
  required by Thomas Aquinas 133
Cenchreae, Greece 200
charismatic
  c. movements 48, 110–13
  c. qualifications for ministry 82
  for Paul, every Christian a c. 23
  ecstatic possession in Montanism
    38
Charlemagne
  crowned 800 first Holy Roman
    Emperor 61

Charles II, king 97
Chicago 264
The Child in the Church 144
Children in the Way 144
China Christian Council
  set up in 1980 118
  ministry and training 119–23,
    273–5
  statistics, 1988 118
China, Christianity in (see also
    China Christian Council and
    C. C. P. A.)
  first N. S. M. ordinations 230
Chinese Catholic Patriotic
    Association
  and the Vatican 117, 187
Chittleborough K. S. 179
Chloe 200
Christian Believing
  C. of E. report, 1976 154
Christian Socialism 107–10
  (see also Maurice F. D.)
Chrysostom, John, bishop
  on the eucharist 53
  on manual labour 227
  on ordination of women 203
Chu, T. 187
church (see also Parish)
  a compulsory society 60
  and empire inseparable 59
  and kingdom of God xiii, 208–9,
    211
  and local community 211–16
  and social action
  associational model of 207–8
  communal model of 208
  controlling whole of life 66
  division of east from west 62
  c. government for Paul 24
  growth of papal government in 62
  growth of c. litigation in 13th
    cent. 63
  in England in 13th cent. 66–70
  union of c. and state 159
Church and Politics Today 212
church buildings
  adaptation of 209
  at Cirta, AD 303 57

church buildings – *cont'd.*
At Dura Europos, AD 200–231 55
basilica 56
in N. Africa, 3rd and 4th centt.
57
in Rome by AD 150 54
no special ones built for first 3
centt. 54
places for clergy in 56
secular buildings adapted 54–5
term used by Clement Alex. 54
*The Church in the Mining
Communities*
(Church of England report,
1988) 142, 144
Church of England 92–100
and ordination of women 205
and vocation 246–7
both catholic and reformed 92
failure of Methodist re-union
with 192
the national church 207
Church of North India 191
Church of South India 191
Church of Scotland
mixed polity in 16th cent. 95
rejected Bishops' Report, 1957
191–2
Cicero 227
Cirta, Numidia
basilica at, before 284 57
Clement of Alexandria 39
Clement VI, pope 64
Clement XIV, pope 116
clergy (see also Minister, Presbyter,
Priest)
as channel of supernatural
authority, 11th cent. 61
celibacy of 68
clerical ideal realised in 14th
cent. 61
clerici at Thamugadi, 363 57–8
definition of by Constantine 58
exemption from law-courts and
taxation 61
home and glebe in 13th cent. 68
number of c. in England in 13th
cent. 68

number needed in England today
266
recent decline in numbers xi, 214
used in government in 14th cent.
63
The Clerical Profession 163
Clichtove, Josse van
Roman priesthood shaped by 91
Coke, Thomas
appointed by Wesley for America
102
Colenso, J. W., bishop 103
Coleridge, S. T. 107
Collège de Montaigu 87–8
confessor
admitted to clergy without
ordination 43, 45
Congregation for the Doctrine of
the Faith 191
Congregational Federation 191
Congregationalists
favoured 'gathered congregation'
80
joined Presbyterians to form U.
R. C. 191
use of deacons 133
conscience, appeal to 176
consensus fidelium 175, 272
Constantine, emperor
and Council of Nicaea 174
legalised church 51
policy of religious toleration 51
support for church 55
Constantinople
quota of clergy under Justinian
158–9
Contarini, Gaspar, cardinal 88
continuing ministerial education
(see Adult Education,
Training of Clergy)
Convocation
suppression of, 1717 178
Corinth 200–202
Cornelius, bishop of Rome
list of stipendiary staff, AD 250
55, 131–2
'*corpus Christi*'
semantic shift 66

Council of Basle (1449) 87
Council of Chalcedon (451)
    not universally accepted 194
Council of Elvira (c. 304)
    canons concerning clergy 53
Council of Jerusalem (Acts 15)
    tradition broken at 174, 202
Council of Nicaea (325)
    acceptance of 189
    Athanasius at 132
    bishop Spyridon at 228
    canons defied 59
    Constantine and 174
    on bishop of Rome's authority 58
    on celibacy 54
    on consecration of bishops 152
Council of Trent (1545–1564)
    89–91
    and a conservative approach to
        Scripture 89
    and the establishment of
        seminaries 91
    and holy orders 90–91
    and the *Imprimatur* 89
    and the language of sacrifice 90
    and Latin as the language of the
        mass 90
    and private masses 90
    and transubstantiation 90
    throwback to Trent 191
Counter-Reformation 87–91
Cranmer, Thomas, archbishop
    and baptismal regeneration 101
    and Ordinal 246
    and Prayer Book of 1549 97
creation
    stories in Genesis 1–2, 196
Cromwell, Oliver 97
Cynic philosophers 227
Cyprian, bishop of Carthage 42–46
    and counsel of clergy and laity
        44, 177
    and martyrs 45
    and Novatian 42
    and penance 43–6
    and teaching authority 45
    death in 258 43
    doctrine of church 43

doctrine of episcopacy 44
doctrine of ordination 43
in Decian persecution 42
influence of 46

Darwin, Charles 103
deacon (Greek *diakonos*) 127–37
    dd. and laity 135
    as apprentice for priesthood
        136–7
    as authoritative spokesman for
        God 129
    as bishop's aide 131–2
    as an order 24–5, 129–32
    derivation of term 4, 128
    for Luther and Calvin 133
    for Thomas Aquinas 133
    in *Apostolic Tradition*, Hippolytus,
        Cyprian 131
    in *Didachē*, *Didaskalia* 131
    in England in 13th cent. 68
    in Ordinal of 1549 133–4
    in Polycarp, Ignatius 129
    in Pliny 130
    in Presbyterian and
        Congregational traditions 133
    permanent or distinctive order
        135
    proposed abolition of 136
    seats for dd. in basilica 56
    dd, subdeacons and archdeacons
        at Rome 131–2
    training for 137
    women as, in New Testament 5
    diakonissa 5
deaconess
    diakonissa and *ministra* 5, 130
    anomalous position in C. of E.
        134
    in Germany in 19th cent. 134
    dd. ordained deacons in C. of E.
        134
    order founded in C. of E., 1861
        134
Deacons in the Church (C. of E.
    report) 136
Deanery, rural 214
Deng Yiming, archbishop 187

Department of Health and Social
Security 236
Diet of Augsburg (1510) 87
Dillistone, F. W. 257
Diocese
Roman origin of term 57
Anglican unit of authority 178
Diocletian, emperor 55
Doctrine in the Church of England (C.
of E. report, 1938) 154
Donation of Constantine 61
Donatism
Caecilian and D. 132
D. basilicas in N. Africa 57
D. bishops in N. Africa 56
doulos (Greek, slave) 4
Downham, George 96
dress of ministers
in first four centuries 53
for Calvin 79
in C. of E. 105–6, 139
Durham 252

Eastern Orthodoxy
and ordination of women 195
and Roman primacy 186
beginnings of 47
in ecumenical conversations
193–4
Ebionites 37–8
Ecclestone, Alan 106
ecstasy, in Montanism 38
ecumenism
Anglican-Reformed reunion
191–3
ecum. aspects of ministry
185–194
and ordination of women 204–5
reunion failures xi–xii, 110
education (see also Adult
Education, Training of Clergy)
modern principles of 257
elder (see also Presbyter, Priest)
as a class in 1 Pet. 25
embryonic system in N. T. 24
for Calvin 77f.
in Ep. James 26
in *1 Clement* 27–8

'the elder' in 2 and 3 John 32
Eleutherus, bishop 152
Eliot, George 103
Eliot, T. S. 100
Elizabeth I, queen 95–8
Epiphanius, bishop
and non-stip. ministry 226
and ordination of women 203
Episcopal Church of Scotland
191–2
Erasmus 84
*Essay on the Development of Christian
Doctrine* 199
eucharist
as main Sunday service 139
Augustine's teaching on 52–3
Chrysostom's teaching on 53
Cyprian's teaching on 51
first sung service in C. of E. in
19th cent. 105
lay presidency at 140
understood as sacrifice 52
vestments at 139
Euodia 200
Evangelical Movement 101–4, 113
evangelism (see Mission)
Ewart G. 161–2
excommunication 60

Fabian, Pope 131
Faith in the City 211
family
as model of ministry 166–8
Farrer, Austin 168
Feminine in the Church 204
Ferard, Elizabeth, deaconess 134
Ferrar, Nicholas, deacon 100
Fleming, Launcelot, bishop 217
flesh
in incarnation 197
folk religion 209
forgiveness of sins
at Peter's confession 32–3
commission given by Jesus 32
in 1 John 32
in Pastoral Epp. 33f.
in Polycarp 33
in *Shepherd* 33

Fountain Trust 111–12
Franciscans 63, 69
Franco, General 160
Frankenhausen,
    peasants defeated at, 1524 83
Free Churches
    and ordination of women 205
Frere, W. H., bishop 106, 195
fundamentalisms
    biblical, ecclesial, patristic 194

Gaudium et Spes 188
Gengis Khan 114
Giberti, Gian Matteo, bishop 87
Gladstone, W. E. 103
God
    became man in Christ 197
    God's action in Christ 208
    plurality in Godhead 196
God's Reign and Our Unity
    (Anglican-Reformed report,
    1984) 192
Graham, Billy 103
Grantly, archdeacon 265
Gratian, emperor 59
Greene, G. 265
Gregory I, pope (the Great)
    critical of a non-stip. bishop 228
    father of medieval papacy 159
    his civil service 159
    'servant of the servants of God' 159
Gregory II 61
Gregory of Nazianzus 203
group ministry 217–220
Guidelines for Local Non-Stipendiary
    Ministry
    (C. of E. report, 1987) 237

Hall, Joseph, bishop 96
Hall, R. O., bishop 195
Harper, M. 111–12
Harris, Barbara, bishop 195
Harvey, A. E. 140
Hastings, A. xi, 174, 265
Headlam, Stewart 109
Henry VIII, king 84, 97
Henson, H. H., bishop 163
Herbert, George 99, 142

Hereford 214
hierarchy 163
hiereus (see Priest)
Hilborough
    group ministry established, 1961
    214, 217–20
Hippo Regius (Algeria)
    3 catholic basilicas at, in 5th
    cent. 57
The Historic Episcopate 236
A History of English Christianity
    1920–1985 265
Hitler, Adolf 160
Hoffmann, Melchior 83
Holy Roman Empire
    Charlemagne its first emperor 61
    ideals and deficiencies 65
    successor to Roman Empire 60
Holy Spirit xiii, 37, 38, 43–4,
    110–13, 176–7, 199–203, 250,
    267
homosexual clergy
    ministry of 179–84
    C. of E. bishops and 183–4
Homosexual Relationships
    (C. of E. report, 1979) 180
An Honorary Ministry
    (C. of E. report, 1977) 233
Hooker, Richard 175
    and the 'godly prince' 92–3
    Laws of Ecclesiastical Polity 92–4
    on church and state 207
Hooper, John, bishop 97
The Hospital – A Place of Truth
    148–9, 222
hospital chaplain 221–3
    ministry of 148–9, 221–3
    training of 145–7
House Church Movement
    heirs of radical reformers 82, 112
Huddersfield 102
Humanae Vitae 181, 185, 188–9
Hunter, Leslie, bishop 223
Huns
    Rome sacked by, 410 59
    Pope Leo I parleyed with, 452 59
hupēretēs 5
Hutter, Jacob 84

Ignatius, bishop
    doctrine of episcopacy 28—30
imperial model of ministry 158—61
indelibility (see Ordination)
indulgences 63—4
Industrial Mission 223—5
Industrial Mission — An Appraisal
    (C. of E. report, 1988) 223
industrial model of ministry 161—3
Industrial Revolution 134, 206
infallibility 176, 187—90
informed consent 210
Innocent XIII, pope 115
Inquisition 159
The Integrity of Anglicanism 256
Irenaeus, bishop 151—2, 203
Islam
    captured Constantinople, 1452
        62
    in Sicily and Spain 60
    removed 3 patriarchies 61
Issues in Human Sexuality
    (C. of E. bishops' statement,
        1991) 183

James, the Lord's brother 19
jester
    a model for ministry 266
Jesus Christ
    his authority 11—16
    his blood-relatives 19
    inclusive humanity of 205
Jeunesse Ouvrière Chrétienne 224
Jewel, John, bishop 93—4
Joanna 197
John, king 159—60
John of Montecorvino
    Franciscan missionary to China
        115
John XXIII
    and Vatican II 187—91
John Paul II
    visit to England 110
    and A. R. C. I. C. 191
Jones, A. 196
Judaeo-Christian tradition,
    pluriformity of 258
Julian, Dame 196

jus divinum
    in A. R. C. I. C. Final Report
        186
    Vatican's response 190
Justinian, emperor 158

Karlstadt
    colleague of Luther 75
Keble, John 93, 104
Khubilai Khan
    Mongol ruler in Beijing 114—15
The Kingdom of Christ 107—9
kingdom of God
    i.e. God's kingly rule 173
    and non-stipendiary ministry 236
    industry and 224
    Jesus' proclamation of 244
    obedience to 209
    parish and 211
    the commanding vision 268
Kingsley, Charles 103, 108, 252
Küng, Hans 155, 188

laity, ministry of
    (see Lay Ministry)
Lambeth Conferences
    1908 on contraception 153
    1920 on deaconesses 134
    1930 on deaconesses 134
        on non-stipendiary ministry
            232
    1948 on authority 174, 270—2
    1958 on contraception 153
        on non-stipendiary ministry
            232
    1968 on non-stipendiary ministry
            232
    1978 on lay presidency at
        eucharist 140
        on ordination of women as
        priests 154, 175, 205
    1988 on ordination of women as
        bishops 175, 205
Lambeth Quadrilateral (1888)
    (see Appendix 1) 269
    on ministry 136, 264
Lambourne, R. A. 146—7
Lang, C. G., archbishop 105—6

Larkin, Philip 209
Latitudinarians 101
Laud, William, archbishop
    on divine right of bishops 95—6
Laurentius, archdeacon 132
lay ministry xii, 135
    and baptism 140—1
    importance of 251
    in countryside 215—16
Lee Tim Oi, Florence
    ordained priest, 1944 195
leitourgos 6—7
Leo I, bishop of Rome (the Great)
    and Petrine monarchy 59, 152
Leo III, pope
    crowned Charlemagne, 800 61
Letters and Papers from Prison 232
levitical uncleanness 204
liberalism 113
Lightfoot, J. B., bishop 162
Lincoln 214, 238—9
Linnell, Charles, priest 168—9
Little Flock
    Protestant group in China 121
Liturgical Movement 139
liturgy (see Worship)
Liverpool 241
Local Ministry 237—43
    in Bethnal Green 237—8
    in Lincoln 238—40
    in Liverpool 241—2
    in Manchester 241
    the Brandon Scheme 240
    training for 241—3
love
    in parish 211
Ludlow, J. M. 107
Lumen Gentium 189
Luther, Martin 73—7
    and the authority of the Bible 73
    and bishops 94
    and the congregation 74—5
    and the magistrate 75
    and the radical reformers 81
    at Ratisbon 88
    his 'Tower' experience' 76
    on grace and faith 76
    on ordination 74

on the pure gospel 76
on vocation 246
Lydia 200

Macaulay, T. B. 103
Manchester, local ministry in 241
Manning, H. E. 103
Mantz, Felix 83
Mao Zedong 117—18
Marian dogmas 190
Mary and Martha 197
Mary Magdalene 197
Mary the mother of Jesus 200
Mary Tudor, queen 97
Mathers, J. R. 147
Matthias 245
Maurice, F. D. 107—10
    and J. M. Ludlow 107
    and Charles Kingsley 108
    on baptism 167
    on bishops 151—2
    on ministry 109—10
    expulsion from King's, London
        108
    unsystematic theologian 257
Melanchthon, Philip
    Luther's lieutenant 82
    at Ratisbon 88
*The Meaning and Unity of the Anglican
    Communion*
    (see Appendix 2) 270—2
Methodism (see also Wesley, J.)
    disapproval of Christian
        Socialism 107
    pastoral strategy 215
Milan, Edict of (AD 313)
    provision for religious toleration
        51
military model of ministry 160—1
minister(s) (see also Clergy, Priest,
        Presbyter)
    meaning of word 7
    celibacy of 54, 68, 91, 133
    definition of clergy 58
    distinctive dress of 53, 79,
        105—6, 139
    excused civic duties by
        Constantine 58

minister(s) – *cont'd.*
  Origen's view of 41—2
  sexual morality of in 4th century
    54
Ministerial Priesthood 110
ministers in secular employment
    226, 233
ministry
  and sacraments 46—7
  in classical period 47
  collaborative m. 220
  family model of 166—8
  flexibility built into 47
  imperial model of 158—60
  industrial model of 161—3
  larger than the local church 248
  loss of confidence in xi
  military model of 160—1
  professional model of 163—4
  a second-order doctrine 173
  secular terminology of, in N.T.
    3f.
  shared m. 210
ministry, stipendiary (see
    Stipendiary Ministry)
ministry, threefold
  in Clement 28
  in Ignatius 29
  influenced by Old Testament 51
  influenced by Roman *ordines* 57
mission and evangelism 144
La Mission de France 219
Missionary Methods: St Paul's or Ours?
    230
Moberly, R. C. 110
Montanism
  and ordination of women 203
  condemnation of 39
  in Phrygia 38—9
Moravians
  J. Wesley's debt to 101
More, Thomas 84
Morrison, Robert 116
Moule, C. F. D. 176—7
multi-parish ministry 215
Münster 83
Münzer, Thomas 82
Mussolini, Benito 160

The Nature of Christian Belief
  (C. of E. report, 1986) 153
Nestorians in China 114
New Zealand
  C. of E. in 178
Newman J. H., cardinal 103
  and apostolical succession
    104—5
  and *Tracts for the Times* 104
  and tradition 199—200
  left C. of E. for Rome, 1845 104
Nicene Creed 197
Nicholas IV, pope 115
non-stipendiary ministry 226—36
  advocates of 229—30
  and D. Bonhoeffer 232
  and worker-priests 230—1
  Bishops' Regulations for, 1970,
    1987 232—3
  different terms for 226
  first 15 training courses 232
  for the Fathers 227—8
  for St Paul 226—7
  in the E. Orthodox church 228
  in the Middle Ages 229
  suspect as unprofessional xii,
    166, 244
  theological foundations of
    235—6
  work of 233—6
Northern Ordination Course ix
  (formerly North West Ordination
    Course) 253—4, 259—61
Norwich 214, 217—18

*The Ordained Ministry: Numbers, Cost
    and Deployment*
  C. of E. report, 1988 266
ordination
  growing sacralisation of 37, 43
  indelibility of 43, 74
  link with local community
    lessened 66
  Luther on 74
  numbers for in C. of E. xi, 233
  rite of, in Pastoral Epistles 47
ordination of women 195—205
  and Free Churches 205

and subordination of women
201—5
and Vatican 190
as priests, at Lambeth
Conference 1968 205
as priests, at Lambeth
Conference 1978 154, 175, 205
as bishops, at Lambeth
Conference 1988 175, 205
Christological aspects of 197—9
pneumatological aspects of
199—203
political aspects of 205
psychological aspects of 204—5
sociological aspects of 203—4
theological aspects of 195—6
*The Ordination of Women to the
Priesthood*
(C. of E. report, 1972) 203
Origen
founded Catechetical School at
Alexandria 39—40
view of ministry 40—1
Oxford
theological training at, 19th cent.
252
Oxford Movement (see also
Anglo-Catholicism)
achievements 113
permeated by Christian
Socialism 109

Packer, J. 103
Papacy (see Rome, bishop of)
papal primacy 185—91
Paphnutius 54
parish 206—16
country village p. 213—16
importance of 265—6
inner-city p. 212—13
number of pp. in England 206
origins of 66, 206
p. church as a focus of meaning
209
pp. in U.S.A. 216
purpose of p. church 209f.
variety of pp. 207
Parish Communion

and Parish Meeting 106
in rural village 215—16
seeds sown by W. H. Frere 106
supported by C. G. Lang and W.
Temple 106
Parker, Matthew, archbishop
97—8
parson's freehold 163
pastor
in hospital setting 148—9
pastoral care and counselling
145—9
Pastoral Epistles
as treatise on church order 30—2
Pattison, Mark 252
Paul, Saint
and apostolic leaders 17—18, 21
apostle to the Gentiles 20—1
call of 20
and collaborative ministry 22
and congregations 21
and elders 24
and moral issues 22
and the Spirit 24
and women at worship 201
P.'s personal qualities 21
Paul VI, pope 188
Peasants' Revolt 75
Peel, Robert 103
penance
priest's influence through
sacrament of p. 69
Pentecostalism 110—12
People of God
includes laity and clergy 122, 127
Perrin, Henri 231
personality traits
feminine and masculine 204
Peter
as leading apostle 18—19, 186, 190
pope as guardian of P.'s body 61
Philip, Saint, evangelist 200
Philip of Hesse 82, 84
Philippi
Paul and church at 227
Phoebe 200
Pius II, pope
overtures to Mahomet II 62

Pius XI, pope 188
Pius XII, pope
  and dogma of the Assumption
    187—8
Pluralities Act, 1838 229
pneuma (Greek for spirit, q.v.)
poimēn (Greek for shepherd, pastor,
  q.v.)
Poland 161
Polish Minor Church
  became Socinian Movement 85
Pontifical Council for Promoting
  Christian Unity 191
Pope (see Rome)
Prayer Book of 1928 106
preaching 141—2
presbyter (see also Priest, Elder)
  meaning of word 7—8
  bishop delegates duties to 56
  seats for pp. in basilica 56
  term preferred by Hooker 94—5
Presbyterians
  favoured territorial ministry 80
  in England 95
  in Scotland 95—6, 191—2
  union with Congregationals to
    form U. R. C. 191
  use of deacons 133
priest (see also presbyter, *hiereus*,
    sacerdos)
  meaning of term 7—8, 9—10,
    244
  absentees 67
  as *animateur* 170
  as cultic figure 91
  as icon of Christ 198
  as leader of worship 139—41
  as minister of the kingdom 138
  as presider over a congregation
    138
  authority 138—49
  children instituted as pp. 67
  Christians as royal priesthood 25
  daily prayer of 141
  in hospital setting 148—9
  Luther on priesthood 74
  parish priest in England in 13th
    cent. 66—70

personal qualities of p. 168—70
priesthood as personal state 66
priests in Old Testament 9—10,
    244
Rome's clerical hierarchy 90—91
sacerdotales at Thamugadi in AD
    363 57
Principles of Church Reform (1833) 229
private masses 66
professional model of ministry
    163—6
prophet (Greek, *prophētēs*)
  meaning of word 8—9
  in Old Testament 9—10
  in New Testament 23
  false prophets 25, 38
  in *Didachē* 24—5, 38
  in Montanism 38
  Jesus as a prophet 13—16
  pp. of Zwickau 82
  testing prophets 38, 113
  prophetesses among radical
    reformers 82
province
  Roman origin of term 57
psychology
  of groups 210
Pusey, E. B. 103

Quixote, Monsignor 265

Rahner, K. 186
Ramsey, I. T. 196
Ravenna 158, 160
Radical reformers 81—6
radicalism
  and social involvement of the
    Church 113
Ratisbon, Colloquy of (1541) 88
Reader, ministry of 140
reason, appeal to 175—7
reception
  of a papal pronouncement 189
rector(s)
  origin of term 67
  in England in 13th cent. 67
Reformed Tradition
  beginnings of 47

The Relevance of the Church (1935)
   230
Religious Language (1957) 196
Ricci, Matteo (Li Matou)
   Jesuit missionary to China 115
Robinson, J. A. T., bishop
   doctrine of ministry 235—6
   and Southwark Ordination
      Course 232
Roman Catholicism (see also
      Rome)
   beginnings of 47
Rome (including Bishop of Rome)
   and shared church government
      127
   and the Counter-Reformation
      87—91
   and the Donation of Constantine
      61
   and vocation 247
   authority of R. over surrounding
      area 58
   authority of R. as empire
      disintegrated 59
   Lateran palace handed over in
      312 56
   Leo the Great and Roman
      imperialism 152
   papal assumption of title 'Vicar
      of Christ' 62, 110
   papal claim of plenitude of power
      63—4
   papal control of appointments
      64, 187
   papal infallibility 176, 187—90
   papal presumption condemned
      by Cyprian 44
   papal primacy 185—91
   papal willingness to grant
      dispensations 70
   parochial organisation at R. in
      3rd cent. 55—6
   R. sacked by Alaric in 410 59
Romero, Oscar, archbishop 157
ruach (Hebrew for Spirit, q.v.)
   196
Ruskin, John 103
Russell, Anthony, bishop 163—4

Sabaudia, Peter de 67
sacerdos (Latin for Priest, q.v.) 9, 51
sacred and secular 236
sacrifice
   as interpretation of eucharist
      51—3, 90
Santer, H. 204
Schillebeeckx, E. 155
Science and the Modern World 268
Schwenckfeld, Caspar 85
sector ministry (see Specialised
      Ministry) 221—5
selection for ministry 247—8
   by conferences 247
   C. of E. and 247—8
   personal qualities needed for 248
   sense of vocation needed for 247
Selwyn E. G. 201
Selwyn, George, bishop 178
Sense and Sensibility 252
servant (see also Deacon)
   aspect of ministry 128f., 138
Shaw, G. B. 164
Sheppard, David, bishop 152
Simeon, Charles 102
Simon the Pharisee 197
Simons, Menno 82
slavery 202
Society of Jesus (Jesuits) 88, 115
Socinus 85
Son of Man
   as title of Jesus 15—16
South Ormesby 214
Southwark Ordination Course 232,
   253
specialised ministry (see also Sector
      Ministry) 221—5
   definition of 221
   hospital chaplaincy 221—3
   industrial chaplaincy 223—5
Spirit, Holy
   and discerning of spirits 23
   and synodical government 178
   and tradition 199—202
   flexibility of 267
   graces of (charismata) 23, 110—13
   source of apostles' commission 20
   working of 176—7

spirituality
  central for ministry 267
  for non-stipendiary ministers 235
  in clergy training 250
  Origen's stress on 40
Spirituality in Ordination Training
  (C. of E. report, 1981) 250
Spyridon, bishop 228
Standonck, Jean 87
Stephen, Saint 200, 129
Stephen, archdeacon 132
stipendiary ministry
  at Rome c. 250 55
  favoured position of C. of E. 267
  income of English clergy in 13th
    cent. 67—70
  Origen's stress on 40
Stockwood, M., bishop 232, 253
Storch, N. 82
Stübner, Marcus 82
Student Christian Movement 103,
  146
Sturminster Newton, Dorset 70
Suhard, Emmanuel, cardinal 170,
  231
A Supporting Ministry
  (C. of E. report, 1968) 233
Susanna 197
Sweden 96
Swiss Brethren 83
Sykes, S. W. bishop 256
synodical government
  bishops in synod 152—3,
    177—84
Syntyche 200

The Tablet 186, 190
Taylor, Jeremy, bishop 96
teacher (see also Adult Education)
  clergy and teaching profession in
    England 229
  first teachers linked with
    prophets 39
  in later 2nd cent. 39—40
  teaching office of bishop in 1
    Tim. 31
team ministry (see also Group
  Ministry)

definition of 218
in city 218
in country 219—20
Temple, William, archbishop 106
Tertullian 37—38, 203
Thamugadi (N. Africa) 57
Theatine Order 87
theological colleges (residential)
  249—62
  Nestorian c. in Beijing 115
  set up by Calvin 81
  set up by Council of Trent 91
  in China 119—20
  in England —
    Kelham 106
    Mirfield 106
    Peache's 103
    Ridley Hall 103
    Wycliffe Hall 103
    19th cent. foundations 252—3
  and degree awarding 165
  and teaching of doctrine 265
  sign of professionalism 164
theological courses
  (part-residential) 259—62
  first 15 in England 232
  and teaching of doctrine 265
Thessalonica, Edict of (AD 380)
  51
Theveste (N. Africa) 57
Thirty-nine Articles 93, 246
Thomas Aquinas
  as basis for R. C. ministerial
    training 257
  disallowed ordination of women
    203
  disapproved of trade 63
  last of medieval systematisers 62
Thomas, R. S. 169—70
three-fold ministry
  ages for entry in 4th cent. 132
  C. of E.'s commitment to 136,
    269
  in B. C. P. Ordinal 127
  in Cyprian 132
Three-Self Patriotic Movement 117,
  273—5
Timothy 200

Ting, K. H., bishop 118—21
Tokyo 255
Tracts for the Times (1833—41) 104
tradition
    against Gnosticism 36
    and lists of bishops 37
    and spirituality 35
    both apostolic and prophetic xiii,
        263—5
    hardening of concept, 2nd cent.
        36
    in Ep. Jude and apostolic fathers
        36
    interpretation not fixed 263—4
    pluriformity 258
    t. living and dead 200
training of clergy
    and study of the world 250—1
    and systematic theology 256—7
    as induction into a tradition
        249—50
    colleges set up by Calvin and
        Trent 81, 91
    continuing training 155
    for local ministry 238—42
    founding of colleges in England
        for 253
    founding of courses in England
        for 253—4
    in countryside 217
    in 18th cent. 102
    in 19th cent. 252—3
    importance of 266
    integration of subjects in 258
    low standards in 13th cent. 69
    part-residential courses for
        259—62
    pattern of training exported 255
    personal growth in 251
    residential colleges for 254—62
    residential training compulsory
        for 253
    re-training of clergy leaving
        ministry 156
    spirituality and 276
    student protest about 255—6
    suitability of universities for 165,
        254

Trinity, Holy
    the basis for ministry xiii, 267—8
The Twelve (see also Apostle) 15,
    17f.

'Unequal treaties' 116
Unitas Fratrum 84
United Reformed Church 191
Universities Test Act 252

Valentinian III, emperor 59
Vandals 59
Vatican (see also Rome) 190—1
Vatican I
    and divine right of Pope 186
    and papal infallibility 187—8
    current standing of 191
Vatican II 106, 187—91
Venn, Henry 102
vicar
    origin of term 57
    representative of abbot 67
'Vicar of Christ'
    and Petrine texts 186
    title assumed by popes in 14th
        cent. 62
vocation
    in O. T. 244
    loss of 156
    meaning of 244—7
    numbers needed 266—7
    through the congregation 237

Wesley, John 101—2
Whalley Abbey, Lancs 67
Wheale, Gerald 212—13
Whitehead, A. N. 268
Whitgift, John, archbishop 92—6
Wickham, E. R. 223
widows
    as an order in the Church 30
    care of, in the east 55
Wilberforce, Robert, priest 105
Wilberforce, William, M.P.
    102—3, 105
Williams, Rowan, bishop 107
Wilson, Michael, priest, physician
    148—9, 222

Women, ordination of xii, 82,
195—205
Worker-priests in France xii,
230—1
World Council of Churches 194
Worlock, Derek, archbishop
152
worship (see also Church, Church
buildings, Eucharist)
for Paul, not organised 24
in *Didachē* becoming prescribed
24—5
in English churches in 13th cent.
68—9
leading w. 139—42

modern w. 210
Reformation changes in 98
The Worship of the Church
(C. of E. report, 1918) 105
wrath of God 173
Wycliffe, John 101

Xavier, Francis 88
Xian, China 114
Ximenes, Cardinal 87

Zeno, bishop 228
Zephyrinus, pope 131
Zwickau 82
Zwingli 83